Oracle®
Data Processing
A Manager's Handbook

Graham H. Seibert

Windcrest®/McGraw-Hill

NOTICES

1-2-3® — Lotus Development Corporation

Compaq™ — Compaq Computer Corporation

Compuserve™ — Compuserve Information, Inc.

Crosstalk™ — Crosstalk Communications

DEC™ — Digital Equipment Corp.

dBase® — Ashton-Tate

ERwin™ — LogicWorks.

Excel™ — Microsoft Corp.

IBM® — International Business Machines

Lotus™ — Lotus Development Corporation

Microsoft™ MS-DOS® — Microsoft Corporation

Oracle and **Oracle*Card ®** — Oracle Corp.

PICK™ — Systems Management, Inc.

SQL*Calc SQL*Forms SQL*Language SQL*Loader SQL*Menu SQL*Net SQL*Plus SQL*ReportWriter SQL*Start and **SQL*123®** — Oracle Corp.

Timeline™ — Breakthrough Software Corp.

Windows® — Microsoft Corporation

VAX™ — Digital Equipment Corp.

FIRST EDITION
FIRST PRINTING

© 1993 by **Windcrest Books**, an imprint of TAB Books.
TAB Books is a division of McGraw-Hill, Inc.
The name "Windcrest" is a registered trademark of TAB Books.

Library of Congress Cataloging-in-Publication Data

Seibert, Graham H.
    Oracle data processing : a manager's handbook / by Graham H. Seibert.
       p.   cm.
    Includes bibliographical references and index.
    ISBN 0-8306-3687-9 (hard)   ISBN 0-8306-3686-2 (pbk.)
    1. Relational data bases.   2. Oracle (Computer file)   I. Title.
 QA76.9.D3S42   1992
 005.75′65—dc20   92-24352
                                                      CIP

Acquisitions Editor: Ron D. Powers
Editor: Bert Peterson
Director of Production: Katherine G. Brown
Book Design: Jaclyn J. Boone
Cover: Sandra Blair Design and Brent Blair Photography, Harrisburg, Pa.   WR1

Contents

Acknowledgments

In the past five years, I have been blessed with excellent long-term clients, with whom I have learned Oracle and expanded my knowledge of management. I would like to extend thanks to John Harned, Sue Manion, Rich Weiskopf, Greg Druffel, and Andrew Mc-Whinnie of Computer Sciences; Cheryl Smith of HFSI, Inc; Bill Mountjoy of the Service Employees International Union; Jack Johnson, Frank Gould, Jenny Brake, and Moira Dolan of the Central Pension Fund of the Operating Engineers; Steve Lyman, Hillary James, and Prakash Sanghvi of CDSI; and Bob Evans of the Army Corps of Engineers.

The people of the Mid Atlantic Oracle User's Group have been a constant source of encouragement and a wealth of technical expertise. Kathy Christian pushed me to write my first book, *Working with Oracle Development Tools*. Others who helped on this project are Warren Capps and Dale Lowery (both of whom preceded me as chair of the organization), Gloria Miller, John Duncan, Mike Venerable, and Matt Comstock. Oracle consultants Ulka Rogers, Charles Peck, Dewey Allen, and Helene Thoreson offered valuable review and comments.

In writing this book, it was essential that I get a broader perspective than I had purely through client experience. I would like to thank the people who provided interviews: Will Gessner of ARINC, Mike Prince of Burlington Coat, Bob Bain of Connie Lee Insurance, Mike Armer and Tim Donohoe of GHA, Jim Weingart of John J. McMullen, Kent Smith of the U.S. Navy, Tom Reddin of Parklawn Computer Center, Mary Serafin of EDS, Frank Schlier of Blue Cross/Blue Shield of Tennessee, and Ulka Desai and Mukund Agashe of World Bank Financial Operations Division.

As before, the Oracle Corporation provided wholehearted support for this writing effort. I would especially like to thank Renee Taylor, Director of CASE Marketing, Richard Barker, Senior Vice President in charge of Oracle CASE; Alan Gater, Vice President of Oracle CASE Development; and Mike Burkett of Oracle Consulting Group.

I would also like to thank the software firms whose products are used in the examples: Ben Cohen and Barbara Bogart of LogicWorks, for the copy of ERwin used to create entity/relationship diagrams in the book, Paul Bodnoff of Corel Systems for a copy of their wonderful Corel DRAW! used to produce the illustrations, Symantec for the copy of Timeline used to illustrate the chapter on project management, and to Bill Sautter of Business Objects.

Acknowledgments

Introduction

What is a missionary to do when the natives' religion works better than his own? It calls for some soul searching. A number of Oracle shops have jettisoned the orthodoxies of the business, especially those that involve paper, and developed good systems incredibly quickly. Oracle is leading a revolution in systems development. Knowledge of the evolving methods is mostly folkloric; the same people who dislike system documentation have avoided documenting their new processes on paper.

The reason for this book

This book is an attempt to document techniques that work in Oracle development shops. The successful new practices turn out really to be only evolutionary, a synthesis of several threads of contemporary thought. The most profound is the concept that quality and productivity are bound up with the software process. Individual people within an organization understand and commit themselves to the processes they use. In fact, they should define them. The most visible result is that they do without superfluous documentation. The management question is how much is truly dispensable?

Custom programming is an expensive way to solve a problem. Henry Ford's genius was to devise one car that fit a variety of needs. Licensed software packages can satisfy more and more business needs, more fully and more reliably than custom software. Service vendors know certain applications and tools better than a user organization could hope; using those tools reduces costs and risks. The role of the data processing professional is changing to that of a shopper, integrator, and contract administrator. This book provides guidelines for performing those roles.

People-intensive businesses invite automation. The largest people costs in our industry are programmers. CASE (computer-aided software engineering) is the machine that threatens to replace them. The replacement won't be sudden. CASE is driving ADP (automated data processing) professionals toward people-oriented work (like analysis) and toward specialist roles in service to the machine (CASE experts, algorithm programmers, database administrators, and data administrators). Management must prepare the largest cohort within the organizations for the new jobs as the role of applications programmer shrinks away. This handbook offers points to consider in hiring, training, and career planning.

Methodologies

Carnegie Mellon's Software Engineering Institute, a leading computer science think tank, has adopted the total quality management school's insight that the individual people within an organization will produce quality products when they understand and commit themselves to the processes they use. Having people define the processes they use is the best means of achieving that understanding. The fundamental issue of management is getting people to work effectively in teams. Team members depend on each other's work. People within an organization depend on their peers to adhere to standards and procedures, whether written or implicit, as they generate work products.

The task of completing a prototype is at the limit of what needs to be done in a team. The foundation of a system—data design, business rules, and system structure—must be established by agreement among the users, the analyst, the designer and the developers. A system cannot tolerate major changes to the foundation; major changes undo any programming built upon the foundation. The programs that make up a system, which in Oracle consist mostly of forms and reports, are pretty much independent of each other. Once the foundation is stable, a developer can become cloistered with the user and complete the prototype rapidly until, by mutual agreement, the programmer and user have the program product they want.

The critical discipline for a successful prototype is to recognize that the job is far from done when the prototype is complete. A prototype shows how the mainline process will look when everything works. A production system is capable of dealing with a full range of exception conditions and user errors. Prototype development must be integrated with systematic design, configuration management, and testing methodologies to yield the level of quality required of production systems.

CASE is a potent tool for prototypes that carries a lot of the needed discipline within itself. CASE inverts the role of narrative documentation. A functional requirement now consists of CASE outputs supported by text to explain the exceptions, instead of text supported by diagrams. It might not be necessary to reduce a requirement to paper. CASE interactive displays are the ideal tool for presenting a CASE design.

It is easy to see CASE as a magic bullet solution by itself. On the contrary, it is only a tool that people use to fashion a solution. To achieve their objectives, those people need to thoroughly understand the CASE tool and use it within a context of complementary procedures. CASE printouts establish de facto standards for certain requirements and design deliverables. The remaining requirements still must be described in installation standards.

Sources

Though Oracle is a billion-dollar corporation, the user community is close enough to greet one another by name at conferences. Users are served by a manageable number of magazines. It is possible to get to know the major Oracle trainers, integrators, consulting firms, and even independent consultants in each geographical area.

Oracle operates according to a sort of unified field theory of DBMS (database management system) software. The company has a plan for almost every functionality niche. The beauty of their plan is that the parts are all orchestrated to work with one another. The downside is that there are problems to solve now, but Oracle's solutions might be a ways in the future. Third-party vendors have been very creative in filling the voids. Chapter 16 on sourcing addresses the trade-offs between Oracle and third-party software.

It is almost irresponsible not to research licensed software before developing an application system in custom code. At the very minimum, look at packages to help you clarify your requirements and show designers some techniques worth borrowing. Applications vendors can be somewhat more difficult to find and their offerings more difficult to assess than DBMS software. This book offers shopping techniques—how to find and evaluate packages.

In writing a book about the Oracle community it is tempting to name names, as in "See Ulka Rogers or Dave Hay for CASE support." or "Charles Peck is the fellow to call for performance tuning help." or "Dewey Allen is the best I know for configuring client/server installations." Because Oracle is an international company and new people rise to prominence quickly, this book focuses on the process of finding expert help rather than naming the experts.

People

Whether by genius or serendipity, Oracle anticipated the sea-change in management philosophy from the structured bureaucracy exemplified by IBM to the small, self-directing teams like those at Microsoft and at Japanese companies. Using a military metaphor, the industry went from conquering DP problems with Roman legions to guerrilla bands.

The use of teams raises a number of issues. How do you staff a guerrilla band? How should team success and individual success be recognized? How should rewards be handled? What management functions need to be given to the managed? To what extent is it possible to manage the data processing department according to a different philosophy than the rest of the company?

It would be presumptuous for any book to answer these questions definitively. The chapters on personnel and staffing and those on generalists and specialists raise the issues, cite expert opinions, and offer suggestions.

Audience

This book is intended for data processing managers who use Oracle and for members of their staff who develop and implement policies and procedures. By the management philosophy expressed here, the audience includes the first-line managers and all journeyman analysts and technicians within a shop.

Why is this book needed?

This book is unique in several respects. Most obviously it focuses exclusively on Oracle. Although most data processing management texts assume that a data processing requirement is resolved by writing a data processing system, this book assumes that writing code is a last resort only when the function cannot be bought. The methodologies presented here include shopping. This book recognizes and encourages the use of prototype and CASE tools in the Oracle environment and defines procedures to support them.

1
Development models

The process of system development was formalized to meet the major system development requirements of 20 years ago. Software has changed more rapidly than development philosophies, and Oracle is at the forefront of software evolution.

This chapter is a brief review of the waterfall model, the prevailing paradigm for system development, with a discussion of how it does and does not relate to Oracle systems development. It includes a section on the anatomy of an Oracle system that shows in a graphical way why the prototype process works. It interprets the meaning of the Software Engineering Institute's process maturity concept within an Oracle environment. Also, it demonstrates in a short history why the IBM model for multiuser data processing worked so well and why Oracle's model is rapidly unseating it.

The discussion serves as a prolog to the rest of the book. It introduces the themes of small development teams, essential documentation only, and empowering the developers to define their processes.

The waterfall development model and documentation

A model is useful to the extent that it reflects reality. The traditional waterfall model shown in Fig. 1-1 depicts a linear development process from requirements through operations. It accurately depicts the phases of a from-scratch system development. The loopbacks show that major steps, such as data design, remain open or are revisited periodically throughout the whole development process. The model does not address existing elements, such as purchased and previously written code, to be integrated into a system.

The waterfall model is accurate but dangerous. Traditional methodologies based on the waterfall model see the main current but ignore the eddies. It is true that you must study the requirements in order to perform analysis and that you must perform analysis to do the design. The eddies indicate feedback. The process of analysis educates the people who establish the requirement, the process of design can change the analysis, programming can change the design, and so on.

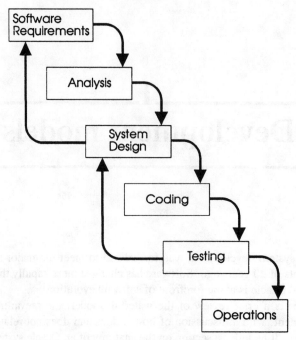

1-1 Waterfall model of system development.

The danger is in the notion that each step must be completed definitively before the next can begin. Standards that support the waterfall model usually dictate that the analysis must be done and approved before design can start, and design must be done before coding or programming can start. Wrapped in with this concept is the notion that different specialists handle different steps along the way. The baton is passed from design to programming with a heavy pile of specifications that management and the programmers ratify by their acceptance. The designer's work is done and he or she can presumably leave the project.

The assumption that a whole project must be carried from one phase to another by documentation alone leads to piles of paper called life-cycle documentation. A corollary assumption is that desk checking documentation along the way is the best way to find problems. The reality is that users cannot visualize most problems until they see them in code. Producing stacks of paper takes time away from writing the code. The documentation assumptions underlying the written standards for most installations were often inapplicable even in 3GL development environments. They can and should be scaled down for Oracle developments for the following reasons:

- Internal communications are better on Oracle projects because staffing is significantly lower per quantum of work. 4GLs like SQL*Forms provide much higher productivity. Verbal communication can handle a larger fraction of information transfer within a team.
- Users are more involved in Oracle developments and analyst/developers more fre-

quently stay with a project from beginning to end. Verbal communication provides a higher proportion of the required corporate memory and continuity.

- There is no need to specify what doesn't have to be written. CASE and Oracle's 4GLs eliminate great quantities of what would be repetitive code in other development languages. File opening and closing, matching routines, fetch routines, and record descriptions are handled by the relational database management system (RDBMS) directly or do not exist at all.

- Analysts and users collaborate on the data design and business rules that underlie any development. The graphical design conventions are simple enough for users to understand. Pictures replace narrative, especially with CASE and design tools like ERwin.

- Processes built upon a data design are largely isolated from one another, as depicted in Fig. 1-2. This independence makes the use of a prototype the best way to develop unique processes for routine functions such as updates and reports. The processing is predictable, and the risk of a mistake having a serious impact elsewhere in the application is low.

- Oracle's 4GL tools are largely nonprocedural. The tools are inherently self-documenting because, by Oracle's architecture, they describe what to do instead of how to do it.

- Life-cycle documentation trades present pain for a future payoff. The pain is always real. With Oracle, much of the future payoff evaporates. Program maintenance is relatively straightforward with the 4GLs, SQL*Forms, and SQL* ReportWriter because there is simply less code. What code exists is isolated into small, single-purpose nuggets within the 4GLs. When CASE generates the code, maintenance is a matter of updating the design and regenerating the source. Users working with the programmer in a prototype mode can quickly identify program shortcomings that might or might not have ever been considered in a specification.

Oracle is a fast-moving train that doesn't carry a lot of baggage. Many shops have abandoned extensive design documentation under the banner of the prototype process, citing the efficiencies listed above. These shops court other risks, the most significant being a temptation not to think the problem through before setting about to solve it and assuming that a system that looks done is done.

Certain elements of documentation are essential. They include strategy and analysis documentation, data design, and the design of all aspects of function and appearance that will be common throughout the system. Every shop needs to take a hard look at other documentation that might be required by their methodologies to evaluate whether it applies to Oracle.

The anatomy of an Oracle system

Oracle systems are oriented towards the user. Figure 1-2 shows the structure. The major structural elements are forms processes to maintain the database, report processes to write it out, and menu processes to control access and organize the processes.

It is possible to use the Oracle database management system in third-generation code and in batch-mode systems. It works better than most other alternatives. However, the

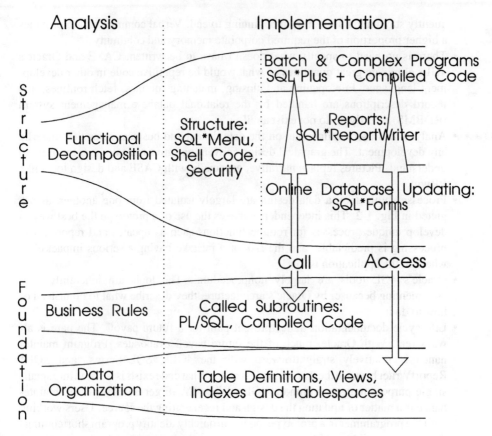

Analysis

Implementation

Structure

Functional
Decomposition

Structure:
SQL*Menu,
Shell Code,
Security

Batch & Complex Programs
SQL*Plus + Compiled Code

Reports:
SQL*ReportWriter

Online Database Updating:
SQL*Forms

Call   Access

Foundation

Business Rules

Called Subroutines:
PL/SQL, Compiled Code

Data
Organization

Table Definitions, Views,
Indexes and Tablespaces

1-2   Structure of an Oracle application.

greatest gains in productivity are to be realized in integrated systems that use fourth-generation languages as well.

The elements that all programs within a system share are labeled *Foundation* in Fig. 1-2. Included are the data-design and common subroutines. These modules usually implement business rules or formatting procedures. The system designer writes specifications for the called subroutines, which when programmed become part of the toolkit from which prototype developers build the structure of the system. Figure 1-3 shows the relationship between subroutine libraries and the mainline modules that appear in the functional decomposition of a system and on the menu.

A menu process provides the structure shown to users. It usually follows the functional decomposition of the system, except that each user sees only the subset of functions that are appropriate to his or her role. The menu invokes online update, reporting, and batch processes. Oracle's 4GL tools for these functions are SQL*Menu, SQL*Forms, SQL*ReportWriter, and SQL*Plus. Any or all of them can of course be written in compiled code. Many users write menu systems in *job control language* procedures (shell

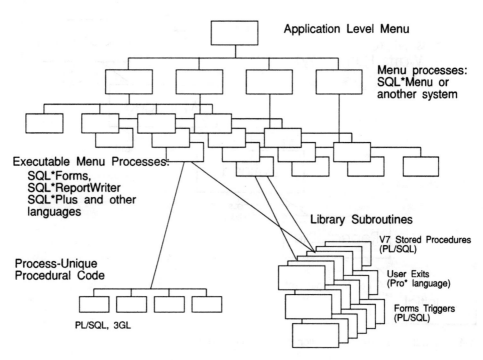

1-3 Top-down decomposition of an Oracle system.

scripts). There are a number of third parties that provide 4GL forms and report tools for Oracle.

The long vertical arrows in Fig. 1-2 imply that each structural module is very dependent on the subroutines it calls and the data it uses, but they are relatively independent of one another. This independence is why the prototype process works so well with Oracle. There is no need to write specifications for modules in the structural area because nothing else depends on them. The developer and user are free to develop whatever suits their needs. The programs communicate via the database, and the 4GLs and Oracle RDBMS take care of relational integrity.

Process maturity

The Software Engineering Institute (SEI) of Carnegie Mellon University is a think tank. Watts Humphrey (1989), Director of the Software Process Program, developed the process maturity level concept as a model for organization and control of software development. The operative principle of the model is that a software organization improves to the extent that the work it performs can be measured, managed and forecast. Figure 1-4 shows the maturity levels in their scheme.

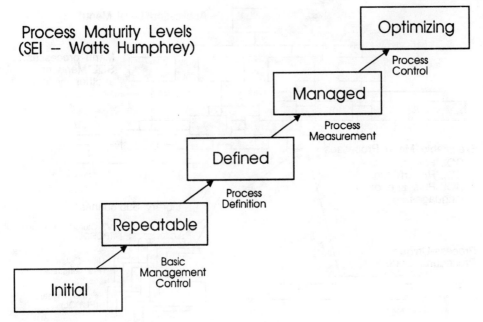

**Process Maturity Levels
(SEI – Watts Humphrey)**

Optimizing

Process
Control

Managed

Process
Measurement

Defined

Process
Definition

Repeatable

Basic
Management
Control

Initial

1-4 Software organization evolution from chaotic to ideal.

The kernel of the SEI's message is that a DP shop must have control over the development process. That control takes the form of rigorously defined procedures, carefully observed, throughout the requirements, design, and development processes. The evidence of such control is predictability: a software group can estimate the amount of resources required to accomplish a given task. At the highest levels they can draw on their database of development experience to modify procedures and optimize their process.

Watts Humphrey (1990) observes that he has rarely seen teams, and never an entire organization, at the managed or optimizing levels. The slope is hard to climb, and so many factors—changes—can set you back. The concept of optimization assumes that there is enough continuity from one project to another to make statistical inferences as to what works and how productive people are. But change, even radical change, is a constant when working with Oracle! It begs the question of whether the definition of *maturity* as *predictability* makes sense to an Oracle shop.

A predictable process assumes understanding and control of the development environment. The manager of an Oracle application shop does not have the degree of control enjoyed by major software houses such as Microsoft and Oracle itself. Among the differences are:

- The software tools change, often significantly, between projects and even during the implementation of one project.
- Applications often use or at least interface to existing code written in other disciplines. They involve conversion, interface, or bridge software.
- The best way to implement a new system is often to build on a base of purchased software. Doing so cuts implementation time; but at the same time it dictates a

system design. Buying a packaged solution means, at least to some extent, letting the software dictate the requirements instead of the other way around. It is cheaper to adapt the business to the software than vice versa.

- The processes that are subject to process maturity, those that can be predicted and repeated, are often the same ones that can be automated using CASE tools. The thrust of the industry is to automate the tasks that, if performed by people, would place an organization high on the maturity chart. What remain are the arts: interviewing, entity-relationship modeling, making the trade-offs in data design, and the political skills of keeping the client sold on the project. The maturity of the process will remain closely tied to the maturity of the particular group of practitioners.

- Software is only a means to an end in most businesses. In software houses, licensed software is the end product. There it gets upper management's full attention. To the average business, software systems are merely a means to meet other goals. Schedules for applications software systems, therefore, are most frequently dictated by the needs of the business rather than the MIS department's ability to produce. Tight budgets and deadlines often mean skimping on configuration and quality control; these economies usually turn out to be false in both the long and short term.

The upshot is that most applications programming environments, Oracle installations included, continue to struggle to pull themselves out of the chaos of Humphrey's level 1—the initial stage. The Oracle 4GL tools don't advance a shop along the SEI's path to maturity. They are intended for productivity more than software engineering. But productivity is the key! When used in an environment with a reasonable set of administrative controls, the productivity of Oracle's tools more than compensates for the absence of a high degree of forecasting accuracy.

CASE tools and methodologies are Oracle's contribution to software engineering. They are succeeding because they make an immediate payoff for doing a project "the right way." A good job of analysis is rewarded by a default design that actually works. A good design generates a system that actually works.

Software development is destined to remain unpredictable. As Fig. 1-5 shows, the aspects of the process that lend themselves to predictability also lend themselves to automation. CASE tools are able to turn business requirements directly into designs and even into code, with varying degrees of accuracy. Academicians develop theories for controlling the software development process. Their graduates put the theories to work brilliantly at major software houses, managing legions of programmers. The DP manager of a typical Oracle shop cannot afford and does not need that level of control.

The DP manager's job in a medium-size applications shop might be described as managing middle-tech. He or she is driven by a budget. He or she wants to use modern, but proven, products and technologies. The DP department employs a cadre of journeyman programmers mostly lacking in advanced degrees from MIT. The manager makes judicious use of outside consultants in areas in which it is not cost effective to have an expert on staff. The manager will prosper if he or she successfully applies decades-old data processing management principles to the middle-tech operation, and will fail if he or she grasps a magic-bullet solution as a substitute for sound management. The challenge is to interpret those principles in light of Oracle.

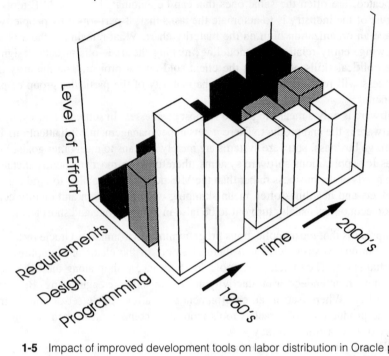

Front-end Shift of System Development Effort with Improvement of Development Tools

1-5 Impact of improved development tools on labor distribution in Oracle projects.

An historical perspective on Oracle

In the 1950s, applications were machine dependent. New machines meant reprogramming. Hardware costs dominated ADP decision making despite the fact that software technologies were embryonic.

IBM pioneered the concept of migration within a product line with their 360 line of computers in 1964. Their intent to have a single operating system across the entire product line devolved into three standard operating systems that are today's DOS/VSE, MVS, and VM. IBM's concept of an operating system included the full suite of software necessary to support an application: the supervisor, compilers and assemblers, link editors, sorts, and utilities. The system was a powerful model because it protected a shop's software investment—so long as they stuck with the IBM hardware standard. At this writing, it remains the dominant paradigm in multiuser computing despite the fact that it has been losing appeal, at a now accelerating rate, for 20 years.

In the 1960s, the United States Congress became distressed that IBM's standards gave them control of the government marketplace. Federal agencies were loath to write truly competitive requests for proposals (RFP) because in their experience only IBM systems would work. The government wanted to protect their software investments by fostering portability among vendors within a competitive marketplace. They established industry-wide committees that produced standards for COBOL, FORTRAN, network databases (CODASYL) and a host of other common software. These were published under the auspices of the American National Standards Institute (ANSI). The government formalized certain standards as requirements in their Federal Information Processing Standards (FIPS). The result was that a user could reasonably easily move batch processes written in standard languages from one processor to another.

At the same time, users went to more extensive online systems, all of which used telecommunications and terminal-support software provided by the manufacturers. Portability again went out the window. The problem was in vendor-proprietary systems software that resisted standardization.

There have been several challenges to the hegemony of proprietary operating systems. The PICK operating system included both operating system and database functions with its proprietary language. It achieved good portability across machines but was difficult to integrate with outside software. It has been widely used for turnkey solutions. Unix is a full-function operating system in the public domain. Most types of applications, including online transaction processing, can usually be moved (*ported*) from one Unix environment to another without great difficulty. Unix is available at little cost to any hardware vendor who wants to use it. It has enabled small, innovative hardware manufacturers to challenge mainframe and minicomputer manufacturers' proprietary operating systems and the expensive hardware that hosts them.

Unix solves the problem of the operating system but does not address the database function. Oracle recognized that applications written in the 1980s would mostly need database management systems. Portability, therefore, would mean that the application code, operating system function, and database function must be portable from one platform to another. It was an insight shared with PICK. The critical difference was that PICK's decision to build its own operating system excluded other processes. Oracle's decision to use the native operating systems but standardize the presentation of their functions within Oracle made it possible to coexist with other systems, including those it would replace.

With Oracle, the need for job control language (JCL), 3GL programs, and other operating system-dependent code diminishes significantly. Applications become truly portable and are spread across multiple machines. As hardware is becoming a commodity and operating systems a given, the RDBMS and tool set are becoming the major determinants of the environment.

Futurists predict that RDBMSs will become commodities, with all vendors' front-end tools linking to everyone else's database engines. Users will be able to mix and match environments. Such a future appears several years away as Oracle and the other major vendors grapple with distributed databases, networks, and the problems of coordinating multiple processors.

Today's applications lag behind the DBMS and other technologies that support them. They are held back by the dead hand of history—every shop's installed base of older code. The present problem is integrating code. The systems are written in different languages and file systems. To make them work in concert, bridges must be developed from one scheme to another. The bridging considerations are low level and tedious.

More and more, major database management systems can read each other's files.

However, the lowest common denominator medium for format exchange remains a flat file: an indexed or database file on one system is unloaded to sequential format and then reloaded into the other file system. An exchange of data requires compatible media on both ends. The normal media for data exchange between systems are operating-system disk files, hand-carried tape or diskette files, and communications.

Systems that are already implemented are hard to integrate because they are locked into data formats, hardware, languages, and protocols. Effective integration has to start at the analysis and design level. Computer-Aided Systems Engineering (CASE) does just that. Its promise is to generate code for any object directly from design specifications. Once all systems have been abstracted to a design level, integrating them will be a far simpler proposition.

Summary

Oracle is successful because it has taken over IBM's "total solution" franchise. What made IBM unique in the 1960s was that they alone could deliver the combination of hardware, software, and service that made it possible for an average company to use computers profitably. Like the IBM of yore, Oracle competes on the breadth of its product line and service. Other vendors today can offer elements of a total solution for less money, but in users' minds, Oracle is worth whatever premium it charges because it minimizes risk. Oracle's tools will be compatible with and able to take advantages of new Oracle features. Oracle's RDBMS can be counted on to support all of a client's hardware and network environments with all of the functionality needed on each one. Oracle is a major beneficiary of the fear, uncertainty, and doubt occasioned by the demise of the IBM standard.

2
The Oracle DP manager's job

The DP manager is the appointed leader of those in the data processing department. Planning, organization, staffing, management, and control are needed to assemble and direct a competent team. The department's success ultimately depends not only on the capabilities of the staff but on the tasks they are set to accomplish. The DP manager is responsible, as a technology leader, for seeing that users select the right information systems strategies for the enterprise.

Leveraging power through delegation is a matter of course within the DP organization. Project and first-line managers are responsible for developing and maintaining software systems. Cadres of specialists maintain the hardware and software environment and provide them with expert support. The people delegated to work with user departments share in the DP manager's mission of forming information systems strategies for the whole broader concern.

This chapter outlines the internal and external roles the manager of an Oracle shop has to fill personally and by delegation. The smaller the shop, the more roles each person must assume. This chapter is an overview of the management job. Subsequent chapters cover the substance of each role.

Technology leadership and strategic planning

The root meaning of *corporation* is "becoming a body." The first dictionary definition is "a group of people acting as an individual." A successful corporation takes on many of the characteristics of an individual: personality, look, and goals in life. Like a person, a corporation uses its intellectual facilities to analyze its environment and formulate plans. Its operations groups execute those plans.

Information is the nervous system of an enterprise. The corporation gathers raw data for analysis and planning, sends requests for action down the line, and sends feedback up the line for further decision making. A corporation's ability to act as a person is as good as its ability to figure out, and let its people know, what to do.

In recognition of the central role of data processing, IBM started preaching business system planning more than 25 years ago. Their message was and is that information systems are central to the success of a company. Corporate executives must put supporting information strategies in place at the same time they develop product and market strategies. Chief information officers who fail are those who aren't included in the strategic planning process.

The Oracle manager's job is to support the business. He or she must first understand top management's strategic objectives and second produce systems to carry out those objectives. The obvious third part of the job is to inform or convince management what can and what cannot be done.

Knowing the business

Most DP managers, those in Oracle environments included, rise from the ranks of programmers rather than MBA/general-management programs. Like guildsmen of old, they have tended to identify more with the profession of data processing than their employer of the moment. This mind-set is becoming perilous. Automation is automating automation itself! CASE tools will supplant programmers in writing code. At the same time, the concept of scientific management is being reassessed as the academicians revert to the view that management is more a matter of people than financial abstractions (Deming 1991). Data processing managers with a user orientation will survive.

Our great business successes, people like T.J. Watson at IBM, Hewlett and Packard, and Sam Walton of Wal-Mart excel because they are closely attuned to every aspect of their businesses. Being attuned to the business is a formula for success in data processing as well.

The data processing director needs to serve as the bridge between technology and the needs of the business. He or she needs to know the business. Learning it is a matter of spending time with and listening to the operating department directors and their subordinates, reading and acquiring whatever formal training is to be had, and of course understanding the information systems that support the business areas. The way to make effective use of a knowledge of the business is through participation in planning and strategy sessions.

All these steps break down the "us and them" distinction between data processing and other departments. The rest of the company often sees data processing as programmers, and programmers as overpaid and out of touch with the realities of the business. Winning the trust of other departments is a big first step toward understanding user department requirements. Trust becomes essential when you begin to broker the interests of one user against another.

Know the history of the company's legacy systems

The term *legacy systems* has caught on rapidly. Major data systems form a legacy in that they are the nucleus of business operations. Each one has a story to tell. Somebody in the user department had a problem long ago and accepted what they got as a solution. The battle scars on the system tell of reorganizations, new businesses, and power shifts.

Old-time programmers (may the shop be blessed with many) will wryly tell anecdotes of the system changes they have implemented over the years. A frequent theme is that they had a good application until the users contorted it unnaturally to handle some off-the-wall requirement. The systems can be a legacy of woe for people who have to maintain them and pick them apart like a pile of jackstraws so they can be put together again straight.

Business applications are for the most part quite predictable. Accounts receivable is accounts receivable; payroll is payroll. This premise is the cornerstone of the packaged software industry. The programmers' tales indicate the nuances of the application within the installation. They provide clues as to why a packaged software solution might not work—or be accepted. They will illuminate users' claims that they have unique problems that demand special attention.

Mike Armer of the Group Health Association recounts that GHA's staff of COBOL programmers was considered mediocre before the decision to go to Oracle. The DP department had been slow to implement new systems. When Frank Schlier, the new CIO, introduced Oracle and a prototyping philosophy, the old timers' stock rose dramatically. The applications knowledge they had acquired over the years gave them the understanding needed to develop prototypes. The users with whom they teamed quickly discovered that the programmers' knowledge of GHA made it possible to develop with a minimum of written specifications.

Participate in general management

The DP manager is the lead ambassador to user departments. The information management department exists to serve, and service starts with helping the organization select intelligent goals. A major defense contractor wrote a bid to deliver tens of thousands of microcomputers. Their traditional business was selling and servicing mainframe systems a few at a time. Microcomputers represented a new strategic direction. The DP department was left out of the business decision.

The proposal managers did not listen when the analysts, only tangentially involved in the proposal, questioned their legacy systems' ability to process the expected volume of orders. The two years between the time the opportunity was identified and the contract award slipped by with no action to improve the data systems. Once the award was made there were only six months until the first delivery. The six months were half gone before upper management fully appreciated that their systems—order entry, billing and receivables, and assembly management—were inadequate for the task.

To its credit, the contractor did not blame the DP department alone for the fiasco. Every department pitched in to find a solution. With help from a delay on the government side of the contract, the sale turned out to be a success. The rank and file in the DP department who gave nights and weekends to the project are fully aware, however, that better planning would have meant a better product with much less left to chance.

The DP manager understands better than anyone that information strategy is essential to corporate strategy. Knowledge, however, is worthless unless it is translated into action. The manager must be in a position to be heard. The top priority has to be establishing the best possible communications with the rest of the company: the users.

The DP manager can invite users in to talk data processing or get invited out to talk business with the users. Most organizations bring users to data processing. They establish a data processing "board of directors" to represent departmental needs and concerns and to help the MIS department set priorities. These information systems boards, management systems counsels, information systems strategy groups or whatever they are called might take the form of standing committees or ad hoc work groups. The life cycle of such committees, shown in Fig. 2–1, is independent of the form they take.

The model of bringing users into data processing falls down because user management will not understand data processing. Best efforts of data processing are frustrated. Even senior DP managers have to leave technology up to specialists on their staffs. The discussion of strategic issues that user managers do understand often devolves into details that they prefer to leave to their staffs, such as the composition of part numbers and what to use in place of a social security number for noncitizens.

The DP Manager has to break the model and go out to the rest of the corporation to be really successful. Having learned the business by making contacts and studying its history, as described above, the DP manager must move into a position of being involved in setting company strategy, at least to the extent that it depends on information resources. This proposition remains true across the gamut of roles played by the DP manager.

Outward orientation by the DP manager sets an excellent leadership example. Systems analysts, the people who assess user requirements and design systems, must gain the trust of their clients to succeed. Every person in the DP shop deals with users to some degree or another. Peters and Waterman (1982) cite being close to the customer as a fundamental value in America's most successful companies. The same philosophy, in an intramural interpretation, marks successful DP operations.

Include information management in strategic planning

Most organizations big enough to have multiperson data processing shops, be they businesses, government agencies, or nonprofit organizations, have instituted some form of strategic planning. The mechanics of the process vary as widely as the practitioners them-

1. A major event precipitates the formation of the committee. More often than not the event has more to do with the DP department than the company. The mainframe is running out of gas, or there has been a major implementation fiasco, or a large systems implementation is being scheduled.
2. General management appoints high level players, Vice Presidents and department heads to the committee.
3. All hands attend a kickoff meeting where the long-standing problem of communications between data processing and user departments, and the specific problem at hand, are discussed.
4. The Committee is given a charter to provide advice and counsel to Data Processing.
5. The Committee appoints working groups to study specific issues. The issues of the day include development of a corporate data model, distributed processing philosophies, and software package acquisitions.
6. Various Vice Presidents and Department Heads tune out after a meeting or two. They don't understand this technology stuff. They send the departmental technology buff (if they have one) in their stead.
7. The Committee agrees on directions for the DP department. The VPs and Directors see paper to that effect as it crosses their desks.
8. The DP department, pleased to have some direction, goes to work. They report progress back at Counsel meetings -- which seem to take place at more distant intervals, with smaller attendance and lower-level participants.
9. The organization stumbles into another crisis. It forms a new committee or breathes new life into the old one and begins again at Step 1.

2-1 Life cycle of an information systems steering committee.

selves. Executive management sometimes sees data processing as an internal support function having little to do with strategies that address the external world. They bring data processing into the discussion when it is time to implement the strategy. These executives are often disappointed when data processing does not come through.

Management is by definition management of resources: people, money, and tangible assets. A successful strategy is one that can achieve its intended objective by deploying its planned assets. It fails if the execution is too expensive or cannot be done. Timing is critical to strategic thinking. Assets cost money over time, and the value of an opportunity can shrink over time. Lastly, as any manager knows, data processing systems are notorious for not being delivered on time.

Top management takes into consideration the risk areas in any strategy. Information support is almost always among them. Any redeployment of people means changing the lines of communication among them, and those lines more and more frequently lead through automated systems. It often means that the nature of communications will change. An order entry system might need to process service orders as well as product orders, or a shipping system might have to service international orders.

More than examining the impact of a strategy on technology, top management also needs to assess the value of technology in a strategy. Burlington Coat Factory, one of the earliest and largest Oracle users, has aggressively used information technology in improving their retail operations. The system they are implementing will continually analyze company-wide sales and inventory information to spot and exploit sales trends and to avoid being stuck with slow-moving merchandise they will have to mark down.

The interdependence and interaction of what is called the business domain with the technology domain is a central theme of *Information Strategy and Economics* by Parker, Trainor, and Bensen (1991). Figure 2–2 shows the concept.

Business strategies require information technology to support them. Once in place, the databases and data communications facilities that are built to support one strategy drive the next. Customer information is a classic example. Businesses started automating information about their customers years ago to manage credit and handle accounts receivable. As every postal patron knows, that automation led to a strategy of tracking what people buy and flooding their mailboxes with targeted sales promotions. Technology led the business strategy.

The DP manager should provide expert assessment of the cost and risk of the information systems element of proposed strategies. He or she will be committed to the budget and deadline once the strategy is adopted. The costing and sizing methodologies used in strategy are the same as the DP department uses internally in sizing projects and evaluating vendor offerings.

There are a great many players in the corporate strategy game. The CEO calls on the heads of the operating divisions of the company, the financial people and often outside consultants. The outsiders bring with them a portfolio of experience from other companies that were faced with similar decisions. Consultants from Price Waterhouse or Booz, Allen are very convincing. The firms' worldwide exposure is enormous, and they are very skilled at distilling the elements of a strategy decision into a succinct presentation that the CEO can digest easily.

It would be out of place for the MIS department to maintain its own stable of consul-

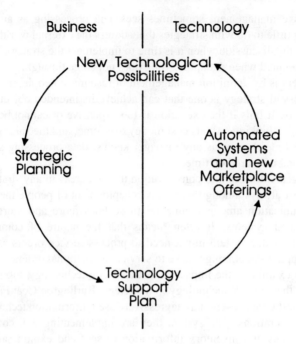

Business | Technology

New Technological Possibilities

Strategic Planning

Automated Systems and new Marketplace Offerings

Technology Support Plan

2-2 Interplay of strategy and technology.

tants to put together flashy presentations. There are other ways to make sure the MIS department's position is heard. They all depend on the DP manager's credibility. His or her advice has to be respected in the councils of the mighty. The devices the DP manager can use to make his points are:

- Participate personally in evaluating corporate strategies, and personally represent the DP department. The informed advice of a trusted DP manager will carry a lot of weight.
- Make sure the DP staff is represented on the team that evaluates strategy options. Needless to say, the representative must be a well respected analyst.
- Participate in the selection of consultants. Most MIS departments have ongoing relationships with consulting firms and independent consultants who are schooled in proposals and presentations and who know the firm's data processing operations.
- Engage consultants to perform research on behalf of the DP organization and help prepare top management presentations.

New technologies translate to new opportunities. Client/server and CASE tools are technologies that significant numbers of Oracle shops are implementing now. Those lie just over the horizon for most Oracle users (as of 1992) include a windowing environment for end users, massive amounts of data available through optical storage, and the integration of text, voice, and graphic images into database applications.

Only large MIS departments have the luxury of dedicating people to evaluating new technologies, but no shop is exempt from the need to do it. Bringing in new technology is one of the most effective ways to improve productivity. Oracle might never solve the problem of keymaps in the Unix environment or block-mode operations in an IBM environment, an issue that burns up immeasurable amounts of time. However, the new client/server technology makes it go away. New development tools, especially CASE, are reducing application development time significantly. End user tools such as Business Objects and Programmed Intelligence Corporation's IQ make it possible for end users to put together their own reports, which translates to less effort bringing up Oracle applications.

The DP manager must estimate how much it will cost, and how long it will take, to support any proposed strategy. A knowledge of the available technologies is essential. The state of the art demands it. All the systems that would be cost effective to implement in batch-mode COBOL have already been done.

Chapter 16 covers in detail the techniques for keeping up with technology. The short-form exhortations are "Read!" and "Network!". ARINC's Will Gessner says "We read like crazy. I require that senior people read. We circulate articles all the time."

Maintain a data model of the business

The data model drives data processing. Every shop manager interviewed for this book stresses that a complete and valid data model is the *sine qua non* in the Oracle business. In environments that use prototypes, where the disciplines of specifications, documentation, configuration management and project management go by the boards, the data design alone is done with rigor. The principal elements of data modeling are data dictionaries that describe the data being modeled and entity-relationship diagrams that show data relationships pictorially.

Entity relationship (ER) models are the heart of the data design. Every Oracle designer should have standard references available on how to do it. Richard Barker's *CASE*Method: Entity Relationship Modelling* is widely used by Oracle developers. The method is totally independent of the Oracle CASE tools, though naturally they incorporate its concepts. Developing ER diagrams on paper is an excellent way to start. You quickly come to appreciate the value of the technique and how essential the CASE tools are in projects of any size. It is a question of the medium.

Paper is a two-dimensional medium the size of which is bounded by the shop's largest windowless wall. It is tedious to draw longhand and tiresome to tape together. Erasure tears it. There are so many formats for the paper representation of a system that any one of them is bound to leave out useful data. In net, it is time to abandon our traditional paper medium for video techniques for representing systems.

In a CASE tool, the video display tube is like a kaleidoscopic magnifying glass for examining designs. The display can focus on any portion of the design and can zoom to any appropriate level. The designer can specify exactly what is to be displayed. A few of the choices are:

- Display the entity (table) name only.
- Display a textual description of the table.
- Display the data elements.
- Indicate which data elements are key fields.
- Display data element characteristics.

- Display data element descriptions.
- Display textual descriptions of relationships between entities.

In a design of any magnitude, the view through the tool is the only one that adequately represents the design.

Full-blown CASE tools are not the only ones that can successfully represent a design. Less expensive entity/relationship diagrammers can represent relationships very well. What distinguishes CASE is the data dictionary standing behind the diagramming functions.

Establish long-range information system plans

Corporate strategy establishes the need for information systems support. A long-range information systems plan is a road map for providing that support. Such a plan provides the context for MIS department operations: its budget, staffing and project definitions. The plan evolves from corporate strategic planning exercises described above and uses the same disciplines.

Define projects and timetables

Some projects are defined at top levels of management. These usually arrive with a priority and a deadline. Most projects take form further down the hierarchy. Though many writers have established rigorous, scientific methodologies for establishing priorities among projects, among them Parker, Trainor, and Benson (1991), in reality they are almost always determined by a more political process.

The DP manager can serve in the role of an honest broker among competing projects. Top management and the DP manager must ask user departments to quantify projected benefits, both tangible and intangible. Users need MIS department help in projecting the expense to implement a project. Putting cost and expense together yields a projected return by project, a preliminary means of ranking them.

There is usually a preferred installation sequence, the logic of which is visible to the DP department alone. One system might depend on the database maintained by another. Two systems might share the same local area network (LAN) setup, or several systems should be developed by the same team for the sake of efficiency. The net is that one implementation sequence involves less cost or risk than another. Every project depends on the availability of staff. The DP manager should handicap projects accordingly.

A DP shop's implementation schedule is a compromise involving resource, technical, and political interests. It holds up best, and the DP organization enjoys the most stability, if the decisions are widely based and understood in the first place.

Schedule technology insertion

The schedule for updating the environment has to shadow the project implementation schedule. Most major applications require some change in ADP resources. The master schedule has to coordinate changes in hardware, networks, the development environment, systems software, data base management systems software, applications software, standards, and every other factor that affects development and production. The ongoing implementation of purchased technology—new replacing old—is called *technology insertion*.

Each technology insertion involves some measure of selection, acquisition, installation, and training. The preliminary steps of researching the marketplace, making a choice, and waiting for the vendor to release a product take a significant amount of time. It helps to coordinate the timing through project management, as described in chapter 17. It is demoralizing to a project team, and wasteful as well, to be idle waiting on new hardware or a new Oracle release.

Acquire and deacquire assets

In most companies, the MIS department is responsible for deciding what they need to acquire and the purchasing department is responsible for negotiating a price and getting it. The comptroller of course provides input through the budget process.

A formal procurement procedure may be desirable or required depending on the size of an acquisition. The escalating levels of formality usually include:

- A management decision: let's buy it.
- In-house selection and evaluation using vendor literature.
- An IFB (invitation for bid) with subjective evaluation of competitive vendor presentations.
- An RFP (request for proposal) for written proposals to be evaluated using a quantitative methodology.

The amount of effort that goes into procurement should be proportional with the amount to be spent. It is typically worth 3 percent to 10 percent of the purchase amount to make sure a large purchase results in the best alternative available.

The DP manager and purchasing department jointly decide on the mechanics of a selection and parcel out the tasks to be done. MIS is usually responsible for writing the technical requirements and locating sources. Chapter 16 describes the techniques, and chapter 10 describes technology shopping as one of the more significant roles in today's DP department.

Managing project managers

The most important ingredient to success in management is having good subordinates. As the manager represents MIS to the rest of the company, he or she has to have full confidence in the lieutenants charged with getting the job done.

Projects present the most interesting management challenge because each one is unique. In contrast, the operations manager is charged with a repetitive process that can be measured by throughput, outages, and statistical quality. The metrics for maintenance coding are the number of system change requests processed, mean time to accomplish a change, and mean level of effort per change. To a much greater degree, a project manager defines the interpretation of success for the project.

Though DP projects fall into broad categories, each one needs yardsticks appropriate to the disciplines being used. How long will design take? How many months to select an order entry package? How long will it take to bring up a LAN using a Sequent as the Oracle file server? How long will it take to convert the 83 screens in an application from Application Foundation to Forms 3.0? It is difficult to estimate project cost and duration at the beginning of a project; estimates of time and effort to completion improve along the way.

The DP manager must ensure that the project manager diligently updates the project milestones and the estimate to completion. Each estimate to completion is an improvement because productivity can be projected based on the effort to date and because future tasks become better and better defined. Chapter 18 covers estimating techniques, and chapter 17 covers project management.

One of the hardest but most necessary disciplines is deciding when to kill a project. An out-of-control project can be death. It steals resources and costs the MIS department credibility with the users. The DP manager must have monitoring tools in place for all projects that allow him or her to recognize and pull the plug on the duds.

An occasional failed project is a sign of a vibrant and healthy DP department. The easiest way to find out if something will work is often just to try it, not study it to death. Far more organizations have seeded Oracle in their environments by getting a copy and trying it out than by minutely scrutinizing its features. A corollary of the try-and-see philosophy is that the DP manager must be ready to deliver the *coup de grace* to failing projects quickly and humanely, freeing the staff for more fruitful pursuits. It requires good intelligence, which only a well-conceived project management system can provide, and a good standing with the user who wanted it in the first place.

The measure of a project manager is not only how well the project goes but how well it is managed. Anyone can look good by setting and making easy targets. A good project manager is one who makes reasonably accurate forecasts, knows where the project stands at all times, and completes the project using a minimum of resources.

Managing the software process

Quality, productivity, and predictability are the holy trinity of software development. They are hard to achieve. The joke goes "I can do it fast. I can do it cheap. I can do it well. Which two do you want?" The biggest determinant of these factors other than the staff themselves, is the development environment.

A development environment exists by default whether or not management pays it any attention. The programmers have their tools and do their job. It is surprising what abominable tools and working conditions programmers often tolerate. Figure 2-3 shows Barry Boehm's view of the relative importance of modern programming practices and the development environment on programmer productivity. Taken together, practices and environment make almost as much of a difference as the programmers themselves. Because good programmers gravitate towards satisfying work environments, establishing an environment is probably the most important action management can take to maximize productivity.

With a little encouragement, the staff will take it upon themselves to obtain a good

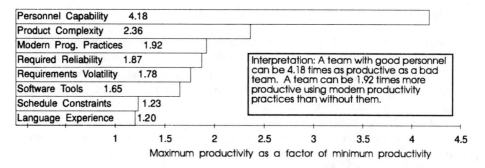

Personnel Capability	4.18
Product Complexity	2.36
Modern Prog. Practices	1.92
Required Reliability	1.87
Requirements Volatility	1.78
Software Tools	1.65
Schedule Constraints	1.23
Language Experience	1.20

Interpretation: A team with good personnel can be 4.18 times as productive as a bad team. A team can be 1.92 times more productive using modern productivity practices than without them.

Maximum productivity as a factor of minimum productivity

Excerpted from Barry Boehm (1985)

2-3 Exerpted COCOMO (constructive cost model) software-development productivity ranges.

software and hardware environment. Every professional enjoys working with state-of-the-art tools. The DP manager can support them by making sure whoever investigates new tools does good research. He or she also must arbitrate between competing requests and make sure they fit within the budget.

Establishing and enforcing modern programming practices, especially when it comes to documentation, is a lonelier job. Programmers love software tools because they can see an immediate return. Standards are always a matter of delayed gratification, about as popular as dental checkups. The pitch is that adhering to standards up front will make the job easier over the long haul.

"Right," breaths the programmer into his beard. "In the long run I'll be three employers down the line. In the meantime I have a four-week deadline for an eight-week project. Give me a break." Whatever standards might be on the bookshelf, expediency dictates which get used. Those standards used are usually the ones with short-term benefits.

A wise manager makes every endeavor to make standards and expediency coincide. Among the steps to take are:

- Go with the flow. Minimize documentation requirements. When possible adopt a prototype standard for system development.
- Use software tools to implement standards. Designers love CASE tools because they do a beautiful job of drawing pictures. It is a lot easier to ask them to enter a few narrative paragraphs as they describe objects within a CASE tool than to get a specification written on a word processor.
- Let software tools enforce standards. As an example, programmers cannot introduce surprises into production runs if they don't have access to production code. When the DP manager evaluates project managers according to weekly status reports produced by a project management system like TimeLine, those managers will learn to take credit for their accomplishments.

However painless the DP manager makes the standards and procedures, they fall into disuse without consistent management attention. Among the hardest DP roles to staff and manage, but also the most necessary, are quality control and configuration management.

Quality

The threat of Japan has data processing managers responding to requests to implement TQM (total quality management) programs in their operations. Central tenets of TQM are that quality goes into a product rather than being added on, and that it is less expensive to do a quality job than a shoddy one. How does a manager fit TQM in with the traditional QC (quality control) function in a data processing shop? Aguayo (1990) cites Dr. Deming's findings that workers are only responsible to a minor degree for product quality. Management, which controls the work environment, is the only agency that can make it possible or impossible to do a quality job. In data processing this means:

- Providing enough time to do the job right.
- Providing (hardware and software) tools appropriate to the job.
- Providing training in the tools and technologies to be used.
- Providing an adequate physical environment.
- Providing a well-understood set of requirements (that is, standards and procedures).

Quality control is not on Dr. Deming's list of ways to ensure quality! TQM assumes that most workers are motivated to produce a quality product and that they fail to do so only because their work environment makes it impossible. This concept dovetails with Boehm's findings (1985) that tools, practices, and working environment are major determinants of productivity.

The term *quality control* in a properly run data processing organization is a misnomer. The developers themselves control quality. What a QC section does is to audit it, keeping statistics on how well the shop is adhering to its declared practices. There are several staff functions to ensure quality in a DP organization, among them configuration management, project management, and a software process group, usually made up of developers who oversee standards, procedures, and tools.

Organization

Organization follows function. The reporting structure that an Oracle manager puts in place reflects his view of his or her mission. The missions of the Oracle managers interviewed for this book vary greatly. Many are service bureau operations with little responsibility for system developing or data administration. Others are developers for whom service bureaus handle the machine environment and DBA work. Figure 2-4 shows an organization chart for a complete Oracle shop.

Development activity in most shops is organized into projects. The biggest projects often involve rewriting most of the systems in an organization. Medium-sized projects might involve installation of a package, implementation of a small application, or upgrading an existing application. Small projects are tasks that need no organization and can be assigned to one or two people.

Small projects are best handled by a static organization in which each individual might have more than one assignment. People are most productive when they have several tasks in their queue. They can pick up on another when one has to wait for some outside action.

Somewhere in the medium-size project category, it becomes advantageous to establish a project organization. The indications are:

- The project involves enough people to require a manager.
- Most of the project staff spends most of their time on the project.
- The project has high visibility outside of MIS.

Project organization dedicates a team to a single mission under the leadership of a single person. It provides, at the expense of some overhead for project management, the tight focus needed for major new development and enhancements.

Maintenance programmers and craft experts, the staff gurus who keep things running, are almost always in permanent staff organizations. Their workload is mostly made up of short-duration tasks associated with permanent assignments. Their assignment is to handle whatever comes up rather than to accomplish a given piece of work, as is the case with project people.

Several concepts advocated by the TQM school push for flatter management structures. A traditional shop of 30 people has three or four first-line managers reporting to the MIS director. Each of these carries the personnel jackets for the people reporting to them. They spend their time in management functions such as handing out assignments, reviewing work, and chairing meetings of their groups. Creating that form of management structure may be counterproductive for several reasons:

- It disengages some of the most productive people from doing actual work.
- Managers start to justify their existence by managing—meddling in their subordinates' work.
- It makes rising to the level of a drone the model for success within the organization.

The alternative is to have team leaders without permanent managerial titles at the first level. This sort of environment is more fluid. It makes it nontraumatic for a person to assume leadership responsibility on one task and serve as a team member on the next. It encourages teamwork. The team leader, not being anointed with a title, has to lead by consensus.

The team leader concept ideally suits the needs of projects. It works well for maintenance programming, in which the analyst is a logical team leader. But it is usually desirable to have one person permanently responsible for the group that handles computer operations who, depending on the size of the organization, might be a candidate for a permanent management title.

The flat organization philosophy is consistent with other TQM precepts. Letting the workers control the development environment by maintaining their own standards, procedures, and tools relieves management of one traditional task. Doing away with management by objectives and formal annual reviews removes some more. Letting the whole team share such tasks as meeting with user organizations and interviewing candidates for employment pushes even more of the managerial workload down to the workers.

The organization structure in Fig. 2-4 can be satisfied with or without managers to

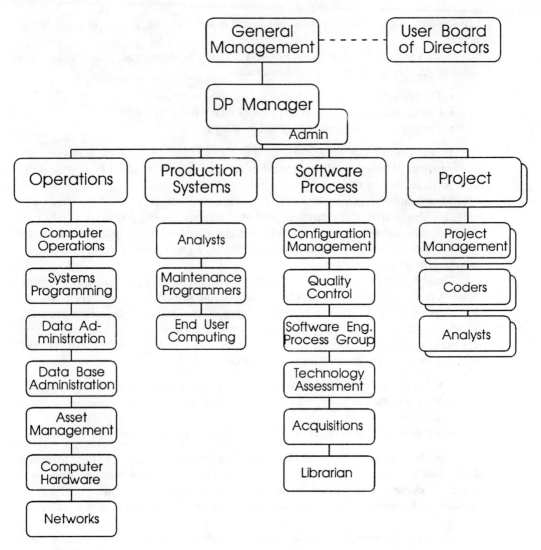

2-4 Organization of roles in an Oracle shop.

head each group. How many are named is a function of the size of the organization and its management philosophy.

Administration and personnel management

Data processing managers bear the same administrative responsibilities as their peers throughout the organization. They have to budget, hire, evaluate personnel, give raises, and obtain office space like every other manager.

The unique character of data processing people makes this aspect of the job interesting. DP employees are better paid than the average worker in most companies. The diverse nature of their skills can make them hard to evaluate. A manager has to be careful not to confuse technical dazzle with productive work. The differences in productivity among data processing staff are dramatic. A responsible DP manager regularly goes to the mat with personnel to get the salary increase which will keep a good person.

Summary

Data processing suffers more disasters than almost any other part of an organization. A good many are caused by unrealistic expectations and commitments. A substantial part of the data processing manager's job is dealing with the rest of the company, making sure that the work the department gets is well conceived and possible to do.

The role of information within an enterprise makes the MIS Director's job unique. There is an information processing facet in almost every major decision top management will make. An effective MIS director has to know the operations of the whole company well. He or she needs to develop and maintain a strategic information plan that parallels the enterprise's strategic plan. He or she needs the qualities of an ambassador or a broker, balancing the needs of different divisions of the enterprise against one another and balancing them all against the MIS shop's ability to produce.

Apart from the unique character of information, running a data processing organization is similar to other management assignments in the technology arena. There is nothing unique about managing a mixed group of specialists who must work together to accomplish a complex mission. DP management boils down to planning and organizing, finding good people, establishing an environment in which they can produce to the maximum, defending them when necessary, and making sure they get credit when it is due.

3
The Oracle environment

No set of standards can hope to apply to all Oracle installations. The breadth of the product line and the versatility of individual products makes for an extremely broad spectrum of users. The section below describes five archetypes that demonstrate the need for different types of organization and management disciplines.

Though individual shops' needs vary, the theme is consistent. Oracle, especially when used with CASE, makes it possible to streamline development procedures and shrink documentation requirements. Certain bedrock disciplines, however, cannot be ignored in any installation. This chapter helps you determine how much is needed beyond the bare essentials.

Operational models for Oracle installations

Oracle's most cherished objective has been to be available in every popular computer environment. They ring up new platforms like McDonald's rings up hamburgers. Oracle's aggressive sales strategies pushed the product to a similarly diverse group of users. No set of methodologies would apply to all of them. Oracle shops have to pick and choose management procedures just like picking software.

The Oracle shop

A distinct minority of Oracle's customers are major installations that use it for backbone systems. However, their numbers are growing fast. These are the pioneers in developing standards and techniques, such as the American Banker's Association, ARINC, and the Group Health Association. These shops have confronted all of the management issues covered by this book in the course of developing and fielding major applications systems.

The most common model for Oracle shops is a heavyweight central processor, typically a large DEC processor or cluster. In most such shops, both development and production are migrating from the mainframe to PCs in a client/server environment. A significant challenge for major Oracle users is controlling the computer horsepower and software dispersed throughout their environments.

Oracle shops have several advantages, the greatest of which is freedom from the dead hand of history. They can forget COBOL and standardize on techniques that work in an Oracle environment.

Oracle applications shops

An Oracle applications shop has end users but no major development activity. The applications include licensed software packages, systems written elsewhere in the company, and minor systems that are totally in the hands of end users.

The database administrator (DBA) is master of this realm. The major issues are tuning, space management, keymaps and other end-user issues, and providing technical support.

Whether or not it is planned, any active Oracle installation generates some programming activity. End users can do it using SQL*Plus, SQL*Calc, SQL*123, or Programmed Intelligence Corporation's Intelligent Query (IQ). A motivated DBA can program on the side to support his or her users. Either way, unless the company has provided development guidelines, the DBA's techniques will become a de facto standard.

Service bureau environments

Oracle is one DBMS among many in the service bureau. IBM mainframe installations often operate in this mode. Oracle is installed because some users need it to run an applications package or need to migrate a database up from PCs.

The service bureau will install its Oracle guru in one cubicle within a row that is also home to IMS, CICS, VTAM, and RACF experts. He or she helps users with nuts and bolts issues like allocating tables, importing data and debugging forms. The larger issues of standards and methodologies are either left to the user or codified in a life-cycle development methodology promulgated in the 1970s.

Users in a service bureau frequently wonder how people can get excited about the Oracle product. The Oracle they see is often filtered through block-mode terminals, driven by small slices of CPU power from overworked proprietary mainframes, and subject to inappropriate development and operations methodologies. These users are often the last to get new products such as Forms 3.0. The upgrades cost money and represent more burden on the already-saturated CPU.

The Food and Drug Administration's Parklawn Computer Center is an example of a well-run Oracle service bureau that has overcome these problems by tuning their DEC/IBM environment for Oracle. They achieve tremendous economies of scale as one of Oracle's largest single customers. Their users' operations are quite independent of one another. Each defines its own data structures and administers its own data.

Stand-alone PC users

Selling Oracle developer kits to PC users for $199 was one of Oracle's boldest moves to gain market share. It brought mainframe-class database functionality to everyone, and spawned a number of back-room Oracle operations. As has been the case with dBASE and every other PC-based database management system (DBMS), many Oracle applications have grown to the point that whole departments and even companies depend on them. What separates Oracle users from the others is that Oracle developers are not boxed in by the PC environment.

Even confirmed stand-alone users, a vanishing breed in this age of networking, can benefit from appropriate management methodologies. If they do not have version control of their database tables, forms, and reports they can cause themselves lots of embarrassment and rework. PC-based packages often involve significant numbers of machines. Just being PC based does not make the problems of distributing software, managing software configurations, and purchasing software any simpler.

Oracle software houses

Developing software for sale is a much more rigorous process than programming for in-house use. When money changes hands, it raises the users' expectations.

Software houses have to rigorously control product versions so that all of the software installed at a single user works together and can be maintained. They have to be able to manage multiple versions of database designs and programs concurrently, from past versions that are still being supported through new versions just being designed. Applications software houses have to be able to manage code they have customized under contract to support major customers.

Software houses tend to manage the software process better than applications shops. It starts with managing people. The entrepreneurs in charge are usually confident enough to recognize and compensate genius, because that genius contributes directly to the bottom line. They also recognize the benefits of modern development philosophies. Software houses are among the earliest and most enthusiastic users of CASE and object oriented technologies.

Management disciplines needed in different Oracle environments

Management implements the disciplines described in this book to save effort and money. There is a trade-off: the disciplines themselves take time and money to enforce. The more people there are to coordinate and money is at stake, the more control is justified. Table 3-1 shows generally which categories of Oracle shops need to formalize which management disciplines.

Integrated organizations need an integrated view of their data. Budget and general ledger systems represent the bottom line for private companies, and most business systems eventually tie to them. Manufacturing companies must tie together information from sales forecasts on one end to raw material suppliers on the other. Central data planning using CASE tools and centralized data administration are essential here.

At the other end of the spectrum, databases belonging to service bureau users and PC users tend to be independent of one another. A small application can exist without extensive data administration even if it is resident on a huge Oracle host.

Table 3-1   Management disciplines appropriate to Oracle environments.

Discipline	Oracle Shop	Oracle Application	Service Bureau	PC User	Software House
Project Management	Yes	No	Some users	Usually no	Yes
Configuration Management	Usually Yes	Usually no	Some users	Some-times	Yes
Formal Data Design Disciplines, such as CASE	Yes	No	Some users	Usually no	Yes
Articulated acquisition methodologies	Yes	Usually No	Yes	No	Yes
"Glass room" operating environment: backup/restore, disaster recovery	Yes	Yes	Yes	Depends on appli-cation	Yes
Password Security	Yes	Yes	Yes	Usually no	Yes
Assigned DBA	Yes	Shared	Yes	Shared if any	Yes
Data Administrator	Yes	Shared	Some-times	No	For in-house systems
Published life-cycle development standards	Yes	No	Some-times	Some-times	Yes

A shop can have standards without writing them from scratch. One approach is to do them by reference. Let standard software packages (such as ERwin for entity-relationship diagrams) define documentation standards. Let a book (such as this one) describe the standard approach to software acquisition.

It is often convenient not to be too specific about standards. In some environments, extensive system documentation standards are a barrier to writing code. The standards for design documentation assume a distant, adversarial relationship between developers and users: the specification had better be right, because that is what will be delivered. Federal sector managers who were interviewed get a lot of mileage out of prototypes. Working closely with their users, they shape a system until it is within a whisker of being complete; then they incorporate the prototype into the system design by reference.

Excessive standards serve their purpose of improving communications in an oblique way. They are such a bother that users and developers work closely to circumvent them.

Oracle overcomes the handicaps of a rigid environment

Standards suited to the application

Thomas Peters (1982) observes that people in the trenches, working outside the bureau-cracy, are responsible for most innovation in large corporations. Written standards reflect the scars of past experience—projects that were years late because the developers did not know what they were developing. Mainframe environments make it easier to enforce standards because computer materials are held hostage to the central processor.

Downsizing undermines standards. Individual users often have enough computer know-how and budget to do their system their way on their own machine. These users won't tolerate much control from the MIS department. Oracle is wonderful for them because it offers full-blown mainframe functionality on a small platform with none of the fetters.

Backroom tinkerers brag, rightly, that they are able to bring systems up much quicker than their MIS departments. Things get sticky when they try to integrate them into the corporate data processing scheme. The litany of "Oops" phrases often sounds like these:

- "I thought I had the whole thing backed up on the diskettes in this drawer."
- "How come your forecasting system doesn't take our order backlog into account?"
- "Why do we have to rekey the line items from the proposal en masse into order entry?"
- "I didn't know you needed those transactions. The system let me delete them."

The MIS department's inevitable and somewhat smug answer is that none of the problems would have occurred if the system planners had only followed standards.

Management's challenge is to sustain the creative drive which gets systems developed but at the same time make sure they fit into a global scheme. Corporate management and MIS management both must be involved, because the innovators often don't belong to the MIS department. The MIS department has to maintain a set of standards that make sense for the company and are palatable to the user departments.

Oracle's beauty is in its clean design and simplicity. The data design is key. If an application database recognizes the true relationships among the data elements with which it works, programming the application is a cookbook function. In fact, Oracle CASE can do it automatically. If the application database uses data-element definitions consistent with other applications in the enterprise, the applications can usually be integrated.

Oracle systems, provided they are properly conceived, can be subjected to standards control as they grow. Different types of Oracle installations need different sets of standards, and even a single installation has to use judgment in enforcing standards on all systems.

Stealth acquisition

Assembling a development environment requires innovation. The best programmers are constantly tinkering. A PC developer will have box upon box of licensed software on the shelf and will be pleased to tell you which are fabulous and which are duds that are never used.

The economics of PCs are wonderful. It is cheaper to buy and try a package than to conduct an exhaustive evaluation. The packages that do get used will more than pay for the ones that get thrown out.

Software houses now write most of their products in C. Just about all major hits in the PC marketplace are available in the home territory for C—Unix. A development shop can buy the Unix or LAN server version of the really worthwhole software and make it a shop standard, available (inexpensively) to all users.

This process rationalizes software acquisition in an Oracle environment. The PC versions of most software products for developers cost under $1000. A programmer's immediate manager should have the authority to buy them. When a developer complains of the tedium of redrawing entity-relationships by hand or using Paintbrush or Corel Draw, let the developer buy ERwin. It makes better use of expensive time and lets the employee know the organization cares. A Unix shop that forces programmers to use the vi editor just because it comes free with the system is as backwards as a PC user who sticks with EDLIN. The economics call for creative shopping. Chapter 16 describes the standard means of finding out what's on the market.

4

The implications of CASE
for Oracle developers

Computer-aided software engineering, or CASE, has grown out of the observation that a data system can be abstracted into an expression much simpler than its software implementation. Most of the code is overhead, which is incidental to the main function of the system. The overhead component is predictable; every program needs to open files, check for errors, check for end of file, report errors to the operator, and so on.

The abstracted expression of a requirement or a design has a number of useful properties. Human minds can grasp a much larger design that is absent the fluff of programming. The pure design lends itself to several kinds of cross validation. Also, an abstracted design can be expressed in whatever source language is most useful for a given implementation environment. It is portable.

The CASE process has far-reaching implications for Oracle developers. Developers can achieve the truest-form of integration at the level of design. The functional benefits of licensed software can at last be realized without paying a significant penalty in adapting it to the environment. The most significant implication of all affects employment: programmers are being automated out of a job. Each MIS manager and professional needs to prepare to staff the jobs that will remain after CASE realizes its potential.

CASE is the name applied to both a development philosophy and sets of tools to implement that philosophy. This chapter explores the implications of CASE for the industry; the management issues in using CASE are addressed throughout the book.

CASE components

Data about data itself, and by extension about data systems, is called *metadata*. Developing a metadata design complete enough to fully represent a generalized system has been the major challenge for the CASE industry. Their models continue to evolve. Metadata models carry data on:

- Entities, tables, and data file records, as collections of related data are variously known.

- Attributes, columns, and data items, the individual elements of data within entities.
- Relationships among entities that are expressed through shared fields.
- Processes that use data and create information.
- Business rules, the logic used within processes.
- The flow of data among processes.
- Formatting rules and preferences that govern the physical layout of data on screens and reports.

All vendors now handle data modeling reasonably well. They are not as far along on representing business rules, procedural logic, and presentation formats.

The database of metadata is at the heart of a CASE system. Oracle calls it the CASE dictionary; IBM calls it the data repository. As Fig. 4-1 shows, the rest of CASE consists of processes that maintain and exploit the dictionary. These include design tools to graphically represent data dictionary contents, reverse engineering tools to abstract metadata from previously coded systems and insert it into the dictionary, and generation tools to express a design in compilable source code.

It is no accident that Oracle has been a CASE pioneer. The concept of CASE fits especially well with the philosophy expressed in the whole Oracle product line, which can be stated as, "Tell me what you want, not how to do it." Oracle's nonprocedural tools are a natural output language for CASE generators. The tools are definitional like CASE itself.

Oracle is in a unique position among the major CASE vendors. The others, Texas

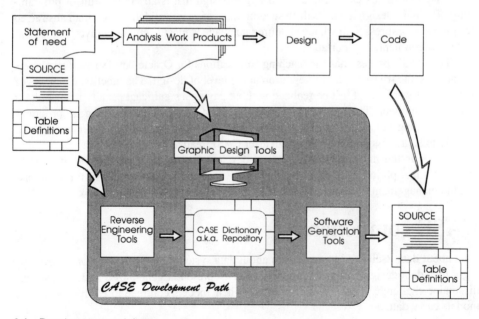

4-1 Development work flow.

Instruments, Knowledgeware, Intersolv, and Bachman, are conceived to support the whole data processing industry. They have taken on the hard problems of extracting logic from existing third generation (mostly COBOL and C) systems and generating COBOL and C code. Oracle has set itself an immediate task of reverse engineering and generating only Oracle code. The idea is that a comprehensive solution within the confines of the Oracle universe will be worth more in the marketplace than a partial solution within a broader sphere. Even Oracle's partial solution has been challenge enough that ample room remains for improvement.

Oracle's 4GL languages eliminate the need to generate the table and file handling logic that a compiled language would require. Most of the exacting and repetitive database-handling code required for managing data integrity and presenting error messages is handled in standardized fashion through relational database management systems (RDBMS) and tools. The source code that CASE generates is definitional like CASE itself. Specifying to SQL*Forms 3.0 that table A and table B are in a master-detail relationship with cascading deletes elegantly sums up what would take several pages of COBOL to accomplish.

CASE tools' metadata implementations have had much better success with data design than procedural logic. Other vendors' products that generate compiled languages like C and COBOL have to handle logic modules. Not surprisingly, their design-level expression of procedures closely resembles COBOL or PASCAL IF-THEN-ELSE phrases. Measured against the CASE objective of using abstraction to simplify a design they are not very successful. The CASE source is almost as verbose and obtuse as its expression in generated 3GL code.

Oracle's structure has allowed it simply not to deal with procedural code. As Fig. 4-2 shows, nonprocedural languages invert the relationship between definition and procedural logic. The body of an Oracle program is definitional code, within which exists discrete nuggets of procedural logic. Conversely, third-generation languages set nuggets of definition within a procedural context. Oracle's CASE approach up to now has been to generate procedural code only to support functions which are described nonprocedurally within CASE. Data integrity, editing, lookups, and lists of values processing head the list of such functions in SQL*Forms. Their handling of the unique logic which represents business rules is:

- Users will incorporate most business rules into standard subroutines. CASE does not deal with the definition or generation of such routines, but it will record which functions call them. In the future, the product might manage the source code for such subroutines.
- Programmers can modify generated code to add whatever logic is unique to a single module. It is more machine efficient and almost as design efficient to write it in the target language source instead of a pseudolanguage at the CASE design level. CASE regeneration will preserve the custom modifications.
- Oracle is devising a systematic approach to handle logic from its capture as business rules through its implementation as code. As this is difficult work and the efficiencies gained in such abstraction are not overwhelming, Oracle does not feel great pressure to rush it to the marketplace.

ORACLE 4GLs

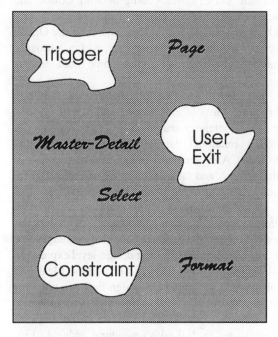

Islands of procedure in a sea of definition

PRECOMPILED 3GLs

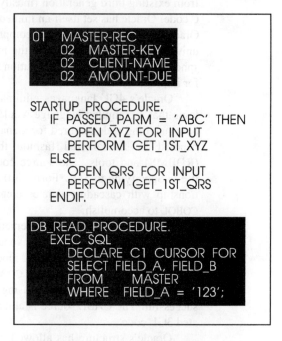

```
01    MASTER-REC
   02    MASTER-KEY
   02    CLIENT-NAME
   02    AMOUNT-DUE

STARTUP_PROCEDURE.
   IF PASSED_PARM = 'ABC' THEN
      OPEN XYZ FOR INPUT
      PERFORM GET_1ST_XYZ
   ELSE
      OPEN QRS FOR INPUT
      PERFORM GET_1ST_QRS
   ENDIF.

DB_READ_PROCEDURE.
   EXEC SQL
      DECLARE C1 CURSOR FOR
      SELECT FIELD_A, FIELD_B
      FROM      MASTER
      WHERE   FIELD_A = '123';
```

Islands of definition in a sea of procedure

4-2 Inversion of definition and procedure in Oracle's 4GLs.

The CASE products available today are merchantable even if they are a long way from complete. They provide a standard protocol for analysts and designers to express their work. They and their application users can share their thoughts much more efficiently using CASE conventions and outputs. CASE cross-reference checks surface anomalies that would otherwise be hard to find. Even though the code CASE tools can generate usually has to be modified, it does a good job with the voluminous and exacting tasks of dealing with data. Figure 4-3, which shows the relative maturity of the different aspects of Oracle CASE, applies fairly well to other vendors' products as well.

Fortified by the native capabilities of their RDBMS, SQL*Forms and SQL*ReportWriter, Oracle's CASE does a good job handling data relationships, formats and edits. Presentation formats were greatly improved in Version 5 of the product. It now accepts global specifications for how screens and reports should look. These can be overridden as required by module and even field-specific definitions. Oracle is working on presentation issues like pop-up windows, tiling, multipage blocks and multiline rows. As of now they have accommodated procedural logic without implementing support for it. Their CASE tools leave the definition of user roles and data security issues up to the analyst and DBA.

Implications of CASE
for systems integration

CASE will make it possible to raise the overall level of integration among applications. Integration is much more a matter of data than processes. Several applications usually share the same data files or tables. There is normally one owner application responsible for maintaining it. That owner lets other applications refer to the data to avoid redundancy, inconsistency, and duplicate work.

The most common medium of data exchange between applications remains a flat file of sequential records written to an operating system file. The bottom diagram in Fig. 4-4 illustrates the fact that it usually requires an interface program to collect and reformat data along the way.

The quest of hierarchical and network database designers in the 1970s was a fully integrated database. Their vision of Nirvana was that when someone on the assembly line dropped a screw, the automated systems could automatically adjust the reorder quantity and simultaneously compute the effect on the bottom line. It never happened. Today's programmers are working furiously to unravel what they wrought when they got close— huge lumps of code that mightily resist efforts at piecemeal replacement of subsystems.

Relational databases made it easier to integrate applications that were not conceived to work together. The essential improvement was to do away with structural elements such as pointers, which were distinct from the data itself. The result was that if it looked like two databases used the same definition for a customer name (for instance), they could probably be made to share the same master table without redoing the database. The RDBMS became the common denominator. The middle diagram in Fig. 4-4 shows how two applications written for the same DBMS, each having its own logical database schema, can communicate by sharing views.

Sharing views has its limitations. It can only overcome minor differences in data structures. For example, it works when an application that keeps 20-character names

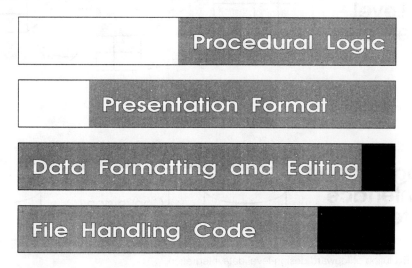

4-3 Maturity of different elements of Oracle CASE.

INCREASING DEGREES OF DATA INTEGRATION

First Application   Exchange Medium   Second Application

Design Level Integration

Common Tables

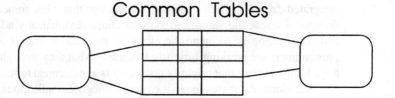

Database Level Integration

Exchanged Views

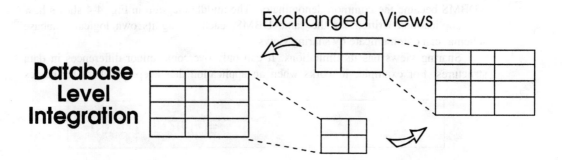

Programmed Interface Integration

Exchange of Reformatted Files

Conversion Program

4-4 Evolution of topward design-level data integration.

shares them with an application that expects 24, but it works only to a limited extent when it is 24 into 20. It works more or less when an application that keeps separate last and first names shares with one that expects a combined name field, but hardly at all the other way around. The single truly satisfactory way to have two applications share database tables is to design them to do so.

The only practical means until now to achieve design-level integration has been to buy an integrated suite of applications software from a single vendor, write whole suites of applications in house, or build a mixed system using one vendor's package as a base. Because large bases of installed applications have made these alternatives unworkable for most shops, today's norm for data exchange remains swapping files. The high standard is sharing tables through the use of views.

Design-level integration, now possible through CASE, resolves these problems. When all of the systems to be integrated are available in CASE, rationalizing the data design to suit the needs of each is a straightforward matter. Getting them into CASE is the issue. The alternatives are:

1. Design the system in CASE to start with. This works with new code.
2. Reverse engineer the system into CASE. This is practical with simple to moderately complex Oracle systems. It is possible in a very limited way using other vendors' reverse engineering tools on code from other sources.
3. Acquire a CASE design along with source code from a package vendor.

Options 2 and 3 are just beginning to be viable. Large-scale integration at the DBMS level will grow significantly as they evolve over the next few years.

Design-level integration will make packaged software more attractive. Packaged solutions almost always enjoy a tremendous advantage in function over custom systems because their developers can afford to be thorough when the cost of development is spread over many users. The disadvantage is in customization and integration. The cost of force-fitting purchased software into an installation might negate the advantage in function. Both these liabilities disappear when the package is delivered in CASE format. Integration and customization can be done efficiently at the design level.

Distributing packaged software at the design level can also make proprietary software more efficient. Package vendors today resort to some unusual tricks to generalize their software. Oracle uses "flex fields" in its accounting software. McCormick and Dodge (now D&B) uses a black-box runtime module to handle support for all the terminal environments in which it operates. Most package data designs include more fields than any single customer is likely to need. CASE will make it possible to sort these issues out at the design level so the generated source code doesn't carry any extra baggage. Figure 4-5 shows how the customization process will change once licensed software is distributed in a CASE format.

Version control is a major headache for package vendors. Each customer wants the package to work a little differently. Oracle's CASE regeneration facility will make it easy for either the vendor or customer to perpetuate customized changes from one release to another. The problem of maintaining multiple versions of a package for multiple languages and platforms will be greatly diminished when CASE generators are available for the different target environments.

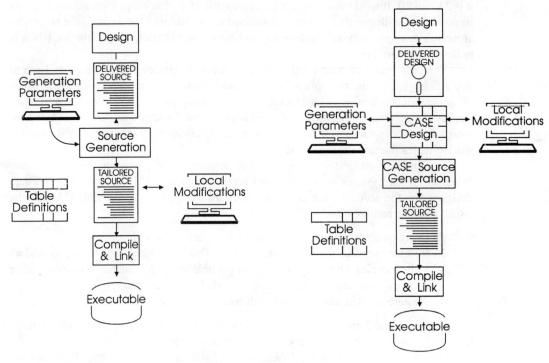

4-5 Licensed software design-level distribution under CASE.

Oracle's CASE Version 5 makes it possible to distribute some Oracle systems in CASE source. The new regeneration facilities are necessary to preserve the customized triggers and screen formats that are essential to any software for sale. Its menu and report generation facilities give it the means to produce the three elements of a basic system: a system structure, database maintenance procedures, and report processes.

Changes in life-cycle documentation procedures with CASE

The user of any piece of software is forced to adopt procedures compatible with that system. A CASE tool forces structure on the development process. There are standards and procedures inherent in its operation.

The standards mean that the changes which an MIS shop makes in moving to a CASE approach have to extend to its standards and procedures. It used to be that documentation carried the sum of all knowledge about a system from one development stage to another. CASE assumes most of that responsibility now. Developers need narrative documentation on an exception basis because CASE tools still capture only the *what* and not the *why* of a system.

Data gathering in the strategic planning and analysis phases of a project is the same as ever, except to the extent that reverse engineering is able to abstract requirements from an existing system. CASE dramatically changes how collected data are handled. It provides a systematic means to arrange data about the requirement. It prompts the analyst for statistics that would be otherwise easy to overlook, such as volume, volatility, and *CRUD* (create, read, update, and delete) characteristics of data fields and records (attributes and entities) within business functions. CASE improves the graphic representation of data relationships so much that it profoundly affects how the analyst does business. It is possible, and in fact highly desirable, to print a series of entity-relationship diagrams as the analyst and users work together towards a comprehensive data model.

Functional decomposition in Oracle's CASE is top-down and structured, not object oriented. The analyst can show a system decomposition by major functions. It does not handle algorithms. Business rules and other processes destined to be implemented as subroutines must be described in text. The CASE tool goes no further than capturing the fact that a given module uses the business rule or subroutine.

The data orientation of CASE in general, and Oracle's implementation in particular, is entirely consistent with relational design. Formats, constraints, edits, and lookups are not properties of a program but the data that a program uses. Therefore, in defining the entities and attributes used in the functions, and whether the data are created, read, updated, or deleted (CRUD again), the analyst has almost completely specified the processing in simple to moderate programs. Analysis and design standards need to call for written documents to describe application-specific logic. The standards should also require a written record of the major compromises and negotiations that are reflected in the design. The logic behind such decisions as specifying separate entities for *person* and *corporation* rather than a single party entity with subtypes must be explained.

The main structure of a CASE system design derives directly from the analysis. Only unique features introduced in the design phase need documentation. That includes the subroutines for handling business rules, complex edits, and utility functions. The menu structure usually needs explanation. Menus usually follow the needs of users rather than the logical decomposition of the system. Design specifications have to define access control for both data and processes. CASE does not address testing; the design documentation has to specify test data and testing procedures.

CASE-generated code contains reams of comments. The Oracle shop's standards and procedures have to ensure that programmer-written code measures up to CASE. Most shops will succeed by rigorously applying their existing 3GL coding standards to whatever custom code is needed to modify the CASE-generated modules or in stand-alone subroutines.

CASE makes its primary contribution to user documentation through the CASE dictionary. Describing the data elements in a system and their usage is a major part of the job. Those descriptions are available through CASE for use in online help systems and hard-copy documents. System developers still need to describe how each individual program handles the user's business functions.

The essential disciplines of project management and configuration management are not yet included in Oracle's CASE product. Oracle has put some of the hooks in place. The designer can specify the language and complexity as an aid to estimating the level of effort to code a module. Version control for the design, but not the generated code, is carried in the CASE dictionary. A shop that turns to CASE will find the management of outside factors such as hardware and package software relatively more important as the task of writing custom code becomes easier.

The impact of CASE on Oracle itself

Today's Oracle environment facilitates application of the CASE technologies. It provides a constrained and predictable source of objects for reverse engineering. The target languages for generation are similarly limited and compatible with the CASE tool. The milieu is ideal for nurturing an evolving product. In the short term, Oracle's CASE products will bind customers even more closely to the company.

Oracle is active in CASE industry groups working to develop standards for exchanging metadata. Their objective is to make a design portable from one vendor's CASE to another. Figure 4-6 shows the exchange. By extension this means that reverse-engineering and code-generation tools will have an industry-wide scope. When another vendor develops a plausible reverse engineering product for COBOL, Oracle can take advantage of it to move applications into their environment. Conversely, Oracle users will be able to migrate out. All this assumes a more complete Oracle CASE product, in particular one capable of handling procedural logic.

The company will need a strategy to hold onto its users when leaving Oracle's

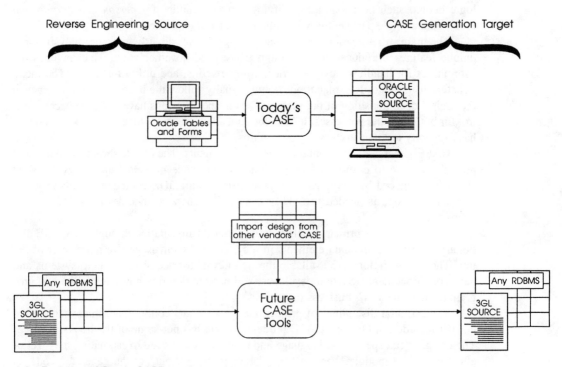

4-6 Evolution of Oracle CASE to other environments.

execution-time environment becomes an option. A user's major incentives to depart are economic. Oracle's 4GL products are interpretive, which means they take more resources to run than compiled code, and they require paying for licensed runtime modules. Oracle can respond to both concerns by developing compilers for SQL*Forms and SQL*ReportWriter. In addition, these would give Oracle the competitive advantage of generating code for a compiled language designed to be compatible with the CASE dictionary. Oracle's metadata language extensions would be more likely to flow through into generated SQL*Forms or SQL*ReportWriter source than COBOL or C.

The impact of CASE
on data processing careers

The premise of CASE is that the substance of a system can be abstracted to the analysis and design level. One hundred percent success would eliminate the need for programmers—everything downstream of design would be handled automatically. Though that

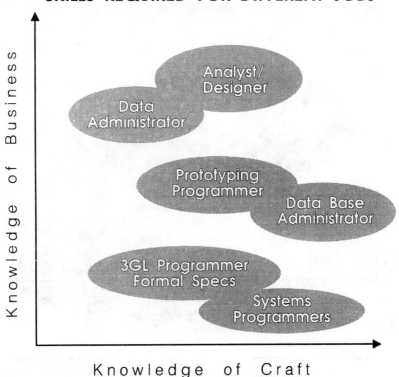

RELATIVE LEVELS OF BUSINESS AND COMPUTER SKILLS REQUIRED FOR DIFFERENT JOBS

4-7 Traditional levels of business and computer skills required for different jobs.

objective will never be completely realized, CASE is going to have a dramatic impact on the mix of job skills required in the workplace.

The traditional mix of job skills align themselves by business and craft, as shown in Fig. 4-7. Programmers have needed craft skills, namely a knowledge of tools of data processing. A remarkable number have shied away from learning about the business problems their code is written to handle. Analysts and designers have needed a knowledge of the business, as well as of analysis methodologies, and some familiarity with the hardware and software in their target environments.

CASE development will require more people with a high level of both types of skills. Figure 4-8 shows them as communications and implementation skills to emphasize the fact that communications with the user on one side and with the implementers on the other is essential to the analysis process. Analyst/designers will do what they have always done in designing systems. What is new is that CASE moves implementation-level decisions up to the design phase. The CASE designer resolves details of screen layout, presentation formats and other details that used to be up to the programmer. Most programs will be 90 percent complete when the designer is finished. Who should logically handle the other 10 percent? Probably the designer.

The most significant benefit of CASE has proven to be in program maintenance. Traditional maintenance has been a three-step process:

1. Reverse engineer the existing code to figure out what it does, where to put the changes and what other parts of the system they will affect.

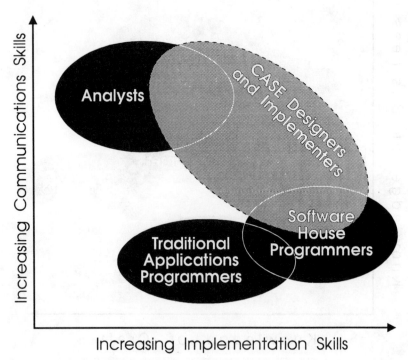

4-8 Communication and implementation skills required in a CASE environment.

2. Code the changes.
3. Perform regression tests to make sure the changes do not have any unexpected side effects.

Writing the code is by far the least part of the effort.

By contrast, making a functional change in CASE involves mainly just updating the design, which the analyst presumably already knows. CASE automatically validates the consistency of the design as the change is made and automatically applies changes to every module that needs to be updated. Re-engineering features ensure that logic that was previously added downstream of CASE remains intact. The net effect is that maintenance is much less work, and it will be done more by designers than programmers.

Programmers' roles will be more specialized with CASE. In place of writing the backbone code of an application, they will do system-level subroutines in PL/SQL and 3GLs from specifications written by the designer. Oracle is still an SQL-based system; there will always be complex SQL queries that are beyond the CASE ability to generate. There will be an ongoing need for programmers—but fewer and smarter. It goes without saying that programmers will have to become familiar with how CASE works and the nature of the code it generates.

Figure 4-9 is a graphic exhibit of the impact of CASE. The left-hand diagram shows that the number of people required to produce a quantum of work will continue to shrink. The right one shows that because programming and maintenance shrink the fastest, analysis and design work will grow as a percentage of the total work load. The solid and dotted lines show implementation and maintenance work shifting forward to designers as a result of CASE. The net is that applications programmers will go the way of blacksmiths, milk deliverers, telephone operators, and plasterers. There will always be a need for a few, but not the legions there are today.

A plan for current practitioners

Managers and technicians need to prepare for the changes CASE will bring. Management needs to plan future staffing requirements and their staffs have to develop skills which will

PROJECTED SHIFT OF SKILL REQUIREMENTS WITH CASE

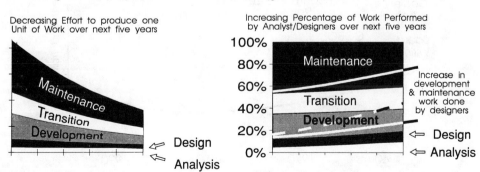

4-9 Increasing percentage of work done by analysts and designers.

be marketable in five years. The unprecedented layoffs of data processing professionals during 1991 and 1992 are only a preview. The industry is changing. There will never be the kind of employment growth seen in the last two decades. Moreover, the level of skill demanded of those who stay in the business is going up. Figure 4-10 shows that amount of brain power, what Microsoft's management calls *bandwidth,* required to work in the field decreased for three decades straight as the industry devised more and more productive tools. The routine tasks are now so easy they are automated—all that is left is the hard stuff—and the curve is climbing again.

Programmers will find they need to reposition themselves into specialties where there will continue to be work. In other words, they must work in the areas where hard problems remain that automation cannot soon eliminate. An Oracle manager should encourage them to:

- Get as much training as possible. Learn relational design and analysis.
- Work closely with end users. Get into as much of a prototype mode as possible.
- Make every effort to learn the users' applications and the company's business. MIS professionals need to broaden their contacts throughout the enterprise.
- Get CASE tool experience. Though employers' greatest needs will be for journeyman analysts and relational systems designers as they move into CASE, most perceive their need to be for people who have used CASE.
- Stay current on technology by reading the trade press.
- Improve credentials as a specialist such as a DBA, Oracle tuner, CASE tools expert, systems programmer, network specialist or any other type of craft expert.

Summary

CASE's objective is to automate the software development process. It will achieve the traditional benefits of automation, a standardized product with improved quality and pro-

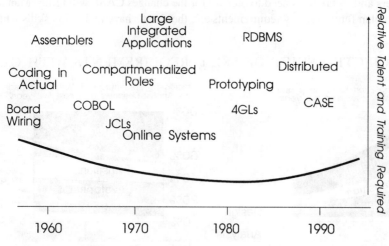

4-10 Data processing trendline in data processing.

ductivity. Standardization will make it possible to achieve integration on a scale that has eluded designers for decades. The productivity improvements brought by CASE will result in a fundamental change to the employment structure of the industry. Programmers especially will need to learn new skills as their traditional functions become automated.

CASE is going to bring unprecedented economies to enterprises that use data processing. It may be the long-sought tool to give them control over data processing system costs, quality, and schedules. It paves the way for other efficiencies in high-level integration and broader use of packaged software.

These economies are achieved by making it easier for analysts and designers to do a thorough job and by reducing the role of the programmer. Data processing managers will be forced to change the way they run their operations and programmers to re-examine what they have to offer in the labor market as CASE becomes a workplace reality.

5
Developing
a data processing strategy

A corporate strategy establishes long-term goals and deploys company resources to attain objectives leading towards those goals. Data processing strategy shadows that of the corporation. The MIS department is one of the corporate resources that figures into corporate planning, and information systems are frequently essential in the execution of a corporate plan.

The MIS department must be part of corporate strategic planning because a modern company moves on information. A corporate strategy is unworkable unless there are information systems in place to coordinate the activities that support it. The MIS department helps the corporation to agree on strategies that are workable from a data-processing perspective. In doing so, they develop application-level strategic plans that show at a macro level how the suites of applications that support a strategy will be implemented. Their departmental strategy derives from the corporate plan. It projects the staff, technology, organization, and management that will be needed to support corporate objectives. In the final analysis, MIS participates actively in three interrelated strategic plans: corporate, application, and departmental, as shown in Fig. 5-1.

A corporate strategic plan goes far beyond data processing. However, the data processing department's input is vital to project the investment, risk, and schedule for many types of projects. The computer experts' estimates go into the weighting process top executives use to balance one alternative against another.

The systems strategy for a given application defines its scope, estimates of the types of hardware, networks, and software needed to support the application, identification of potential vendors of hardware, systems software and applications, and a quantification of the risk factors associated with the project. Applications strategy is the first phase of system development, and as such is described in chapter 15 on procedures.

The MIS department's strategy exists at a higher level. It takes into account:

- The workload forecast, which consists of projects within the strategic plan, lower-visibility projects that will come out of the departments, and ongoing maintenance and production.

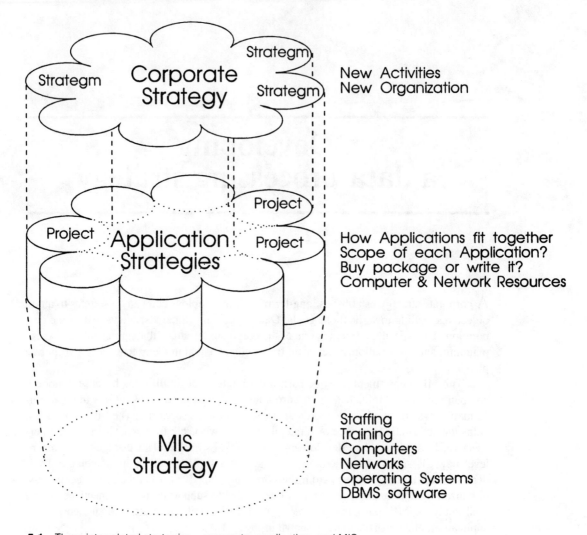

5-1 Three interrelated strategies—corporate, application, and MIS.

- Maintaining and upgrading the installation, including computers, networks, systems software, RDBMS software, and tools.
- Staffing levels by specialty and skill level, including training, hiring, and promotion.
- Organization and management, including the position of DP within the organization, the internal organization of the DP department, and the management methodologies to be used.
- A budget and schedule to realize and support the above.

It derives from the corporate strategy and has to change with it.

MIS support of corporate strategy

Top management needs to borrow on MIS department expertise to estimate the costs of new information systems. The benefits of the systems they can usually estimate themselves. MIS usually needs to put projects in context before they can estimate the costs: what other systems can it build on, when is it needed, and what functions will it do?

MIS and corporate strategic plans are interdependent. Top management suggests a direction; MIS develops feasibility, cost, and risk projections. Then top management decides what they can live with. When the dust settles, the MIS department has a few years' backlog of major projects with which they can flesh out their own strategic plan. The cycle never ends. The executives have to let MIS know when they change direction, and MIS has to let top management know when their estimates of cost, time, and feasibility change substantially.

Data systems always represent some compromise of function, speed, and cost. The MIS experts who support corporate strategic planning cannot stop at merely costing out the ideas that pop out of general management brainstorming sessions. They have to seek the best compromises through a dialog, and they especially have to update management on what the technology can do. MIS supports corporate strategic planning both by answering questions and by making sure they get asked intelligent questions. This process takes some preparation. Table 5-1 shows that the MIS department has to anticipate corporate planning by keeping current on technology and keeping up-to-date models of existing systems that can be used as a baseline for plotting change.

MIS can introduce its own agenda into strategic planning. They can frequently argue that there is money to be saved by replacing current hardware and software systems. Economies come in the form of reduced machine costs, reduced maintenance costs, reduced development costs for new systems, and positioning the company to take advantage of new ADP technologies.

Corporate planning involves planning better ways to support existing functions as often as it does adding new ones. The corporate data model maintained by MIS provides a measure of the integration of a corporation's various strategies. Data systems can be an indicator of discontinuity within an enterprise. Information plunging in and out of departmental computer systems in a serpentine fashion is a fair indication that the various fiefdoms within a company perform overlapping functions or are not coordinating their efforts well. MIS planning tools such as entity-relationship diagrams and data flow diagrams can be as useful for rationalizing corporate operations as for planning data systems.

Neither a company nor a data processing department plans in a vacuum. Any plan has to start with the status quo. It must support ongoing activities; new directions are often expressed by the ways in which they depart from current practice. The same is true in data processing. New requirements must be defined in terms of both existing information systems and new corporate directions.

The information systems strategy

An enterprise's information systems strategy is its blueprint to support its evolving automation requirements. It is made up of plans for the MIS department and other elements

Table 5-1   Procedures for enterprise and MIS strategic planning.

Business Strategy	Information Systems Strategy
	Model enterprise information processes and requirements as reflected by existing systems.
	Continually monitor developments in technology and inform users how they might benefit from them.
Convene a strategy group to reset goals and objectives	
Working in subgroups, develop proposed business strategies: new objectives and the investments and organization to support them.	Interview users to learn about current and proposed business functions.
	Create a modified information model to show proposed business activities, information flows, and data entities and relationships.
Develop financial and philosophical justification for proposed plans in subgroups.	Perform highest-level system design and create a work breakdown structure to generate estimated costs of management proposals.
Reconvene the strategy group to decide which strategies to pursue and set priorities and schedules for them.	
	Develop a technology strategy to support the business strategy.

such as end-user computing, PCs and departmental systems, communications, and outside computing services for which MIS might have staff responsibility. There are usually a project and a continuing operations component. Continuing operations includes support for systems already in place, the normal maintenance and enhancement activity associated with production systems, and development of new systems that are too small to register in the corporate strategic plan. The computer equipment and development costs of major projects are accounted individually. Giving them visibility as individual entities makes it easier to project the effects of a schedule or scope change.

The MIS strategy cuts across all applications. It sums the aggregate requirement of all projects and continuing operations to determine resource requirements over time. Figure 5-2 shows some of the line items that usually appear in the MIS strategy.

An MIS strategy is an exercise in four-dimensional vision. It has to picture the full scope of ongoing activities and the resources that each individual project will demand. Then, the strategy must sum the resources by month or quarter over future years to determine the aggregate demand at each point in time. It is a tough exercise. It is certainly easier when data for individual projects is in a common and tractable format, such as a standard project management system or spreadsheet, as described in chapter 17. A standard format makes it easy to add up conforming items, such as personnel requirements by skill, direct expenditures to outside vendors, and end-user PC requirements to get an overall picture.

Management Methodologies
    Organization
    Development and Maintenance Procedures
Staffing efforts to be managed in-house
    Numbers of people by category and skill level
    Plans to arrive at the above:
        Hiring
        Training
        Promotion
        Contracting
Physical Resources
    Occupancy
    Furniture and Equipment
Computer Resources
    Processing capacity
    Storage capacity
    Technologies to employ
    Software Environment
        Operating System
        RDBMS
        Development tools
        End user tools
    End-user computers: PCs and work stations
Communications Resources
    LAN and WANs
    Remote access computing
    Phones, Fax and voice mail
Contracting Activities
    Systems Development
    Maintenance and Support
    Facilities management
    Software packages
Schedule
Time-phased Budget

5-2   Line items in an MIS strategy.

How the job is done has a large bearing on the kind of resources required. Projecting the workload is only a start. An MIS plan has to be grounded in assumptions about how things will be done. Will the work be contracted or done in house? Will Oracle CASE be used? Is the department free to optimize their standards and procedures to suit the development tools? Are there any staffing constraints such as head-count ceilings, salary caps, or restrictions on training that stand in the way of assembling an optimal staff? Are there any impediments, such as a long-standing commitment to one hardware vendor, to the selection of optimal solutions? The first line item in the MIS strategy sets forth the assumptions about organization and procedures.

People to make it happen are a major element of any strategy, but they may be ignored in the shuffle. Application strategists can easily conclude that an NCR 3700 system will be a better host for an upgraded application than the current IBM MVS system. It is easy to overlook the drag-along implications: the MVS systems programmers are no longer needed, but there will be a Unix requirement, the DBA will need to go to class on Unix and character-mode operations. As chapter 4 indicates, going CASE has a profound impact on the size, skills, and basic talent levels required in an organization. The MIS director needs to find automated tools to help see the ripple effects of strategy decisions on bottom-line resource requirements.

The fluidity of staffing in an Oracle shop often hides a lack of planning. It doesn't make sense to make five-year plans for people whose average tenure is two years. The best organizations, however, offer their employees a work environment in which they are respected and are given good development tools and interesting projects. Those people stick around. They almost demand a personnel development strategy of training, promotions, and varied assignments that will enable them to grow to meet future staff needs. The MIS staffing strategy needs to project how much of future requirements can be handled by current staff (allowing for attrition), and by deduction, how many and what types of hires are needed and when.

Summary

MIS must be involved in corporate strategic planning because almost all corporate activities depend on information support. A strategy is not viable without the needed information support; its cost justification has to include the cost of automated systems support.

MIS must organize to support corporate planning in a staff capacity. They need high-level models and abstractions of the current operation to serve as a baseline for projecting changes, and they need to be able to research the cost and risk in developing support for proposed corporate actions.

Planning to support individual stratagems is the first phase of systems development. It employs the same analysis and estimating disciplines that are repeated at decision points throughout the life cycle of an application. The enterprise-wide management information systems strategy embraces ongoing operations as well as all new projects. It sums the resource requirements of each individual element and projects the staffing and infrastructure requirements to support the whole work load.

The MIS strategy is built on assumptions about organization, management and procedures as well as the projected work load. It is highly advantageous to use an automated process to sum the resource requirements of individual projects and factor in risk and schedule.

6
DP in the corporate hierarchy

Computing and computing expertise is migrating from data processing shops into user departments. Data processing shops have long since lost their hegemony. User departments with a job to do make an open market decision whether it is easier to do it on their own with PCs and departmental machines or put up with corporate MIS.

The MIS department is still essential for company-wide systems. MIS usually defends the company's interests by seeing that data processing decisions are optimized at the enterprise level rather than the department level. They ensure that departmental systems interconnect to the degree necessary and make sure that the company benefits from economies of scale.

A solution that frequently works is to make the MIS department a profit center. As such it competes for business with outside contractors and encourages user departments to make intelligent investment decisions by paying fair value for automation support.

Upper management's evaluation of the MIS department has to include both its operational and staff roles. As an operational entity it is responsible for developing systems and supporting production. As a staff entity it can set standards and procedures for the whole organization, research ADP technologies and contribute to strategic planning in user departments and the enterprise as a whole.

Sharing work with the departments

A company acts as a single entity because its departments coordinate their efforts to achieve a common mission. They tell each other what they are doing by exchanging automated data. The MIS department's charge is to make that data exchange work and to facilitate communications between the company and the outside world.

Table 6-1 shows how modes of sharing data processing functions between the MIS and user departments. The MIS department sets standards and coordinates enterprise-wide planning and data exchange. Beyond that it is a matter of culture and economics who does the implementation.

Table 6-1 Distribution of responsibility between MIS and users.

	MIS	User with MIS support	MIS with user support	User
Strategic Information Plan			X	
Data Dictionary	X			
Data Administration	X			
Data Exchange standards	X			
Computer architecture standards	X			
System Development Methodology	X			
Hardware and Network Acquisition	X	X		
Systems Programming	X	PCs		
Computer Operations	X	X		
Systems Analysis and Design		X	X	
Application Programming		X	X	
Software Package Acquisition		X	X	
End-User Programming		X		X

Is MIS a cost center or profit center?

Most companies started using data processing to keep financial records and to control operations long ago. The MIS department usually belonged to the bean counters. MIS was a cost center because financial management was a cost center. Figure 6-1 shows a typical organization chart from about 1965.

Thirty years ago, mainframe computers were expensive and specialized. It made sense to contain the costs and expertise within an MIS department. Financially, the department was seen as a cost center that supported the whole enterprise.

Departmental minicomputers started chipping away at the centralized philosophy in the 1970s and the PC revolution of the 1980s demolished it completely. Now everybody has computers and they don't need MIS to tell them how to use them. The costs of computers, programming, and operations are spread throughout the company.

The case is made that the MIS department should be a profit center, competing for system development business with user departments or contractors that the users engage directly. MIS departments frequently do not even want to bother with isolated applications, and they encourage decentralized development. Table 6-2 outlines the relative advantages of a profit center approach opposed to a cost center organization.

The federal government runs a number of Oracle shops as service bureaus. Tom Reddin's Food and Drug Administration Parklawn Computer Center is a model profit center. His users are free to shop around for computers and services. Tom promotes the use of his training and DBA services by absorbing them into overhead, making them free to

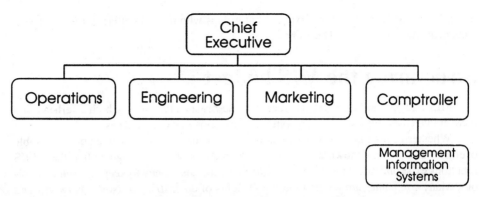

6-1 Traditional position of MIS in the corporate hierarchy.

**Table 6-2 Advantages and disadvantages
of cost-center and profit-center organizations.**

Cost Center	
Advantages	Disadvantages
The MIS department knows all corporate information requirements and can seek global solutions.	Competition for ADP resources is political, because the service is free to the users
	Financial management cannot measure the return on investment in data processing. The MIS department is a target for cost cutting.
	The MIS department has an in-house monopoly. It has little incentive to select the most economical solution to a user's problems.

Profit Center	
Advantages	Disadvantages
Accurate budgeting and costing supports return on investment computations for investments in automation	Internal fund transfers and accounting are complex.
Project costing disciplines promote price competition with outside vendors for system development and computer time.	Time accounting takes time away from the tasks at hand.
Accounting of MIS labor hours within applied to user projects highlights poorly used resources.	There is a motivation to shortchange support functions that cannot be rebilled, such as standards organizations, DBAs, and systems programmers.

users. He makes the natural observation that groups who make intelligent use of the systems make the most satisfied customers.

Structuring the MIS budget

The MIS budget should reflect the fact that the organization incurs both overhead and recoverable costs. Figure 6-2 shows one categorization of expense types.

Whether or not the MIS department is a profit center, there are some nonrecoverable overhead activities as shown in Fig. 6-2. The enterprise has to recognize that these MIS functions exist only to support the corporate staff. It costs money to keep up with technology. Many companies are looking into the benefits of downsizing to Novell networks and using CASE methodologies. Their investment in investigating their alternatives will ultimately benefit the whole enterprise; the enterprise should absorb the expense. Likewise, the way to make sure that the MIS department performs essential but nonrecoverable functions, such as developing standards and procedures, is to designate them as pure overhead within the MIS budget. One litmus test of a nonrecoverable overhead line item is whether it would exist if all data processing work were out-sourced.

The line items identified as recoverable overhead in Fig. 6-2 are incidental to providing services which are recoverable. The more systems are installed the more computers, DBAs, and training will be required to support them. An algorithm can be developed to distribute recoverable overhead costs to users. A sophisticated cost accounting or ledger package such as Oracle's general ledger can distribute overhead costs according to a for-

Recoverable Costs
    System Analysis
    System Development
    System Maintenance
    User Training and Support
    Support of Departmental Computers and PCs
    Computer Operating Expense
Recoverable Overhead Costs
    Systems Programming
    DBA
    Training
    Network Management
    Acquisition Services
Non-Recoverable Overhead Costs
    Maintaining Standards
        Development methodologies
        Documentation Standards
        Computer Environment
    Corporate Data Administration
    Strategic Planning Support

6-2. Recoverable and non recoverable budget categories.

mula. The usual approach is to base the formula on direct charges related to the overhead item.

Major ADP systems are capital items as far as the corporation is concerned but expense lines to the MIS department. MIS charges its expenses to the user department, which carries the capital expense line item in its budget. The MIS department spends capital for computers and software to develop and deliver applications systems. MIS department chargebacks for services should include depreciation on their capital investment.

Measurement of the MIS function

The MIS manager needs to be able to gauge his or her own performance and suggest to upper management how to evaluate performance. Measurements that may apply to the director and his department include:

- Quality of support for strategic decisions. How much does MIS bring to executive decision making?
- Quality of the MIS strategic plan. The quality of the MIS department's long-range plans for development methodologies, environments, and user support.
- Quality of systems being delivered.
- Timeliness and reliability of computer operations.
- Profitability in a cost center, or cost containment in a cost center.
- Accuracy of forecasts, especially development project duration and expense.

The MIS director's greatest contributions are often those that are most subjective, such as helping to develop overall corporate strategies. The director of MIS benefits two ways in making these criteria prominent in his or her evaluation scheme. It ensures recognition for the job which should be done, and it provides entree to all forums in which MIS should be represented.

Summary

Management information systems can easily become isolated within a department by that name and isolated from the mainstream of the businesses it supports. This compartmentalization is dangerous to the enterprise. Upper management can make strategic decisions assuming a level of information support that MIS might be unable to satisfy. The danger to MIS is that they might be perceived as, and might in fact be, expensive and unresponsive to corporate needs. Making data processing a profit center helps ensure that data processing costs are fully figured into investment decisions and that in-house services remain competitive with outside contractors.

7
Staffing plans

For staffing, short-term expediency can mean long-term expense. MIS department staffing, including Oracle, is a proper entry in the long-term data systems development plan.

A hidden liability in migrating to Oracle is making an MIS staff more valuable in the labor market. Oracle is a hot commodity. Successful managers have been able to devise strategies beyond salary alone to keep the Oracle team together. Sly ones exploit the fact that less desirable staff can land somewhere if they are induced to jump ship.

The legitimate objectives of a staffing plan are to get the department's work done with a minimum of expense and risk. Unacknowledged objectives such as empire building and avoiding threats to the boss also of course play a role significant enough to be addressed here. Developing the plan is a matter of balancing staffing sources against requirements. Planning turnover balances the costs of salary increases, training, and benefits against costs of hiring and the disruption caused by departures.

Sources of staff

Every organization has a backbone of employed staff, if only to oversee contractors. Most shops use some outside ADP services. The hierarchy, in rough terms of the longevity of their association with the enterprise, is:

- Employees.
- Leased employees.
- Facilities management contract employees.
- Oracle consultants.
- Consulting house employees.
- Independent consultants.
- "Body shop" consultants.
- Development contractor employees.

Each source has its own characteristics in terms of:

- Hourly labor costs.
- Utilization of the enterprise's overhead resources.
- Cost of acquisition/deacquisition.
- Expertise of the individual.
- Support infrastructure behind the individual.
- Part-time versus full-time availability.
- Long term availability.

The difference in productivity among individuals and situations is such that hourly cost alone cannot be the major determinant in sourcing staff. Where it is, the staff tend to be modestly paid and modestly talented—invariably an expensive combination when measured by overall productivity.

Table 7-1 shows the broad characteristics of different types of staff available for hire and contract. Talent, loyalty, and character are of course vested in individuals and not their employers. This guide can serve only as a broad generalization.

Core staff

The MIS organization needs a core staff to provide continuity to its operations. These people have knowledge of the business. They maintain contacts with the user departments within the organization and with the suppliers who provide the ADP environment. The traditional model has been that the core staff are direct employees. More recently, firms have been using leased employees and facilities-management firms to staff these requirements.

It is not uncommon to find independent consultants among the core staff. This relationship works for several reasons. One is continuity: having already opted out of full-time employment and committed contractually to a client, a consultant is much more likely to be available in the long term. A firm can use a consulting relationship to pay an individual a market rate without consideration of personnel policies, to use an individual only as much as needed, and to maintain the corporate memory of a project after the development team disbands.

Management positions being on the core staff, most people promoted into them come from the core staff. Better managed firms prepare succession plans. A healthy MIS department staff is made up of ambitious people. Their movement creates a need to replace them, which translates into the opportunity to give a promotion to someone junior to them.

Project, peakload, and expert requirements

Peakload, project, and expert requirements do not need to be satisfied by permanent employees. Whether to hire or contract depends on the personality of the company and on the nature of the need. Many companies are uncomfortable laying people off and are therefore reluctant to take on employees for short-term work. Others routinely hire for projects and lay people off when the projects end.

Table 7-1　Characteristics of different types of staff.

Factor Staff type	Hourly labor costs	Overhead costs.	Acquisition/ deacquisition	Expertise of individuals	Support infra-structure	Scheduling flexibility	Long term availability
Employees	Usually the least: typically $15 to $35 per hour for pro-grammers.	Occupancy, full corporate services	Expensive. Headhunters in, outplacement out	Variable.	Other employ-ees and on-site contractors help as needed	Usually a fixed weekly schedule..	Excellent while employed. When they quit, they're gone.
Leased em-ployees	Standard em-ployee plus a percentage	Some covered by lessor	Usually same as employee.	Same as em-ployee	Same as em-ployee	Same as em-ployee	Same as em-ployee
Facilities manage-ment contract em-ployees	Standard em-ployee plus contractor markup; rela-tively inexpen-sive, .	Occupancy and equipment. Other manage-ment handled by contractor.	Handled by contractor	About the same as employees	Contractor often has staff experts available to sup-port contract staff..	Usually same as employees	Subject to continuation of contract, and continued em-ployment of individual.
Independ-ent consult-ants	Moderate. $45 $100 / hour	Desk space, equipment utilization if on site	Cost of contracting	Usually ex-cellent craft skills, depth of experience with Oracle	Most have excellent ties into informal network of Oracle experts	Most flexible. Individuals make their own commitments	Consultant available in-definitely as needed for consultation
Brokered consult-ants	Moderate. $45 - $100 / hour	Desk space, equipment utilization	Cost of contracting	Comparable with employees	Whatever the individual con-sultant brings; brokers typi-cally have none themselves	Very flexible. Brokerage firm does not inter-fere with indi-vidual schedules.	Subject to availability of individual, terms of bro-kerage contract.
Develop-ment con-tractor employ-ees	Moderate. $45 - $100 / hour	Desk space, equipment utilization if on site	Cost of contracting	Comparable with employees	Many have significant Oracle expertise on staff.	Flexible over long term, mod-erately flexible short term.	Subject to continued employment by contractor
Consult-ing house em-ployees	Relatively expensive: $75 - $200 /hour	Desk space, equipment utilization if on site	Cost of contracting	Usually very good craft and communications skills	Many have significant Oracle expertise on staff.	Very flexible. Key people often have other client obligations	Subject to continued employment by consulting firm
Oracle con-sultants	Expensive: $100 - $200 /hour	Desk space, equipment utilization	Cost of contracting	Highly trained and intelligent, often short on experience	Oracle stands behind them. Excellent access to answers.	Very flexible. Key people often have other client obligations	Subject to continued employment by Oracle

There are several advantages to engaging independent consultants and contract per-sonnel for peakload and project requirements strictly related to the time they can apply to the job:

- The acquisition process is shorter. Candidates do not have to pass muster for col-lege degrees or years of experience or satisfy other personnel department require-ments.
- The learning curve is shorter: contractors have to be acclimated to the task at hand, but not so much the corporate culture they are entering.

- Contractors can be excluded from the formal and informal meetings that soak up employees' time.
- More talent might be available on short notice through contracts than through hiring.

The success of a project team depends on the members' ability to communicate with one another. There are several ways in which communications should be taken into account in putting together a project team. The most significant is that communications requirements grow with the size of a team. A 12-person team requires many more meetings, and much more written communication, than a three-person team. One of the many premises on which Oracle's success is based is that highly productive tools result in small teams, which become still more productive because of the meetings and documentation they can avoid.

Following this logic, it makes sense to assemble a project team of a few highly experienced and talented people rather than many average ones. One of the parables floating around IBM years ago was that Tom Simpson, who developed their HASP job-spooling system in the field, was asked how long it would take to develop the successor product if he had a project team of 1000 people. He answered, "Two years." Management was aghast. They asked how many it would take to get the project done in one year. "Ten." answered Simpson. Presumably Mr. Simpson had nothing to do with OS2.

Given that a small, highly focused team is the optimal way to solve most technical problems, choosing the team members is critical. It takes judgment and involves risk. The manager who composes a project team can locate consultants, independent or employed by consulting houses, with resumes well suited to the task at hand. An independent consultant who has been at it two years or more has demonstrated worth in the marketplace, and large consulting houses like Booz Allen or Price Waterhouse cannot afford, at their rates, to offer only average talent. A poor choice can be rectified quickly; an unsatisfactory consultant can be out the door tomorrow. Employees represent a larger risk; a greater long-term asset if they work out, but a much larger liability when they do not.

A project team that has worked successfully before is a decided advantage. They had to learn to communicate and rely on one another. The ideal situation is to redeploy a team of employees from one project to another. Taking a proven team as a group from a contracting organization can be better than assembling people one by one. Independent consultants gain wide experience working with each other. One of the best ways to assemble a team of outsiders is to select an independent consultant as the key technical resource and let him or her help locate and select other people.

A highly talented, tightly focused group of senior people can solve a technical problem more efficiently than other types of team. Without proper planning it can fail to satisfy other objectives. If the senior people are employees, they might leave for a better offer or to take on another challenging assignment. Consultants leave or at least reduce their participation as a project winds down. Unless the firm has an ongoing relationship with the senior project staff, in leaving they remove both application knowledge and the MIS department's contacts with the users.

Management can address the long-term considerations of employee development and continuity through the selection of junior team members. Making maximum use of a senior employee or consultant means propagating their skills. In an ideal situation the senior people spend perhaps three-quarters time giving technical direction to a project and doing the hard work for which they alone are qualified. The rest of their contribution is in working alongside the rest of the team, sharing techniques and jointly solving problems.

Contractors and employees form two classes of staff. Employees, the candidates for promotion, stand in a different relationship to management than the contractors. An employee has to balance self-interest against the interest of the firm. Put another way, he or she must juggle professional instinct against survival instinct. There is a strong motive to avoid risk.

Risk, however, is essential to progress. Oracle is a risk. The amazing fact that the IBM model of monolithic mainframes is dominant even in 1992 is a tribute to risk avoidance. MIS directors find it easy to stick with the status quo. Every MIS manager interviewed for this book risked his or her job in deciding to downsize and use Oracle.

An environment which includes a mixture of contractors fosters innovation and risk. Consultants bring experience of the outside world. Their orientation is more towards the task at hand than the politics of the client organization. Contractors are frequently in the best position to articulate the shortcomings in an MIS department plan, and are more likely than employees to feel free to do so.

Successful companies, according to Peters and Waterman, are those that get things done despite their bureaucracies. They pull together ad hoc groups to solve immediate problems. MIS directors in more rigid companies can use consultants to bypass formal information channels. A skilled outsider, with no vested interest in the organization, can often broker departmental interests better than anyone within the hierarchy. An outside consultant might be expected to make wide contacts in a company that the core staff cannot or is reluctant to attempt.

Oracle shops are more and more fragmented into small groups of experts; some, like analysts, with an orientation towards the business and others, like DBAs, with a data processing craft orientation. Figure 8-1 shows career paths, and Fig. 4-7 shows the skill requirements of the various specialties.

Craft skills lend themselves especially well to outside support. It can take a real expert to install and tune Unix for Oracle or to set up Oracle on a LAN. There is no need for a full-time specialist once the job is done. Unless they double as developers they get bored, they moonlight, and they look for other jobs. When trouble strikes, however, they need to focus intently on the problem until it is solved. Oracle preferred systems integrators (PSI), specialized consulting firms, and independent consultants can handle DBA, systems programming, and tuning tasks especially well. They offer a high level of expertise when it is needed and otherwise don't represent an ongoing expense. Their clients benefit from the expertise and the close contacts with Oracle that they acquire in servicing multiple firms. Outsourcing is also a better assurance of continuity. A consultant with an established clientele typically maintains a client contact longer than an employee stays in one job.

Long-term trends in employment

CASE technologies—Oracle's product and others—will have a profound effect on staffing within the next five years. Work that has been done by applications programmers, the most numerous cohorts within the data processing community, is being split among auto-mated tools, analysts, and programmers. The number of people required to produce a result will diminish, but they will need a higher level of skill than today's practitioners. The job categories which will grow require a high degree of specialization either in the employer's business or a data processing craft.

Oracle's orientation toward using prototypes has already blurred the distinction be-tween analysts and programmers. Programmers and end users work together more than they would if each worked against a formal specification written by an analyst. Analysts will assume the mantle of programmers even more as they are increasingly able to have CASE implement their designs automatically. CASE analyst/programmers will be every bit as much the analyst as they are now, but will also need to master the generation ele-ments of CASE.

As chapter 4 on the implications of CASE indicates, the emerging analyst/designer/developer role will put a premium on analytical skills. It will require a general knowledge of the business and detailed knowledge of selected business areas. The more an individual practitioner can master, the better. These business-oriented people will need support from different types of data processing craft experts.

MIS managers today need to be cultivating the analysts they will need in coming years. Analysts need classroom instruction in technical topics such as relational design and CASE tools. They also need hands-on experience to learn the craft of analysis and the business at hand. Like managers and salespeople, an effective analyst's greatest talent is in communications and the greatest asset is the contacts with whom the analyst commu-nicates. It takes awhile to develop.

Oracle shops should consider hiring programmers with a vision of what they will grow into. An SQL*Forms or SQL*ReportWriter coder who is only a coder will eventu-ally be automated out of business. Fortunately there are enough requirements for niche expertise that any good programmer will find something to do. The criterion for hiring programmers should therefore be "Are they good?" rather than "Do they know SQL*Forms 3.0 (or whatever)?" Tim Donohoe of Group Health Association looks for the ability to learn quickly. His standard approach is to listen to the applicant's description of how he or she uses tools in present environment. His assumption is that a programmer who has fully mastered one set of tools will approach any new set with the same intellec-tual curiosity.

Craft skills, which are independent of the business, are a commodity item. Set the right salary, and the organization will have a good DBA. Economics factors, and the desire to offer a career path to programmers, might favor developing the DBA and systems programmers in house. This can be an especially effective strategy if there are expert consultants on call to support them. In a pinch, the MIS director will always be able to find outside help when it is needed.

Developing managers is more complicated than in the days when the best COBOL programmer rose to manage COBOL programmers. Today's managers must supervise more things they will never fully understand. As MIS moves more up front towards working jointly with users in a CASE environment, more MIS managers will come up through the ranks of analysts. It is a good training ground. Analysis is the art of understanding people, and design is very much the art of brokering competing interests to arrive at an optimum solution.

Making a long-term staffing plan

The strategic plan that MIS follows will name major systems development efforts out to a three to five year planning horizon. The projected cost of the projects will include staffing, usually assuming current technologies rather than betting on productivity gains through new tools. The MIS director can easily aggregate demand for personnel, by position, using a spreadsheet. Factoring in staff members without a project orientation forms the basis for long-term planning.

The MIS director turns two knobs to bring the crystal ball into focus. Future projects have to be discounted for the possibility they will be delayed or not undertaken at all. Also, the staffing requirements have to be adjusted with a best-guess estimate of the implementation tools to be used. There are significant productivity differences between doing a job in C and using Oracle 4GL tools, or between a traditional waterfall development cycle and using Oracle CASE.

The best-guess spreadsheet map of future staffing requirements is a basis for plotting career paths of the employed staff and making hiring plans. The peaks and valleys created by large projects, less than full-time staffing requirements, and requirements for specialists are areas in which the MIS manager should consider using outsiders.

Summary

Staffing to meet short-term requirements has to fit into long-term strategies. In fairness to the employee and to best serve its own interests, a company should foresee some sort of career path for each hire. The most obvious ones are as senior systems developers, such as analysts, as specialists of some sort, and as managers. "Throw away" hires are expensive. More than that, they cost a company in morale and ultimately in productivity.

Every shop needs the flexibility to bring in outside support from time to time. Contractors can help with peak-load requirements and bring in types and levels of expertise that could not be supported among the employed staff. Costs, qualifications, and levels of infrastructure support vary significantly among different types of service providers. People in the MIS department need to familiarize themselves with the services marketplace before making a commitment.

A company needs core staff to give continuity to the business. The function is usually handled by employees, occasionally by a facilities-management firm. Outside consultants sometimes provide continuity for key applications. The MIS department's strategic plan has to provide for training, development, and retention of core staff. The emergence of CASE methodologies and tools will have a profound impact on staffing and training requirements during the decade of the 1990s. A company's technology and staffing plans have to be worked out in concert.

8
Personnel management of Oracle professionals

An MIS director is first a manager of people. Some directors succeed without knowing the technology very well, and some are not especially good at formal disciplines such as life-cycle methodologies. They work through others. Every manager's success depends on his or her skill at managing the people who do have the skills to get the job done.

A network login blurb quoted some DP sage saying "Managing senior programmers is like herding cats." The profession is different. Programmers are highly mobile, the pay is relatively good, and the skill requirements change rapidly. In most companies, the MIS director needs to adapt the company's personnel policies to suit the department's needs.

MIS personnel policies have to embrace several contradictions. The work is performed in teams, so teamwork has to be rewarded. However, the difference in productivity among individuals is greater in ADP than almost any other field. Management certainly needs to recognize individual merit somehow. Many people are so specialized that even their peers do not know exactly what they do, so management can assess their performance indirectly at best. Their peers certainly recognize a dud, however, and management has to straighten them out before they undermine the morale of a whole group.

The contemporary themes of quality run through personnel management. A Japanese inspired school of thought holds that it is counterproductive to grade and rank employees; most are motivated by self respect and the opinion of their peers to do their best—rankings only serve to discourage people of middling ability. Conversely, a few highly productive people far more than carry their weight in most ADP shops, and management has to be able to reward them in order to keep them.

A rational analyst contends that the objective of personnel management is to make sure that the staffing plan is filled with qualified bodies. Furthermore, it must be done in a manner consistent with the organization's personnel policies and at a reasonable cost.

All that is true, but the answer is somewhat larger. An organization's effectiveness is determined by qualities apart from the people who staff it. Spirit, morale, teamwork, and a willingness to experiment belong to an organization's culture. Though everybody contributes to the culture and is influenced by it, the managers have the largest role in establishing it. They do so by their own actions and those they reward and condemn.

The larger objective of personnel management is to create the most effective team to accomplish the mission at hand. Salary, benefits, training, and the allocation of perks should be administered in light of that larger objective.

There cannot be a cookbook answer to managing people. What is effective depends on the nature of the shop, the culture of the corporation and the personalities involved. The following sections raise the issues with which every manager has to come to terms and offers techniques that have been successful for some Oracle installations.

Turnover

ADP career management as practiced is largely a matter of opportunity. People keep their resumes on the street and jump to more attractive jobs when they can. The better people are pulled into management as openings come up. Firms like IBM, which work out long-term career paths within the company, are the exception.

It does not make sense to put time into long-range plans in a high-turnover environment. The questions to ask are what is the cost of high turnover and whether a lack of planning contributes to it. The most successful Oracle shops have relatively low turnover and usually do take a long-term view of careers.

Turnover costs are found directly in the expense to replace the knowledge that goes out the door. There are the obvious costs of advertising, headhunters, and unproductive time as a newcomer is plugged into the bureaucracy. As an indictment of the pay and working conditions, turnover costs are found indirectly in morale and productivity.

Hiring to replace people who leave is becoming more expensive as data processing professionals' expertise becomes more deeply rooted in the business. Relatively few Oracle developers are just plain coders anymore, working from specifications written by others. Most work in a prototype mode in which part of the job is becoming familiar with user requirements. Developers under CASE will often be the analysts themselves. Their knowledge of the business and contacts within the organization are highly specific. A newly hired analyst, even with journeyman level experience, takes a few months to work into the applications.

Career paths in data processing

Data processing professionals have to choose early in their careers whether to be generalists or specialists. Specialists, though well paid for a well defined technical skill, are limited in their career opportunities. A DBA can aspire to be the top DBA in a large shop and perhaps the manager of a DBA section; a systems programmer can become the lead systems programmer. But, programmers and analysts are the ADP generalists who can aspire to become the director of MIS. Figure 8-1 shows a typical pattern of diversification into specialities over the course of people's careers.

The MIS director's options are limited in dealing with specialists because their career progression is more often foreordained by their choice of a niche. Management has a responsibility to advise people early in their career what choosing a specialty does to their

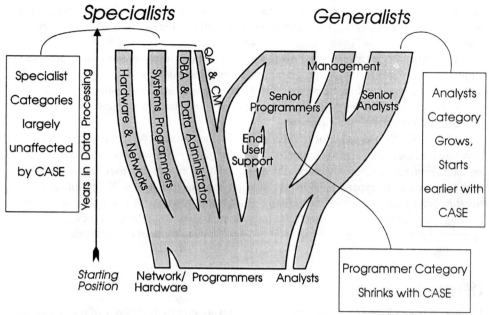

8-1 Typical career paths in data processing.

subsequent career options. Once they have chosen, the challenge is to find the mixture of assignments, training, and salary that will keep them happy and productive.

Specialists are today's guildsmen. They frequently associate themselves more with their profession than their employer. Management has to accept the fact that these people often must change companies to grow within their niche. The effect of turnover is mitigated by the fact that it is usually possible to hire a replacement with most of the skills required to do the job. The new Unix systems programmer might, for instance, have to learn Sequent's flavor of Unix or the new DBA learn Wyse emulation, but the job is fundamentally the same from one installation to another.

The exceptions prove the rule. It is a special challenge to staffing positions that require specialists whose knowledge is highly company dependent. Data administrators, quality control, and configuration management people fall into this category. Managers use the following strategies for staffing these positions:

- Staff them with capable administrative staff rather than programmers. The pay is sufficiently attractive to compensate for a lack of promotion opportunities.
- Staff them on the basis of planned rotation, even making them a stepping stone towards management.
- Staff them with ineffective programmers who are not sacrificing career opportunities in any case.

The last option, which is unfortunately common, shows a lack of dedication to the management controls these people are supposed to impose. The other two are a tossup. Administrative staff need training in some data processing disciplines and active management support to succeed, but are generally appreciative of the opportunity. Rotating people in and out of these positions spreads an appreciation of their importance throughout the MIS department, but it means that the incumbents are usually on the steeper part of the learning curve.

Generalists' careers take more management attention simply because there are more choices to make. Analysts and programmers assume increasing levels of project responsiblity as they grow within the profession. At some point, that responsibility can be formalized through a management title. The option of specialization remains open for those who are not interested in management.

Cheryl Smith, the Director of MIS at HFSI, Inc., makes very effective use of her new hires. In their first year to 18 months of employment, new hires work as programmers on internal projects. Cheryl manages the assignments to ensure that they have the opportunity to work with experienced project leaders, especially analysts. When this apprenticeship period ends, a person can choose among continuing with internal systems, becoming a consultant to HFSI clients, or pursuing a craft skill. Telling the new hire what their options will be a year in advance forces new hires to think in career terms from day one.

Outside the department

Promotions outside the ADP field have been relatively rare in the history of data processing. ADP has been growing, and the money has been good. A more common story has been the user who became handy with computers and transferred into ADP. The skills one developed in the MIS department were not especially relevant to the rest of the business.

Conditions have changed. The percentage of ADP people who thoroughly understand the business is growing steadily. Information systems are more and more vital to the business. Individual departments more frequently control their own data processing resources. Though still rare, it is becoming more common for a career path to lead out of data processing into general management.

An MIS director benefits several ways whenever he or she promotes outside the MIS department. It expands the promotion potential for data processing staff, which has to be good for morale. It improves the working relationship between ADP and the customer organization. Also, it is an excellent way to develop general management with a deep understanding of ADP and ADP management with a good knowledge of the business.

Productivity

People want to do a good job. Productivity is the flip side of the quality issue. High productivity gives people the time to do a quality job. It also implies the use of the standard, repeated processes that are the hallmark of quality. Two very distinct philosophies of management address the quality/productivity issue.

The traditional American school of management counsels the boss to measure the productivity of each individual in the organization as objectively as possible. Then the superachievers are publicly rewarded and promoted when possible, the middle-of-the-roaders receive middling rewards, and the bottom 10 percent or so are subject to reassignment or dismissal *pour encourager les autres* (to encourage the others). Adherents of this school tend to believe that employees control their own productivity, that they give only as much as management demands of them. These managers are prone to increase productivity by executive fiat, pronouncing "We will work 12-hour days, and the project will be done on time," or "We will reduce testing errors by 20 percent this year without increasing staff."

The TQM school counters that individual productivity is not the issue. It is the productivity of groups of people, project teams, and eventually the whole enterprise, that matters. Management's objective must be to help every individual contribute a maximum to the team effort. Aguayo (1991) stresses the importance of training, tools, procedures, and communications in attaining these goals. Rewarding individual achievement is almost counterproductive according to this school. It encourages only the people who are already self-motivated, undermines teamwork by fostering competition, and abdicates management responsibility through the assumption that the workers are capable of augmenting productivity all on their own.

Many of the TQM notions have been in currency in computer management books for years. Brooks, Humphrey, Albrecht, and others have drawn correlations between environmental factors and productivity. Figure 2-3 shows Brooks and Albrecht's conclusions about what contributes to a productive environment. Humphrey and Deming both advocate setting up an environment in which the employees themselves continually improve the process.

People are the question. Deming envisions an environment in which differences in the productivity of individuals is less important than differences inherent in the system. His belief is that team productivity is paramount. Individuals are valuable in that they contribute to a team. He therefore discourages merit raises and percentiles.

Most students of data processing share Brooks' observation that individual capability is the single most important determinant of productivity. Figure 2-3 expresses his finding that there might be a 4:1 difference in productivity among project teams depending on the capability of the individuals who staff them. The fiction that one worker is interchangeable with another might be tolerable in the Army or a labor union, but not in data processing. The management challenge is how to make optimal use of people with dissimilar natural aptitudes. Here are some suggestions:

- Let the leaders lead—teams, processes and tools. Let their salary grow in proportion to responsibility.
- Reward team players. Any person who is willing and able to work on a team will make a positive contribution.
- To the extent practical, let people form their own teams and choose their own projects. People put their heart into the work they choose themselves; control over your destiny makes you productive. Management's role becomes defending these self-directed people against unreasonable demands and deadlines.
- Hire carefully. Qualified, motivated people are the most important determinant of success. Do what is required to get competitive salaries.
- Steer lonely-genius types into areas where solo efforts are tolerable, such as systems programming, networks, etc. At that, encourage them to communicate. Never trust a genius so profound that nobody understands him or her.
- Weed out people who are not team players. Me-firsters, empire builders, conspiri-

tors, shammers, and charletans undermine a group effort despite individual contributions they may make.
- Provide training. Chapter 11 covers the wide variety of ways to handle it.

Productivity and quality work are a natural expression of people's views of themselves. Most people consider themselves above average and look for an opportunity to prove it. The natural outlet is work. Part of being above average, however, is not being stupid. The same above-average people will tolerate only a certain amount of disorder, lack of direction, and lack of appreciation until they decide that management is not making good use of their time. Being too smart to give something for nothing, they slack off.

Management's job, therefore, is to provide an environment in which people can be productive. They need organization, a workplace, tools, training, and well-defined and attainable objectives. Management leads by serving. Most workers' self-direction gives them adequate leadership when they have the wherewithall to do the job.

Characteristics of successful performance evaluation

Evaluating people is so hard that the best measure of a manager might be how well they measure their staff. There is no topic on which the staff is keener than evaluating their own management. Employees respect and produce for a manager who respects their contributions. Morale evaporates in the face of a manager who does not know or care about their accomplishments.

Performance evaluations are a basis for action. They underlie the decisions as to who gets promoted, who gets laid off, and what sort of raises each person gets. The personnel department, if not the employees themselves, will point out any major inconsistencies. The characteristics of successful evaluation programs are:

- Employees understand how evaluations work.
- The employees' objectives in a period are few and clear.
- Management provides frequent feedback.
- Two levels of management are involved in the evaluation.
- Employees accept the evaluation.
- Rewards are real.

A formal evaluation process is so stressful for both the employees and their managers that some business thinkers would do away with it. The alternatives are even more problematic. One alternative is to treat and pay all people in a given job category equally. This flies in the face of experience that there are significant differences in individual productivity. Pay all people the same,and the good ones will leave. Another option, substituting management's judgment or that of a person's peers for a formal evaluation process invites a return to the kinds of abuses that led to formal systems decades ago. The best of managers might do a better job absent any corporate restraints, but average managers might be influenced by personality factors and their own self-interest. The appearance of scientific impartiality is important as an increasing number of personnel actions wind up in court. A company needs a paperwork trail to show that all employees have been treated equally.

The themes below run through most companies' evaluation processes. The discussion relates them to the special concerns in a data processing operation.

Understanding the process

The universal disclaimer "Don't take it personally." is pure hypocrisy in a performance evaluation. Everyone takes criticism personally. How could an employee take criticism to heart, benefit by it and change, if it were not personal?

An evaluation asks the employee to undertake the single most difficult task any human faces, that of looking at him or herself objectively. The human organism has fantastic defenses against doing so. The evaluation process has to disarm a person's denial mechanisms in order to be successful. It has to be credible.

Credible evaluation systems are like school report cards. The process is universal and predictable. It is part of the culture. Everyone in the organization accepts the results as valid. The process is so important that any organization large enough to have a personnel department will probably have a standard procedure. The evaluation process must be written. It must be explained to each new employee in a face-to-face meeting. And, it must be reasonably consistent over time, evolving by degrees, so that past evaluations retain their validity.

Few and attainable objectives

An employee should be able to predict his or her rating in a successful evaluation process. Management sets clear and attainable goals and establishes milestones to show progress against those goals. Performance is a factor of measurable progress against those milestones.

Project managers' goals can tie neatly to a project management system. Though there are more significant reasons to use project managment, it is nice the way personnel management falls out of them. This is the most objective kind of goal possible. If the January commitment is that the system will be operable by year end, the December question is "Is it?"

Too many goals, and fuzzy goals, confuse the process. All fallible mortals have any number of shortcomings to address any time. It does not make sense to establish any goal that is not at least somewhat measurable and that does not tie in with a course of action to achieve it. Any number over perhaps five goals is a cop-out. Most employees will make some, fail on others, and make indeterminate progress on some more and have to accept whatever middling evaluation the manager assigns.

A manager has to understand that objective measures to gauge a person's contribution to an organization are hard to come by. Evaluation points are at best a one-dimensional reflection of the person's value. It is sometimes necessary to pick subjective over objective criteria even though it makes the process more difficult. It would be possible, for instance, to rate a systems programmer by system availability. The more significant measures, though, are probably the support that he or she offers developers and the enhancements he or she makes to the system environment.

Provide frequent feedback

Practice communicating, marriage counsellors recommend, because sometime you might need to say something. Make it a point to provide people with feedback on progress against their objectives even when things are going well. It will make them attentive when you have to offer some criticism. The discipline will reinforce in your mind the things they have done right.

Data processing can be a very satisfying profession. When a techie gets wrapped up in a problem, the rest of the world goes away. The effect on the problem is marvellous. The techie works night and day until it goes away. Sometimes entire teams are transported by shared inspiration and dedication. A frequent effect on management is to ignore these successful workers and focus where the problems are. This gives short shrift to good work.

It is easy to ignore things that are going right, such as people who are productive, users who are satisfied, and projects that are on time. Memory of the good times can slip away. It is hard enough to remember what you were doing nine months ago, let alone what 10 people on a staff were up to. People weigh recent memories more heavily.

The best approach is to provide frequent evaluation feedback. When that is not possible, management should at least make a discipline of making monthly notes on each employee's performance. A quarterly review process is sufficient. If the formal review process is done only yearly, a manager should have each employee in his or her office quarterly to discuss progress against objectives.

Involve two levels of management

The evaluation process needs to filter out the personality factor as much as possible in evaluating employees. It is a given that an employee's direct manager writes the evaluation. Another person, usually the second line manager, reviews, and approves the appraisal. The second person validates the doctrine that it is the institution performing the evaluation. The reviewer can temper an appraisal and "norm" it against other appraisals in the group. In a school where a B average is the norm, a teacher who grades on a curve centered on C will be trouble for the students and ultimately for him or herself. The same applies to a manager who is consistently more lenient or severe than his or her peers.

Employees accept the evaluation

It is standard practice to go over the evaluation with an employee, after which they sign to confirm that it has been done. It does not mean that they like what they hear.

The evaluation has to stand once it is presented to the employee. Allowing employees to negotiate their evaluations would undermine the process. However, most firms allow the employee to write a dissent to the evaluation that will accompany it in the personnel file and be read by at least the second-level manager.

Rewards are real

There is an impressive disparity between the ranges of productivity and the ranges of salary in data processing. Barry Boehm cites a factor of four difference in productivity among teams. The difference among individual programmers is even greater.

The top two curves in Fig. 8-2 show typical spreads of salary and productivity for ADP generalists at the five year mark. The third curve, at the bottom of the figure, shows graph shows the cost per unit of productivity (curve 1 divided by curve 2). The conclusion is that as long as people are paid consistently with their talent, the cost per unit of productivity decreases with more talented people even when there is a considerable salary spread.

The top people in a shop are usually more than merely productive. They are the leaders, the inspiration to their fellows, and the ones who make the shop's reputation. It is good policy to give them good raises. They know their value.

Assuming that people start at more or less equal pay, it takes raises that look extravagant to arrive at the salary spread shown in Fig. 8-2 at the five-year mark. If salary guidelines allow a star performer raises of 5 percent above the average, it will take fourteen years for that person to be making twice the average salary. It gives the employee a long time to shop his or her skills to employers who might recognize real value.

MIS Directors need wide latitude in awarding raises if they are to keep their best people. They need the ability to encourage marginal performers to leave by awarding nothing. It is worth an occasional fight with personnel to do the right thing.

Evaluation and ranking schemes

Though some TQM adherents avoid formal systems for rating employees, most traditional companies use one of two basic schemes. The first is like a school report card, in which the manager rates each employee individually. The second is a ranking report. Every employee in the whole department is assigned a number that reflects their relative value. The person who tops the list is almost indispensible, and those at the bottom of the list had better have their resumes together. A former employer used to call this a lifeboat drill. If the ship were sinking and there was a 20-person lifeboat, who would be in it? How about a 10-person boat?

The Japanese school of management provides a solid rationale for not rating employees. The good ones need no encouragement. Their work shows they are already self-motivated. The middling-to-poor ones can only resent being tagged as average or below. Nobody thinks of themselves in those terms. Rating employees is a difficult process in any scheme. In data processing, however, it is widely recognized that the difference in productivity between top- and bottom-level performers is dramatic, on the order of ten to one in some tasks. It is worth evaluating the trade-offs among rating and ranking schemes.

A formal ranking process makes it impossible to avoid confronting hard facts. The only question is whether the result justifies the pain. A problem in report-card type rating systems is that unless managers make the hard calls and assign below-average ratings, the system is worthless. Ranking can be brutal. It is more palatable to an employee being satisfactory than being 38th out of 50 within a department. The subjective rating is also easier for management to support because it does not involve other personalities. Even

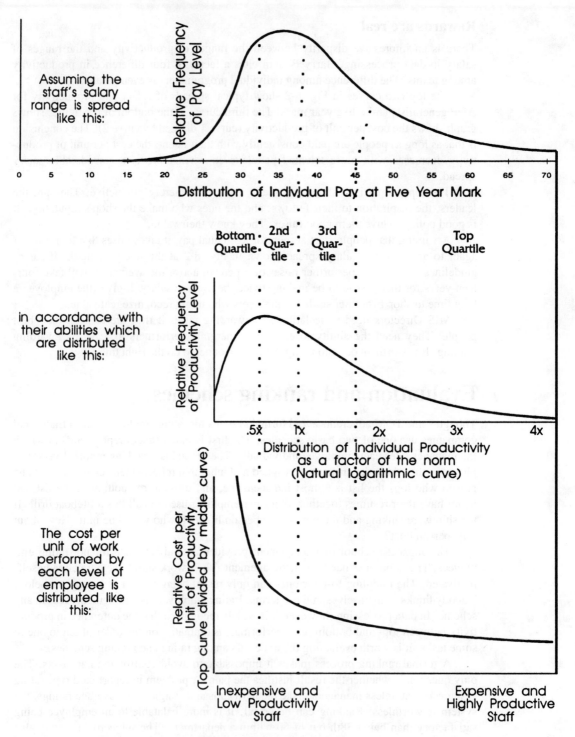

8-2 Salary, productivity, and unit cost of productivity ranges.

companies with ranking systems for internal use usually give employees only their report-card scheme rating.

Normalization in a rating scheme

Evaluation systems have to be normalized to counter the effects of grade inflation. A military officer with a mere excellent rating knows he or she is in trouble. An outstanding rating is nearer the average. High schools and colleges have also experienced grade inflation. Although a grade of C is defined as the average, in many schools it is a solid B. In some places it makes sense to ask "Yeah, he's Phi Beta Kappa, but is he smart?"

Grade inflation starts with lazy or timid graders. Awarding too high a rating to an employee can avoid a scene with a difficult employee. However, out of fairness, other people's rankings also have to be bumped to show that they are at least as good. Rating an entire section as above the average is a cheap way to buy affection, like making up for being gone all year by showering the kids with Christmas presents.

One discipline that forces managers towards the middle is to have them write a comment to justify any rating other than satisfactory. Making them think about exceptions reinforces the notion that the average rating is for people who are average within the department.

The only way to make the numbers meaningful is to force the average. Many firms have a policy that there is some size group, usually 50 to a few hundred, within which the evaluation scores must average to the defined mean. If 1 is poor, 3 is satisfactory and 5 is excellent, it might be all right to have a section with an average of 3.5, but each 200-person department had better average to 3. Otherwise, who's to know what a 3 rating really means?

It is convenient to make the norming group the same as the salary budgeting organization. Salary increase guidelines are based on an average employee. They work almost automatically when the average rating within the department is forced to coincide with the average defined for the rating scale.

It is true that there are outstanding organizations with exceptionally talented people. They attain that position by offering pay and benefits that attract excellent people. As a balm to their employees' egos, a rating scheme could be extended to something like:

1. Unsatisfactory
2. Marginally satisfactory
3. Satisfactory
4. Superior
5. Excellent
6. Outstanding
7. Extraordinary
8. Phenomenal

with an average of approximately 6. The essence is that the organization not deceive itself. In any group of people there will be some who are more valuable to the company than others. Evaluations have to retain their meaning across sections and departments and from year to year to be of use in managing people.

Employees are expected to improve their skills as they move up the ladder. A rating scheme needs to normalize by position or pay grade. A senior person might be superior with regard to the department but only satisfactory in comparison with the people who pull down the same paycheck.

Rating factors in a rating scheme

A good employee is a well-rounded person. Employees should be rated on all of the factors that make them valuable to the company. The following evaluation points figure into most plans:

- Ability to work in a team.
- Communications ability.
- Technical competence.
- Productivity.
- Loyal to the company.
- Organization and leadership.
- Professionalism.

It generally makes sense to give a composite rating that takes all factors into account. Though some firms tell first line managers how to weight each factor, many leave it up to their discretion. The purpose of enumerating the evaluation criteria is to make sure that they consider the whole person.

A management by objectives approach evaluates employees against their goals for a rating period. This approach can be dangerous in data processing. The objective measures, such as completion of a given project, are largely beyond the control of any one person. It creates a conflict wherever the goals of the business are inconsistent with an individual's assigned goals, which is often the case over a one-year period in data processing. Moreover, the leadership and teamwork qualities which are most valuable in an employee are not subject to objective measurement. Management cannot escape the responsibility of knowing and evaluating the whole of a person's contribution.

Ranking techniques

A ranking scheme assigns each person a numerical ranking within the whole MIS organization, most valuable to least valuable. First-line managers often provide the input to the top-to-bottom ranking process. Cheryl Smith describes a process that works in rounds like this:

1. In each round, each manager writes the names of the two best people not already ranked on the blackboard.
2. A scribe writes down the names of all the people whose names are written on the board more than once, in order, with those with the most mentions at the top.
3. The managers as a group discuss the merits of individuals with the same number of mentions, and assign relative rankings among them. The scribe assigns them the next sequence of ranking numbers, moves the names to the list of people already ranked, and erases their names from the blackboard.
4. The process proceeds to the next round. Each manager names two people, presumably including those that they alone named the last time.

John Harned offers an approach that works from the bottom up. He asks first who is expendable. To perform a ranking in a large department where there are several first-line managers he asks the individual managers to rank their own people, then gathers them together to form a consolidated ranking.

Both Smith and Harned implemented ranking schemes on their own, not to satisfy a company policy. They make similar arguments for the utility of rankings:

- The people at the top of the list are candidates for promotion. They may need assignments which give them breadth and visibility.
- The people at the bottom of the list are on the way out the door. It is sometimes necessary to put the spotlight on them in order to document the coming termination.
- It highlights discrepancies in ratings. It bears analysis if the tenth most valuable person has a report card grade of 3 and the 25th is rated a 2.
- Adding salaries to the ranking list highlights major imbalances between pay and performance.

The task of management is to make the best use of the resources at hand. In the case of personnel that resource is salary money. A ranking system shows where it is being well spent.

No rating system

Formal rating systems represented some sort of an advance over their precursors. They brought an appearance of scientific impartiality into the business of personnel. Having to put together a rationale for granting raises and promotions, or firing people, supposedly limits a boss's ability to play favorites.

There is no doubt that formal systems have decreased the level of bias in personnel actions. The documentation they require provides an audit trail for the personnel department and for upper management. They insulate employees and the company against radical changes in salary or title. They protect employees from weak and arbitrary managers who are not doing their job.

Formal systems work against strong managers and employees. They can stifle motivation by forcing half the employees even in the best shop to be below average. They can foster destructive competition among employees for the best ratings. They can tie a manager's hands in moving a really strong person up quickly in an organization.

Doing away with formal ratings takes away the one occasion on which the employee and manager routinely sit down face to face. It is then up to the manager to make sure that informal contact at least replaces that session. Without a rating scheme, the manager has to know employees all the better in order to decide how to recommend people for promotion and decide how to apportion the budget for raises among employees.

Salary and title administration

Data processing usually has to live with the salary administration scheme set by the personnel department, but it is worth noting the elements of a successful plan. It begins with the objective of salary administration, which most simply put is to achieve a maximum of productivity with a minimum of risk and expense.

It takes teamwork to maximize productivity. A company cannot afford a divisive salary plan. One precept of a successful plan is that salaries are private between the individual and the company. Because salaries are based on historical factors as much as current performance, there will always be inequities. A good plan plays them down in the short term and evens them out over the long term.

Many successful salary plans make only loose connections between title and salary range. One person with a given title might make more or less than another. A manager can use this latitude to smooth the path for people moving up and down the ladder. Figure 8-3 shows how rising star can quickly assume new titles and more and more responsibility, but a mature employee can step off the escalator of success and retreat into the ranks of worker bees without necessarily being penalized in compensation.

Hierarchies are not the most efficient structure for addressing data processing problems—it takes teams of people with the best (available) mix of talent for the job at hand. Teams should be able to come together and split up as easily in programming as in pick-up basketball games. This is easy in a flat organization. Employees recognize the natural leaders and technical wizards in their midst and are usually pleased to work with them.

Unmaking an annointed manager is tough. It is easier never to have promoted a person than to move them back into the ranks once the need for the management role is gone. The more flexible approach is to give everyone a title such as *Member of technical staff,* perhaps with prefixes such as *junior, senior, advisory,* or *consulting.*

Minimizing the formal hierarchy puts emphasis where it belongs, on those who do the work. When climbing the management ladder is the only path to a bigger paycheck, people naturally become very interested in accumulating titles. They want to be managers whether or not they are cut out for the work. Good technicians are almost propelled into management positions where their gifts are of less value. It makes much more sense to name them team leaders, a role in which they are expected to share their talent working in a team, than to put them in a position to dictate and second guess the approaches taken by a team under their direction.

Dealing with poor performers

There are good, bad, and indifferent Oracle programmers, but as of this writing very few unemployed ones. A capable manager is usually able to upgrade his staff without tremendous resistance. Poor performers can often be induced to jump to another company and become somebody else's problem. Sometimes it is a matter of moving a person to a situation which is better suited to their personality and abilities.

Bottom-level performers usually have some skills that could be of value to the organization. It is just that harnessing their productivity takes more time and effort than they will return, resulting in a net negative. It is intolerable simply to ignore the situation. Here is a short catalog of the cost of tolerating mediocrity:

- Putting a dud on a team slows everyone else down as they devise ways to work around him or her.

Value of Wide Salary Ranges in Downward Mobility

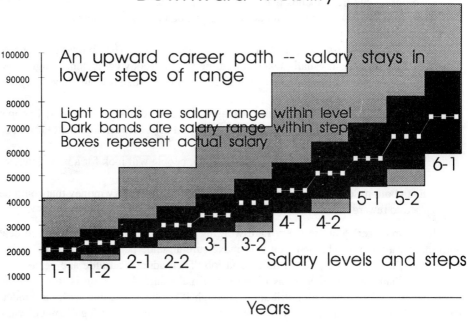

An upward career path -- salary stays in lower steps of range

Light bands are salary range within level
Dark bands are salary range within step
Boxes represent actual salary

1-1 1-2   2-1 2-2   3-1 3-2   4-1 4-2   5-1 5-2   6-1

Salary levels and steps

Years

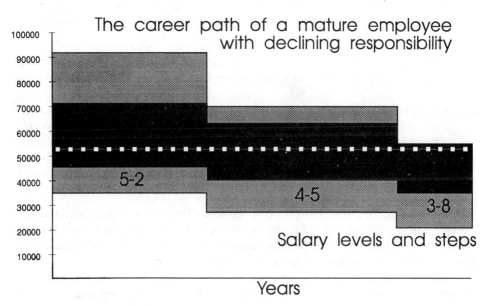

The career path of a mature employee with declining responsibility

5-2   4-5   3-8

Salary levels and steps

Years

8-3 Value of wide salary ranges in downward mobility.

- Most bottom-level performers cannot see themselves as they are. They eat up management time complaining about their treatment.
- Corporate culture demands that everybody get some sort of assignment. It is difficult to take work back from a dud, even when other team members are stuck waiting for their product.
- Bottom performers' work products are like time bombs. They blow up at embarrassing moments. It usually takes more time for somebody competent to figure out what a design or program was trying to do, then fix it, than it would have to do the job in the first place.
- The presence of a dud signals that management tolerates mediocracy. Better people do not have to push themselves to look good in a mediocre environment. They can fall into a 9-to-5 mentality.
- Working with a dud is no fun. The competent people will look for a more interesting environment.
- Even bottom-level people have to be paid. They absorb salary money that could be used to reward the people who do the work.

It is a manager's duty to every hard-working person within an organization to deal with those who aren't. The first step is to make sure an underperforming person has the preparation, training, and tools to do a good job. Then address attitude and personality situations, changing assignments as necessary to make sure the person is in a position where he or she can make a contribution. Though it is out of keeping with the kinder, gentler philosophy of Theory Y/TQM managers, it is essential from a legal point of view to document these actions and the associated counseling sessions which can lead to the last step, firing.

In some environments, it can be a Herculean task to document poor performance and actually fire somebody. Some of the most imaginative ruses in business are used to clean house, such as:

- New sections formed out of deadwood; then reorganized out of existence with a RIF (reduction in force), which terminates the employees with no apparent prejudice.
- Total incompetents given a promotion along with a transfer out. Government and military elements sometimes take the formation of a new organization as an opportunity to clean house. A new Army company will collect every every eight ball in the battalion.
- Glowing referrals to ease an employee into a new job in another department or company.

It takes strategy and luck to get rid of someone. The most straightforward way is to document their shortcomings and counseling sessions in their personnel file and fire them when there is enough evidence. So many employees now sue for wrongful discharge that it is extremely important to document every adverse personnel action.

What an unpleasant topic! Dealing with problem employees is invariably expensive, devisive, and a terrible waste of management time. What it does is emphasize the importance of spending a lot of effort in the hiring process to bring on people who will be assets over the long haul.

Succession planning

Good people advance quickly in an organization and in their careers. They also tend to travel a lot—to job sites, to conferences, for training, and on vacation. Somebody needs to cover for them in their temporary absences and fill their positions when they leave.

Richard Barker, Vice President in charge of Oracle UK and Oracle's CASE product, covers both contingencies with one plan. The second in command for each position is heir apparent, and takes over in the boss's absence. The measure of a successful manager is how long he or she can be gone without being missed.

Hiring

The want ads exemplify the *scientific management theory* that employees are interchangeable cogs in a large machine. A company advertises for an

> ORACLE
> SQL*Forms 3.0
> SQL*ReportWriter
> Client/Srvr a plus
> BS req'd 3 yr exp.

programmer, who once the current project is over, will presumably answer another company's ad demanding four years' experience. Look at what is implicit in this approach to hiring. First, it assumes that the employee's total value is in their technical skills. "We know what we're doing." it seems to say, "Management has everything planned—we just need you to do it." It also assumes that skills are rather immutable, as if a person with four years SQL*Plus and SQL*Forms 2.3 experience would be unsuitable to the task.

The practice is just the opposite. A new hire joins a team. The company needs to invest in any new hire to teach him or her how things are done in the organization. The better the shop, the more the training required to use its specific tools, standards, and procedures. The new hire must become familiar with the business. Moreover, the hiring company is missing a bet if it does not use new employees for cross-pollenization, seeding good new ideas from the outside into their organization. Once a person becomes an employee, they will of course receive ongoing training along with the pre-existing staff. The want ad should probably read something like:

> Education Applications Developer
> Skilled user of several relational tools
> In-depth knowledge related application
> Valued member of development team
> for Oracle Forms/ReportWriter environment

Business Week related two questions Microsoft supposedly asks prospective employees: "Why are manhole covers round?" and "How much astroturf would it take to cover all the stadiums in the major leagues?" One technology company gave a young woman two weeks to come up with an answer to this classic problem: "You have a simple balance that will show that the contents of one pan weigh the same, less, or more than those in the other pan. You are given 12 identical-looking marbles. Eleven weigh the same, and the other is slightly heavy or light. How many weighings does it take to find the odd marble, and how do you do it?"

These problems measure analytical ability: "Lessee—there must be about 16 teams per league because the playoffs take so long, and I know two leagues play in the World Series, and a ballpark must be about as deep as a guy can bat a ball because an over-the-fence homer happens every so often, so. . . ." Furthermore, they recognize that the process of getting an answer can be more interesting than the answer itself. The last one measured a critical business skill, which is the ability to define a problem and find a solution through other people. The answer, incidentally, is three weighings.

When you accept that a manager's primary role is to establish an environment in which employees can be productive and leave it to them to figure out how, you see how important hiring really is. The hirees are the people who will both conceive and perform the work. It is worth relating a number of hiring strategies that have been successful for many years:

- Recruit from colleges with a strong DBMS curriculum in their computer science program. This brings in people with the background to appreciate Oracle and learn the tools.
- Have their prospective teammates interview each prospect. Encourage them to have the candidate describe their current projects in detail, to get an appreciation of whether they understand their business as well as their data processing tools. Ask them to describe the tools they currently use and what they like and dislike about them.
- Have employees recommend people from among their contacts within the industry. Productive employees like to help assemble productive teams.
- Have prospective teammates participate in calling references. Have them engage the reference whenever possible in discussions about specific projects. It is generally fruitless to ask if a person was a good, bad, or indifferent employee, but a reference can indicate volumes in describing the prospect's contribution to a team effort.
- Kick off a project by using consultants in senior technical roles. It takes time pressure off the hiring process, provides an opportunity to see what the real requirements are, and exploits the consultants' industry contacts to find the right staff. Often the consultants are receptive to employment offers.
- Use summer-hire programs to build relationships with promising high school and college students. They more than pay their keep, especially after the first year, and there is no ramp-up when they come on board after graduation.

In contrast to the way newspaper ads are phrased, these real-life strategies are all based on people rather than their specific technical skills. They recognize that character matters over the long haul.

Summary

The fundamental rule of personnel management is that good people, given the opportunity, will make a good organization. The manager's role is to midwife the process. It starts with hiring capable people who can work together in a team. Management makes sure that the employees have the training and tools they need to get the job done.

The chiefs form teams and manage the workload in such a way that the people can succeed. Individual assignments and deadlines might be challenging but should be possible. Salary administration and rating systems should reward employees justly with a minimum of pain and dissention.

Personnel management philosophies need to dovetail with project management, quality control, standards, and procedures. The common sense observation of Watts Humphry and TQM advocates is that employees are most enthusiastic and productive where they have a say in the matter.

9

Generalist roles

Generalists are the people who do the mainstream work of data processing, applying automation to satisfy user-department requirements. Figure 9-1 shows how a data processing staff can be seen in a kind of a three-way matrix as people with position titles, performing roles, and assigned to projects.

In mainframe COBOL installations, titles have usually been assigned and people tasked according to their roles. An analyst was an analyst, a programmer a programmer. Good programmers aspired to become analysts. Their careers progressed within role definitions: junior programmer to associate programmer to senior programmer.

The role-oriented model fit with the waterfall development paradigm of the time. Analysts wrote requirements and let them splash down to the designers. Designers wrote specifications for programs to satisfy the requirement and let them fall through to the programmers. The programmer wasn't supposed to think much about the application— just produce good COBOL.

IBM endorsed the move from the role-oriented model to a project-oriented model in the 1970s with their chief programmer concept. At issue is whether affinities are strongest within a project or among tools. The human brain can absorb a limited amount of information: some of it has to be static. The role-oriented model made knowledge of tools and procedures static and varied the business problems. A project-oriented model makes the business problem more of a constant and broadens the scope of tools and procedures with which a person works. As tools become easier to learn and use, the project-oriented model is more and more appropriate. The roles filled by generalists on a project or maintenance team are:

- Programming
- Detailed design
- General design
- Data design
- Test design
- Test data developer

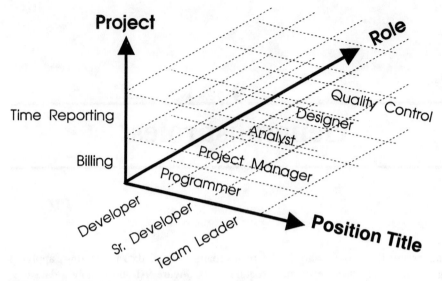

9-1 Three-dimensional matrix for data-processing generalist assignments.

- First-line manager
- Analyst
- Shopper
- Configuration manager
- User support

This chapter discusses the issues of filling roles within a project, training for those roles, and combinations of roles that a single person can assume. It is closely related to chapter 15, which covers procedures for carrying out the tasks assigned to various roles. Chapter 10 describes the roles of specialists on staff to support the generalist developers.

Programming

Oracle's programming tools are extremely powerful. They are easy to use for those who do simple things with them, complex if the applications are complex. The core skills every Oracle applications programmer needs are:

- Relational concepts
- SQL*Language
- The PL/SQL language
- SQL*Plus
- SQL*Forms (less frequently, some other front-end tool or compiled language)
- Skill with some report generator

These are not difficult to master. It takes a few weeks to study them in school. SQL and PL/SQL are the hardest technical skills to learn, though the introduction of PL/SQL has actually simplified matters by eliminating the need to write convoluted nonprocedural statements in SQL to achieve procedural objectives.

Defining the requirement overshadows pure programming in an Oracle tools environment. Oracle presents data to end users primarily via terminals and reports. Both the SQL*Forms and SQL*ReportWriter tools are definitional. The programmer indicates which tables and fields are used in a process, and the Oracle tool generates a process to handle them. The portion that looks like traditional programming, with syntax rules, functions, operators, and all, is buried in small nuggets of procedural code within the definitional framework. It is no misnomer when Oracle calls their SQL*Forms programming tool the forms designer; it concerns itself as much with layout as with logic. The menu and report tools are also oriented towards the designer.

The upshot is that Oracle 4GL programming work is mostly design. It makes sense to assign the roles of module designer and programmer to the same person. That person might choose to write a design specification for a particularly complex program, but will ordinarily code from a higher-level design or even the requirements document. Most form and report processes are largely defined by the tables and columns they use.

A CASE design provides a designer/programmer with the same type of guidance as would traditional design documentation. It specifies the tables and columns and the business rules used within each process. A data dictionary specifies most of the field validation. Oracle CASE generation translates these specifications into a form or report product. It reduces the programmer's job to one of polishing the format, invoking subroutines to handle business rules, and implementing some measure of code to handle logic peculiar to the module being developed. With or without CASE the programming and design roles belong together; there isn't much for a pure programmer to do.

Oracle systems usually involve a degree of intense, head-down programming. Most of it takes the form of support code:

- User exits from SQL*Forms and SQL*ReportWriter.
- PL/SQL and SQL routines to implement business rules.
- 3GL code (usually C or COBOL) to implement business rules.
- Operating system shell scripts for batch processes.

Some application areas require complex batch processes in pro-Oracle languages. Financial modeling, language processing systems, and statistical systems often draw from Oracle databases. The waterfall model still applies to this kind of line-edited code; each module requires thorough planning and written design specifications before anyone starts coding. Especially in coding subroutines, it is more important for the programmer to be skillful with the language than to know the application.

SQL deserves special mention as a programming language. A number of programmers, including many who are otherwise successful with Oracle's 4GLs, find the nonprocedural approach difficult to conceptualize. Working with statements that deal with an entire set of records simultaneously instead of taking them one by one takes a mental shift. A distinct minority of Oracle programmers are proficient with the features that make the language most powerful: subqueries, outer joins, and sets of nested SQL functions. Even fewer understand the performance issues in using these features. The implications for management are:

- Each shop needs one or two SQL gurus to whom the others can turn for help with coding and performance issues. Small shops can fill this role with an on-call consultant. The role will diminish somewhat as PL/SQL reduces the need for complex SQL statements, and the cost-based optimization in Version 7 reduces the need for coders to be concerned with performance.
- Complex SQL for 4GL processes should be worked out in advance, often even written into the module design. This discipline is valuable even if the programmer and the designer are the same person.
- SQL training has to be an ongoing process. Average programmers do not seem to pick it up through usage the same way they learn Oracle's 4GL products or even PL/SQL.

Referring back to Fig. 9-1, the programmers responsible for the mainline 4GL work on an Oracle project usually double as module designers. They need to work with the users and know the application. They can develop their modules in a prototype mode. The programmers who write line-edited code for subroutines don't need to be associated with the project. They can be systems programmers, DBAs, consultants, or other members of the staff with a good knowledge of the tools to be used. This level of programming is often considered more a specialist's than a generalist's skill.

Most people enter the data processing field as programmers. Some come directly from technical curricula in college. Others teach themselves on the job in other departments or at home. Some go to matchbook-cover schools, learn in the armed services, or get promoted from administrative positions. Where they come from is not important, nor is a college degree or any other credential. The skills a person needs to be a successful programmer are:

- Ability to define and solve problems.
- Ability to learn.
- Ability to use tools.
- Curiosity.
- Ability to read well and write passably.

Like all employees, programmers must be able to get along with people and work in a team. The specific computer language skills a programmer needs change all the time. Oracle is accelerating the pace with its CASE tools and new 4GLs; what a programmer needs most is the ability to learn. There is no substitute for hard work in the hiring process. Interviewers have to dig into how well the candidate has learned each new skill in the past and assess how willing and able they are to keep doing so.

Detailed design

Detailed design, the specification of individual modules, is so low level that it usually merges with programming in a high-level language. In contrast, data design in Oracle systems is a high-level process fairly closely tied to data modeling. The database plan for an application has to take all related systems into consideration and has to be complete almost before coding starts.

Most of the time the detailed designer and programmer are one and the same. Standard, recurring elements and hard parts of the system make the exceptions. The following design elements need to be in place preceding the development of individual code modules:

- Standard screen and report formats for the application.
- Application naming conventions.
- Specifications for standard subroutines, often to implement business rules.
- Help routine specifications.
- Specifications for custom security, backup/restore, data integrity, and continuity of operations processes.

These elements must work together and must be consistent throughout the entire application. A design benefits to the extent that it is the product of a single person with a project-wide vision. Because they have global implications, these detailed specifications must be committed to paper and reviewed by the entire project team.

Programmers usually fill the detailed design role. Oracle's 4GL tools are intended to handle design and implementation simultaneously. System-level detailed design, writing specifications to implement common subroutines, interface specifications and formatting conventions, is more the province of whoever handles general design.

General design

An application system must appear both in the total concept and in the details as though it is the product of one mind. It needs to be logical in its organization and consistent in its execution. The pieces need to fit together. Moreover, it needs to function well in its selected environment. A general designer has to put together an overall architecture, outline the common threads that hold the system together, and specify the operating environment in which it will all work.

General design is the most creative part of system development. Analysis is the right-brain process of collecting facts about the requirement. Data modeling and design is a matter of applying skills and experience to the facts acquired during design, and detailed design such an automatic process that CASE tools can do it for you. Synthesizing a system from the requirement, the available tools, hardware, and skills is the major left-brain activity in the development process.

Frederick Brooks (1987) observes that "Great designs come from great designers. Software construction is a *creative* process . . . The differences between the great and the average approach an order of magnitude." Almost all great designs are the product of a single person, however many others might advise and support that individual.

The design process must take into account every element of automation involved in delivering function to the users, whereas most development processes are only a matter of writing software. Figure 9-2 lists a few design considerations. The environment might dictate many of these parameters for small systems. Many or all of them might be open when it comes to enterprise systems.

- Defining the so tware system structure: what processes will be available to each user, how will the choices be presented and how will the processes be invoked.
  - ~ What kind of menuing will be used
  - ~ How functions are grouped or divided into modules
  - ~ What standard subroutines will be needed
- Defining the software environment
  - ~ Operating systems on each platform
  - ~ Oracle and other RDBMS systems products
    - Tools
    - Release levels
    - Distribution of function
- Defining the communications environment
  - ~ Data links
    - Hardwire connections
    - Leased capacity
    - Switched lines
    - Common carrier packet switching
  - ~ Networks
    - LAN / WAN type (ethernet vs. token)
    - Network software (NCP, TCP/IP)
- Defining the hardware environment
  - ~ Processor speed
  - ~ Processor memory
  - ~ Disk configuration
- Distribution
  - ~ Data distribution
  - ~ Client/server distribution of process
- Security
  - ~ Access security
  - ~ Data security
- Continuity of operations
  - ~ Graceful degradation
  - ~ Disaster recovery plan

9-2 Elements of general design.

With smaller systems, the designer usually turns out to be the analyst. The issue is finding a person to define is how to satisfy the requirement with the tools at hand. It is usually less of a stretch for the analyst to learn enough about implementation tools than for tools experts to learn the requirement, so the analyst gets the job. With CASE tools there is no question; the analyst designs because 80% of the design flows directly from analysis.

Large system designs start out much like small ones, with a functional decomposition as shown in Fig. 1-3. These elements are largely independent of environmental considerations. After the outline of a design is in place, the large system designer becomes more of a project and information manager. The designer leads the effort to synthesize expert advice on the topics named in Fig. 9-2 into an architecture that satisfies the functional requirements, performs adequately, is affordable, and presents an acceptable level of risk.

The project analyst(s) often double as lead designer(s). The transition from analysis to design is very direct, and the analyst will automatically think ahead to design in the process of resolving requirements. Project analysts, then, are often the ones to write design specifications with system-wide implications.

Designers rise from the ranks of programmers and analysts. They learn from experience, starting as programmers or analysts on small projects. Designers certainly need to be schooled in modern techniques. Courses in relational design are indispensable. It helps to take courses in whatever technologies apply to a design at hand. Currently these almost have to include local-area networks, client/server architectures, communications, and some RDBMS internal architecture.

A designer is like an artist commissioned to produce a given *oeuvre*. The foundation is a thorough understanding of the requirement at hand, the client, and the available materials. Genius is the ability to spin common materials together to achieve an uncommon result. There is no way to make an artist out of just anybody in either data processing or the fine arts. The trick is to recognize talent where it exists and encourage its possessor to make the most of it.

Data design

A data design is a practical implementation of the analyst's entity-relationship model. What are the practical considerations? They include performance, storage space, the constraints imposed by existing systems, and ease of programming.

A data design is usually the product of collaboration between the analyst/designer(s) and the DBA. The analyst/designer knows the table sizes, transaction volumes, and response time requirements. Oracle's CASE, if used, will have prompted the analyst for these data in the course of capturing requirements. The DBA should know the physical installation and be adept at tuning and making performance trade-offs.

The distributed data designs that are making sense for an increasing number of large applications pose special challenges for a designer. They often run up against the state of the art in RDBMS software, network software, communications bandwidth, and application design. The designer has to be highly confident that systems analysis has accurately shown the nature and volume of both transactions and data. It then becomes a question of the specifications and performance of the hardware, networks, and operating system components. There is not a great abundance of expertise in these issues. Moreover, the state of the art is evolving rapidly in all of the technologies involved. It is usually wise to call in an Oracle consultant or a highly qualified outsider to help in distributed designs.

It is critical to get the data design right. Design is the most important determinant of performance. The data design is also relatively final. Changing it disrupts whatever forms, reports, or compiled programs use the altered tables. Without CASE generation tools, changing the design is a disaster. In a CASE environment, changing the data structure means regenerating the programs within an application. Although the CASE Version 5 re-engineering faculty should preserve most of the logic, the modules need at a minimum to be retested. SQL*Forms and SQL*ReportWriter modules outside of CASE will need systematic changes that in some cases are so laborious it is less expensive simply to recode them. It being the cornerstone of an Oracle system, the data design must be understood and agreed upon by the whole project team. Users need to understand the data model upon which the design is based and should appreciate the performance trade-offs implicit in the design.

Unless there are bona fide experts on staff, it is almost always worth the price to have outside help with the data model and design. The best independent consultants in the business cost about $1000/day. Most of the time, the data modeling and design phase of a project only lasts a few weeks. The staff designers even in large shops only get to do them every year or two. Critical as it is, it makes sense to bring in an expert who has broad experience in the process. Buying two or three days of a consultant's time to ask probing questions during a design review is very cheap insurance against an inefficient or unworkable design.

Test design

The only way to see if a data system works is to test it, and the only parts of a system that can be known to work are those that have been tested. The logic is obvious. However, testing is such a tedious task that otherwise systematic shops are often go about it haphazardly. An organization needs development procedures that identify the test plan as a design task and supporting standards to describe what it includes.

The test designer must specify how to collect representative test data for the data tables within the system. The choices are to invent test data out of whole cloth, using the data design for guidance, or to extract live data records and adapt them to the purpose. Live data is almost always the preferred choice. It looks real, it is available in volumes that would be tedious to invent, and it often contains data combinations that a test designer might overlook. Regardless of the source, the test designer ideally specifies in writing all of the unique data conditions that have to be represented in each file or table and the total number of records needed.

The test designer must specify data entry and update transactions. Again, the design indicates which data conditions need to be represented and why.

Testing is usually planned at the module, subsystem, and system levels. The test design usually provides data for module testing, though the module developers themselves often adapt it to their needs. Subsystem and system level testing follows the designer's specifications more closely.

Testing has several objectives. The most important, universal goal is to confirm that the system works right. Some tests check out the user interfaces, making sure the system flows smoothly and is easy to understand. Stress tests, also called volume tests, validate performance under load conditions. The system-wide tests have to fit the architecture of the system. The test designer works from the general design specifications, consulting with the analyst and designer.

The analyst is the person who knows the data and business rules best. If the test designer and the analyst are not one and the same, the analyst should at least be an advisor.

Looking at the data that a module is expected to process is a useful crosscheck against the written description of functions it is to perform.

The roles of test designer and test data developer are a good ones to rotate among the developers on a team. They are essential but not exactly a career aspiration. When nature follows its course the weakest members of a team are likely to be stuck with the least agreeable work, which almost always involves testing. Not so dumb as to miss the implication, they might not put their heart into putting together decent tests. Unless the process is checked the system can go clear through to installation without a thorough test; after all, nobody really wants to see the system delayed. Installing a system that doesn't work is not in anybody's long-term interest even though it satisfies a lot of short-term concerns. A good test plan protects the developers from their own human nature.

Test data developer

The person who puts together test data needs a high sense of mission. It is important to the process, and important to do it right.

The programmers who will use it are the best candidates for assembling test data. They need to get to know it sooner or later. The test data developer almost always needs ongoing support from the test designer. There are inevitably situations that the test design doesn't describe in enough detail and live data that doesn't appear in the expected format.

A test data developer needs as much help as possible from the user community. They are the ones who can provide source documents and who know the quirky situations that confound their existing systems. An ideal test data development team includes both users and people from MIS.

The more widely used a product is, the more it costs to fix a bug. Half the effort in putting out a new release of the Oracle kernel goes into testing. Oracle is organized in such a way that the testing group is a natural ally of the developers, rather than a traffic cop whose mission is to prevent the release of code. Oracle hires and promotes people within the testing organization in career positions. They take it seriously. The testers' charter is to assemble the most diverse, realistic test suites they can to enable the developers to find bugs early rather than late. Their favorite source is customer data, though they also assemble contributions from the developers and make up their own test data from the program specifications.

Project librarian

Somebody has to keep track of libraries, data designs, modules, specifications, test data, CASE materials, and other documentation at the project level. The MIS departmental document control section usually doesn't want it until the system is somewhat together and they can accept a complete baseline. Until then, the project manager delegates the responsibility to team members by type of documentation according to their roles on the project.

Whoever handles the librarian function for a given type of material makes sure it is available to other team members. An SQL*Forms V3.0 librarian maintains the mother form containing installation standard trigger code. The data designer makes the current baseline version of the table definitions available to the rest of the team. A C or COBOL librarian keeps up copy modules corresponding to Oracle tables.

Project manager

Whoever gets assigned to lead a project is responsible for organizing and coordinating the work. Among the project manager's tasks are to:

- Maintain the work breakdown structure.
- Estimate task cost and duration.
- Assign and manage tasks.
- Manage automated project-management tools.
- Staff the project.
- Manage the budget.
- Manage the schedule.
- Manage procurements.
- Report to management.
- Control quality—the adherence to standards and procedures.

The analyst and designer, the technical leaders of the project, will always have the best handle on the work to be done. Their responsibilities grow in all directions as projects get larger. In larger undertakings they have to pass off some or all of the project management responsibility to other people.

On projects of a few staff-months, management is an informal process that doesn't take enough time even to be budgeted. There is no need to account for management work apart from the technical work. Internal communications are easy: one person making notes.

As projects approach a staff-year in size it becomes useful to break tasks out through a work breakdown structure (WBS) and Gantt chart. Even if only one person is doing the work, the tools are a useful device for organizing the tasks and establishing a development sequence. Performing tasks out of order can cost a lot of time in rework even in the smallest of project teams.

The project manager role needs to be allotted some time when an effort exceeds two staff-years and the team size grows to three or four people. Staffing the team becomes an issue: what types of people are needed and when are they needed? It becomes more important to link the project with outside events. Management wants more in the way of status reports on larger projects. Confusion has its own costs; budgeting time for project management ensures that time devoted to technical work is optimally spent.

Management tasks become a major distraction to technical team leaders for projects on the order of 10 staff-years and up. At this point, they need an administrative assistant to whom they can delegate project management chores. A subordinate can handle running the automated project-management system, keeping the budget and schedule up to date, and preparing management reports. This leaves the technical leader with only true management tasks: staffing, task assignments, and quality.

In truly large projects, the technical leaders usually distinct from project management. The Manhattan Project to build the A bomb is a good example. Dr. Robert Oppenheimer led the physicists to build the bomb, and General Leslie Groves staffed the project, set the schedules, procured what they needed, and made policy decisions for the team.

Regardless of its size, a project needs some investment in management in order to maximize the return on the purely technical energies devoted to it. The technical leaders are the natural project managers, but there comes a point at which they cannot do both. It makes sense to delegate the administrative functions of project management in medium-sized projects, and to separate project management from technical leadership on larger projects. The project manager role is filled, then, by some combination of analysts, administrative personnel, and professional managers.

First-line manager

First-line managers usually occupy permanent positions, as opposed to project managers who are appointed for the duration of a task. The responsibilities that go with the role include among other things:

- Hiring.
- Personnel management.
- Making job assignments.
- Establishing performance objectives.
- Performance evaluations.
- Approving expenses.
- Project management.

First-line management positions exist in many organizations as a matter of corporate structure. If a company is organized in a hierarchy with each manager having a span of control of 5 to 10 people, the data processing shop usually looks that way too. It gives focus to people's ambitions: progress in the company means rising through the ranks. Whether or not first-line management positions are essential to carrying out the data processing department's mission is a question worth addressing.

First-line managers play a vital role when they serve as project managers. The role requires technical skills in the tools used in the project and in the use of project-management tools. To be credible as a leader, the project manager must share with the analyst and designer a thorough understanding of the requirement and solution. Project manager is a good role for first-line management, but only if the managers have retained their technical skills.

How to use time has often been an issue for bottom-rung managers in a hierarchy. The formal responsibility of keeping tabs on 5 to 10 people does not occupy them. They pick up or create other responsibilities to fill the day. Among them are handling staff assignments from the DP manager, performing technical work, and serving as liaison with users. In their capacity as supervisors, they might critique their subordinates' work.

The validity of giving many of the named tasks to a first-line manager is now in question. If the line workers are responsible for the quality of their work and work procedures, who should critique them? Today's consensus is that it should be their peers as much as management. Who should establish performance objectives and do formal reviews? The Deming school (Aguayo, 1991) advocates doing without them. Who should make project assignments? Probably a project manager. Take these tasks away, and there is not much of a job left.

The MIS director of an Oracle shop should consider the alternative of increasing the span of control of card-carrying managers and using project managers and staff to handle most first-line functions. It provides several kinds of flexibility. Never appointing first-line managers means never having to demote them when the need goes away. Letting the senior technical staff have more of a leadership role, and not having a designated manager over them, gives DP more latitude in setting compensation. People at the working level tend to be more productive when their leaders understand what they are doing, as must be the case with analysts and project managers.

An extension of this argument is that a permanent management position should not exist unless the incumbent can spend more or less full time on management, organization, and leadership issues. The technical staff should be trained for and capable of providing a lot of its own management.

Analyst

Analyst as a job title covers a lot more than analyst as a role. The role is to determine user requirements. In that capacity, the analyst becomes the expert on the problem at hand and gets to know all the players involved. A natural result is that people with the job title of analyst wind up filling a number of other roles in most implementation efforts.

The person in the role of an analyst needs an even mix of interpersonal skills and technical skills. Users do not know precisely what they want. Worse, they often think they do. They ask for a system "just like what we have now, only integrated so we don't have to key stuff off of printouts." The analyst's role from a data processing standpoint is to learn and document the full requirement as the basis for a design. His or her business mission is broader. A successful analyst is one who instructs users in the process of analysis and leads them to share in understanding the full requirement. The corollary is readying them to recognize a satisfactory solution. A technically correct design is only half the battle; users have to believe in it to make it work.

Data processing theorists have contended that the analyst should not be concerned with implementation. Some consider it a sin to let the concept of a solution cloud a definition of the problem. "To a carpenter, every problem looks like a nail." goes the saying. There is some justice to their position: an analyst who knows Oracle on Netware might tend to structure problem definitions in Oracle client/server terms.

The other side of the argument is that a successful analyst is one whose systems get implemented. There is nothing wrong with writing a requirement such that a licensed application package, the Oracle RDBMS or some other package can handle the job. Assume an insurance company, for instance, requires access to source documents. The documents have traditionally been stored in file cabinets with a locator key in the database, but the time might have arrived to capture them in machine-readable image format. The analyst is only being realistic to omit it from the requirement with the note "Not yet: technology is too expensive." or note that the implementation should be phased because scanning will be cost effective in a few years. Likewise, an analyst could document a requirement for very simple security controls for a system out of ignorance of the state of the art. Inexperienced Oracle analysts who don't know the power of SQL*Forms tend to see a requirement to update tables one at a time instead of in complex master-detail relationships. There is a lot to be said for anticipating the solution. A naive analysis can be unrealistically complex or too simple.

The analysts in an Oracle shop should know what Oracle can do. They also need to know be familiar with the automated tools used in analysis. Analysts write a lot, so they should be familiar with word processors. They have to do estimation, so they should know how to use spreadsheets. The analyst has to know whatever CASE tools a shop uses. The bottom line is that an analyst must have a mix of technical and interpersonal skills. The job is to convert soft statements about the requirement into a hard definition that can serve as the basis for a design.

Analysts fill all kinds of other roles; what other kinds of people can do the analyst role? On small tasks where the analyst, designer, and programmer are one and the same, that person might have more of a programming bent. The danger is that to a programmer, everything looks like a programming problem. The programmer will listen to a user's requirement and say "I can do that in two weeks." and make good on the commitment. He or she can also claim with justice "You didn't tell me that." when the user asks for 1, then 2, then 10 small modifications to the system. A system developed from a programmers perspective often has no real architecture and soon grows out of control. To answer the question as to who can do analysis, it takes someone with analytical skills. Those skills are usually vested in people who carry the title of analyst.

The topic of how to develop analysts has been debated for years. The majority are ex-programmers whose curiosity led them to learn about the problems they are given to solve. Quite a few enter from user organizations or management consulting positions. They are self-selecting. The people who aspire to be analysts will be good analysts much more of the time than people eager for promotion make good managers.

It does not especially matter from where an analyst comes. The issue is in making sure they have all the training and tools to do the job. The major analytical techniques can be taught. Data modeling, interviewing, project organization, and the use of CASE tools are very systematic disciplines. Analysts should go to school on them. They learn the broader skills of dealing with people and handling political decisions by personal experience and listening to war stories. Developing analysts is a matter of recognizing talent where it exists, then providing training, opportunity and support to help it flourish.

Shopper

Custom code is a very expensive solution to any problem. Turnkey systems with no programmers whatsoever handle more and more data processing requirements. Shops with more unique requirements can keep programming to a minimum using integrated suites of application packages. The initial steps in the development process are similar to those for custom systems, namely setting a strategy and analyzing requirements. The next phase, that of locating, evaluating, and selecting packages, has not until recently been recognized as part of the life cycle. The people who do it often lack training and procedures.

Software is only one among many confusing elements in putting together data systems. The days are long past when the question was "Is a 360/40 big enough, or do we need a 360/50?" A shop can choose among a great many radically different architectures in processors, communications, networks, operating systems, RDBMS, programming languages, and even development methodologies. It requires a methodology for shopping: learn the marketplace, define requirements, formulate alternative solutions, learn values, and negotiate a contract.

Chapter 16 on sourcing outlines the substance of a methodology. It is hard to teach but not too difficult to learn. People in the role of shoppers first of all need some freedom. It takes time, a bit of local travel, and small amounts of money to collect reference materials such as magazines, books, and directories. Subscriptions to information services like CompuServ take a little money and faith in the people who get to use them. The shoppers need freedom to phone vendors all over the country. Most people enjoy shopping. With the support of the organization it is not hard to learn how to do a good job of locating products.

Everyone gets into the act once the designated shopper has found some products. It takes a good understanding of the requirement and a bit of business analysis to pick the right product. The users have to participate in choosing products they will use. In the case of applications software, the requesting departments usually read the literature and sit in on demonstrations. If the buy concerns software tools or computer hardware, the systems programmer, DBA, operations managers, and others should be involved. The shopper generally belongs to one of the interested groups in the first place.

Configuration manager

Any piece of software is liable to fall apart when the assumptions upon which it is built crumble. A development project has to assume a stable foundation, called a baseline, as the environment in which all components of the system will work. The applications element of a baseline includes the various requirements and design specifications. The systems element establishes the hardware, operating system, Oracle products, and release levels, utility programs, networking, and other factors that affect system operation. The task of tracking all the configuration elements is called *configuration management* (CM).

Data design is the most important baseline element in most Oracle projects. Changing the table definitions affects all the programs that use them. Keymaps, called-subroutine specifications, data names, trigger libraries, views, synonyms, global parameters, and a host of other shared elements are also major baseline elements.

The person in the CM role must manage the baseline changes during development and production. The procedure is to accept requests for change, discuss them with the people who might be affected, group the agreed-upon changes into an updated baseline, adopt the updated baseline, and broadcast the changes to everyone who might be affected.

The CM role has to be exercised at both a project and an installation level. Design issues are resolved within an application, but changes such as a migration to a new hardware platform or a new release of Oracle take place across the board. Only very large projects need a full-time person to handle configuration management. The role is usually shared with that of designer, analyst or librarian.

User support

Giving user departments responsibility for running their own systems frees the DP department from having to staff an operations department. The trade-off is a new requirement to support users in their role as operators.

The user-support role concerns itself with tools rather than applications. Analysts must be the ones to help their users with questions that have to do with the application itself, such as how to produce a certain kind of report. This kind of support remains essential to the success of any automated system.

End users today have a decided PC orientation. They demand the ability to get their data down to a PC where they can get their hands on it. If that is impractical, they want tools on the Oracle platform that are as easy to use as a PC. Whoever handles end-user support must be expert in software packages available to the users. It helps to have some understanding of the applications and good analytical skills.

The most efficient way to develop code is to let someone else do it. User departments, wanting control over their data and the way in which it is presented, are willing and eager to take over—even if it means doing programming work that the MIS department could handle more efficiently. The DP manager can improve customer relations and take a load off the developers by putting the right people into user support.

Career progression

In organizations without much formal structure, progress through the ranks is a matter of responsibility and salary more than titles. The most common progression is programmer to analyst to manager. As Table 9-1 shows, it is a matter of learning to handle more roles and responsibility.

Data processing managers are usually promoted from the ranks of the generalists. They are the ones who know the business. The relative importance of analytical skills, and hence general business skills, is rising with the increased use of CASE and packaged software. This will bring data processing more in line with the organizations to which it belongs and might, at long last, enable data processing professionals to move into general management. The converse should be true as well. Users who pick up analysis skills as their areas are being automated might be able to move into data processing.

Summary

Data processing development involves more tasks than there are titles to go around. People cannot afford to overspecialize; teams would get so large that too much time would be lost in communication. The model that works best is a small team of people with overlapping technical skills and a deep, shared understanding of the business. Rigid position titles can hinder people moving into the roles they can best perform.

The two most obvious position titles are analyst/designer and programmer. Even the distinction between them is fading. As technology evolves, it is pushing more work forward to the analysts. With CASE, a well-analyzed requirement is as much as 80 percent

Table 9-1   Common assignments by role and job title.

Role \ Title	Programmer	Analyst	Project Manager	Line Manager
Analysis		•		
Data Design		•		
General Design		•	•	
Detailed Design	•	•		
Test Design	•	•		
Test Data Development	•	•		
Programming	•	•		
Project Management		•	•	•
Shopping	•	•	•	•
Librarian	•	•	•	•
Configuration Manager	•	•	•	
User Support	•	•		

designed and 60 percent coded. It appears that analysts will inherit increasing amounts of design, development and maintenance work as the productivity tools in their hands improve.

Projects need a lot of management, but people not so much. A fluid, task-oriented organizational structure serves best for Oracle development. The DP manager should be circumspect about creating permanent positions that might reduce flexibility and take manpower away from tasks at hand, but quite ready to assign people temporary roles such as project manager.

People need training by the roles they play more than the titles they carry. It is management's job to see that they get formal training where it is available and to devise alternatives where there is not. It can be valuable to track the roles a person plays and even include them in career development plans. A knowledge of the jobs to be done helps as analysts, designers, project managers and first-line managers estimate projects and assign and manage tasks.

10
Specialist roles

The data processing world is put together with fathomless layers of highly technical components. Following the old Navy adage, DP systems are "designed by geniuses to be used by idiots." Nobody in an applications shop has to know the internal workings of a central processor, disk drive, RDBMS kernel, Unix operating system, internal modem, fax card, LAN, SQL*Forms generator, or any of the rest of the tools. They are expected to work as advertised and serviced by an expert when they don't work.

An Oracle shop needs on-call experts in the fringe areas that genius has yet to dominate. Oracle might install and tune itself some day, but not yet: a DBA is needed. Unix might come preinstalled with the machine like MS-DOS or go on with a command like A:install, but not yet: a systems programmer is needed. Some old specialties like tape librarian, keypunch artist, and I/O desk manager are fading away, but not as fast as new ones emerge. This chapter describes the roles of:

- Systems programmer
- System administration
- Expert programmer
- Database administrator (DBA)
- Data administrator
- Network coordinator
- PC experts
- Hardware configuration
- Operations
- Quality control
- Configuration management
- Librarian
- Software process
- CASE expert

Only a very large shop can afford to staff these roles with separate people. Usually one person handles a number of roles. Often the requirement is satisfied using on-call consultant services.

Systems programmer

Operating systems have always been the focus of systems programming. Operating systems consist of code modules for every conceivable situation. The systems programmer's job is to select and tune the ones that are applicable for a given machine and suite of applications. Tuning is largely a matter of allocating main memory and disk storage to achieve optimal overall performance. The more memory the operating system uses the faster it can run, but the less is left for application programs.

Twenty and thirty years ago, the systems programmer had to customize operating system source code, and then assemble and link edit the operating system. It took real programming skill. These days it is extremely rare for anyone to even understand, let alone modify, operating system code. Operating systems provide interfaces for custom device drivers so they can support nonstandard I/O (input/output) devices. Hardware manufacturers and integrators almost always provide the interface code with their product, so all the systems programmer has to do is install it.

The systems programmer is not a programmer at all as far as the operating system is concerned. The job requires a knowledge of how the operating system works, a good ability to follow instructions, an intuition for reading between the lines when the documentation is poor, and a knack for wringing the most out of vendor support.

The systems programmer is usually involved in installing whatever other packaged software comes into the shop. Licensed software often affects or depends on the operating system tuning parameters that the systems programmer has selected. Major packages usually take tuning of their own. Just like operating system packages, the installation instructions for licensed software is sometimes obtuse. The systems programmer's trained intuition and skill in using hotlines comes in handy.

Just keeping up with the operating system requires lots of the kind of specific knowledge that is best taught in a classroom. A month a year is not excessive. The job also calls for lots of experimentation and self-study. A question for small shops is how to amortize the cost of the person and the training over just a few machines. A common answer is to contract for the service. An outside consultant can provide in-depth support to several shops and still have time enough to read and attend classes.

In small shops, the programmer who feels the most affinity with the machine gravitates into systems programming. Somebody has to figure out DOS, or Unix well enough to install it and the other software. They can go to class later.

With larger installations, the process is more formal. Whether home grown, hired in, or contracted, every large installation has to have a qualified systems programmer available. They also need an understudy, which gives a new designee time to attend a series of classes and learn the trade.

Systems programmer is a standard position title. Table 10-1 shows other roles that often go with the job.

System administrator

There has to be a single person in charge of any multiuser system to look after the common good. The major system-level functions are adding and deleting users, allocating resources, and backing up the system.

Table 10-1 Logical combinations of specialist roles.

The person who handles the role below may also handle those indicated with a dot to the right.	Systems Programmer	System Administration	Expert Programmer	The DBA	The Data Administrator	Network Coordinator	PC Expert	Hardware Configuration	Computer Operations	Quality Control	Configuration Management	Librarian	Software Process Coord.	CASE Expert
Systems programmer	X	•	•	•	•	•		•	•					
Install Operating System														
Tune Operating System														
Install licensed software														
System Administration	•	X			•									
User management														
Security administration														
Disk space management														
Continuity of operations														
Expert Programmer			X											
Low-level languages														
SQL & PL/SQL														
4GL tools														
Job Control & Utilities														
Data Base Administrator	•	•	•	X	•	•								
Install RDBMS														
Tune RDBMS														
Consult in Data Designs														
Data Administrator		•			X									
Oracle user administration														
Oracle space management														
DBMS continuity of operations														
Network Coordinator						X	•							
Network Configuration														
Physical Connection														
PC Expert							X							
PC Strategy														
Software Installation														
Hardware Configuration														
Hardware Maintenance														
Hardware Configuration								X						
Multi-user strategy														
Buying peripherals														

Table 10-1.   Continued.

The person who handles the role below may also handle those indicated with a dot to the right.	Systems Programmer	System Administration	Expert Programmer	The DBA	The Data Administrator	Network Coordinator	PC Expert	Hardware Configuration	Computer Operations	Quality Control	Configuration Management	Librarian	Software Process Coord.	CASE Expert
Computer Operations									x					
Scheduling														
Handling Tapes & printers														
Quality Assurance														
Output distribution														
Remote user support														
Quality Control										x				
Development Auditing														
Quality Assurance														
Configuration Management											x	•		
Librarian												x		
Software Process Coordinator.										•	•	•	X	•
CASE Expert														x

Every multiuser system exercises some control over who can use it and what they can do. The system administrator grants access to the system through user IDs and passwords. Most systems provide tools, which let the administrator limit what a user can access and the amount of resources each can use.

Passwords get compromised over time. People write them down or tell them to co-workers to let them into the system on an on-time basis. The system administrator has to force users to change passwords periodically to maintain an effective password-protection system.

Entropy increaseth. It is a law of physics that the amount of chaos in the universe increases over time, a short time in a multiuser operating system. Disk space gets fragmented as users create and delete files. It gets eaten up by permanent files—some needed and some merely forgotten. The system administrator needs to police the users.

It is axiomatic that computer hardware fails and data gets lost. The only protection is to create duplicate copies of the data through a backup process. Usually the most efficient way to handle the requirement is to let the system administrator do it using an operating system utility.

The role is merely administrative if someone else, like the systems programmer, has set up procedures to handle routine tasks. It does not require an extensive data processing background; any conscientious employee can handle it. If the systems administrator is responsible for developing housekeeping procedures, the task borders on systems programming.

Expert programmer

Applications programmers cannot be expert in every type of coding. In Oracle installations, their expertise tends to be in high-productivity languages and the applications they are implementing. Developers often need help when it comes to advanced programming in lower-level languages.

Oracle shops usually need experts to cover:

- Subroutine programming languages, most often C or assembler.
- Writing shell scripts using job control language and operating system utilities.
- Writing complex SQL and PL/SQL routines.
- Using advanced features of the 4GL tools.

Expert programmer roles can be filled by several people with different titles. Although the word *programmer* has been a misnomer in the systems programmer's job title for more than a decade, for historical reasons the assembler or C language expert is often on the system programming staff. The SQL and PL/SQL experts are usually DBAs or sharp applications developers.

Experts are sometimes tasked to perform rather than merely advise. The SQL expert might write START files to drop, create, and copy tables and views within an application. An application designer might write specifications for user exits and called subroutines for the resident C expert to code. There is no economy in having an applications programmer do the work unless it involves a skill they will need to advance their career. Some want to learn everything and others are happy to leave it to experts.

The professionals within a shop know who their experts are and will seek them out. They don't need to be formally named, just recognized. Management's responsibility is to make sure they are there and to acknowledge that their role as experts will take time away from their other assignments.

Staffing the expert programmer positions is part of management's responsibility in setting up a productive workplace. When there aren't any experts available, the natural human tendency on the part of people assigned to a task is to muddle through instead of confessing to management that they need help. The shortage of expertise announces itself through slipped deadlines. A proactive management can take the following steps to make sure people have access to the support they need to work efficiently:

- Identify the areas in which expertise is needed.
- Establish training plans for people in project and support roles.
- Establish the role assignments for shop experts and budget them time to fulfill the role.
- Develop lines of support outside the shop. Even the in-house experts need another line of defense. Oracle hotline support is useful, as are retainer arrangements with Oracle consulting firms and independent consultants.

The use of expert programmers is bound up with the themes of training and technology transfer. Every manager's goal should be to make employees more valuable to the organization—to improve their skills. The questions to ask are the same wherever an expert is used. Would the person who is being helped benefit by learning the skill? Do they have the time, background, and ability to learn the skill? Is it cost effective to have the skill at the requester's level within the organization?

Database administrator

A DBA is like a systems programmer for the Oracle system. At the systems level, the DBA performs the cookbook functions of installing the Oracle RDBMS and tools and the expert task of tuning the system. At the applications level, the DBA provides expert assistance in setting up instances, tablespaces, tables, indices, and views.

The DBA's job parallels that of a systems programmer, except that the scope is the RDBMS rather than the operating system. The same person often serves both roles in smaller shops. As noted above, the person with the title of DBA is frequently the resident expert on all functions of the DBMS. In Oracle shops this means the SQL and PL/SQL languages and 4GL tools.

Oracle functionality is usually spread over a number of machines. Host machines where the RDBMS and tables reside might do all the processing or simply act as servers. End users more and more frequently use PCs, either in terminal emulation mode or as Oracle clients. Either way, the DBA is responsible for making sure the links work. In client/server installations it involves setting up SQL*Net to link the system together. In host-mode environments the DBA has to make sure the emulator programs and Oracle keymaps work together.

DBAs usually serve as tuning experts. Data design is the most significant determinant of performance; the DBA plays a key role in physical implementation decisions such as denormalizing the database, spreading table spaces across available disk drives, and structuring indices. They stay involved during systems testing and production to ensure that the application performs acceptably well.

Data administrator

The data administrator (DA) has overall responsibility for the security and integrity of data within the RDBMS and for managing space. The role is similar to the systems administrator's, except that it is exercised within the purview of the DBMS. The two are often combined. Oracle OPS$ user IDs make it possible to combine the functions of Oracle and operating system access control.

The DA Oracle user has an ID/password system that limits access to authorized individuals and its systems of grants, views, and roles the data and processes those authorized people can use. Most shops use paperwork procedures to manage requests for access to the system. The DBA usually sets up SQL*START files the DA can use to bring new users into the system with access to the appropriate applications.

Managing space is a matter of monitoring space usage within the system and taking periodic action to free it up. It consists among other things of deleting unused tables, migrating old data to a backup medium, and reorganizing the database to improve performance and consolidate free blocks. The DA often uses utility software and routines written by the DBA and third-party software houses to accomplish these tasks.

The DA establishes backup/restore procedures appropriate to each instance and application. Small applications are often designed in such a way that a day's transactions can be reentered. These applications make do with operating system backups of the database files. Larger applications require applying update transactions from a REDO file to bring a restored database current as of the moment it crashed. The DA is responsible for deciding how many generations of backup tapes to keep and how to rotate them in and out of off-site storage. The systems administrator generally executes the backup plan put together by the DA.

The DA role is often shared with the DBA or systems administrator role. Two or more roles taken together make enough work for a full-time position in a smaller shop. The DA often works for the DBA when the role warrants its own full-time person. It can be an administrative position for someone without an extensive data processing background or an apprenticeship for the DBA role itself.

Network coordinator

This role used to be known as the communications coordinator until networks took over most communications functions. Oracle only recognizes a logical network. It takes for granted that the network people have established the environment defined to SQL*Net. It involves everything between any two machines in the system: LAN connections within buildings, WAN connections over leased lines or packet networks, hardwire connections where possible, modems, servers and their software and many more things the average manager and programmer want to work but don't have any desire to learn.

In smaller shops, configuring a network is a one-time affair. Out sourcing is an obvious way to handle it. The network coordinator, systems programmer, and sometimes the DBA act as the points of contact with the vendor. Small-shop network coordinators are usually handy with a screwdriver. They will run cable, install network cards, install LAN software, and do the other small tasks needed to add new users and move machines around within established networks.

Communications issues become highly complex in large shops and applications. The network coordinator is really an integrator, working with LAN hardware and software vendors, the common carriers who provide WAN service, the modems, packet assembler/disassemblers, switches, and multiplexers associated with leased lines, and as always the software interfaces. The role is a natural for out sourcing to a firm that employs people with the different kinds of expertise required to service a complex network. Just as in smaller shops, there is always a need for people with screwdrivers and diskettes who can set PCs up on LANs.

PC expert

PCs are part of the environment in the corporate world. More often than not, the data processing department is responsible for tracking, configuring, maintaining, networking, and loading them with software. The job has little to do with Oracle beyond the fact that the machines sometimes serve as terminals or clients to Oracle systems.

There is a policy role that calls for PC expertise. PCs represent a significant fraction of the automation budget, and standardization issues in hardware and software are important. Whether or not it is the person who deals with them at the physical level, someone needs to coordinate PC policy with an organization's long-term automation strategies.

The same people often handle the roles of PC expert and network coordinator. At the working level, they both involve a lot of hands-on with hardware. They are usually the contact with the organizations that maintain networks and PC equipment.

Hardware configuration

Hardware technology is always new, dazzling, and confusing. It takes a real expert to figure how well different vendor offerings relate to the needs of the business. The game becomes an order of magnitude more complex as Oracle dissolves dependence on specific vendors and architectures and straddles networks of dissimilar machines.

The problem of configuration was tough enough within a single product line. Proprietary architectures have long bound shops to the major hardware vendors. It has often been too wrenching of a change for an IBM AS400 or DOS/VSE-SP user to move to another vendor. As a result, though IBM users anguish over what to buy, the initials on the box are often not in question. Configuration for them is a matter of the right IBM offering.

Oracle's chosen mission is to eliminate dependency on the (hardware) vendor. Portability has always been one of their primary claims to fame. A pure Oracle installation can now choose among almost all major architectures in the marketplace: traditional mainframes, traditional minis, client/server on PCs, massively parallel Unix machines, RISC machines, and distributed combinations of all the above.

A staff hardware expert can usually make decisions within a manufacturer's product line, such as between RAID (redundant arrays of inexpensive disk) storage versus traditional Winchester type units, streamer tapes versus nine-track, or what size VAX box to buy. Systems programmers often double as hardware experts because they are the ones who have to install new devices. Their expertise is usually good enough for upgrades and peripheral devices, but the expertise of the whole shop should be brought together for major architectural decisions.

The relative merits of different hardware configurations depend on the applications they will run. The process of selecting a systems architecture has to be as holistic as possible. What are the applications? How will they be distributed? What is coming up? What are the costs of conversion? What expertise does the staff have, and what would they need to learn under each alternative? Hardware experts, staff and consultants, participate with all the other staff experts in putting together specifications.

The experts don't exist who can pronounce with certainty exactly which architecture and configuration is optimally suited to a given requirement. At best, the configuration process for a large project works through a series of estimates and approximations:

- Applications strategists project approximate processor, storage, and network workloads by time and location.

- The MIS department adds new projects to the existing workload to come up with projected totals by time and location. MIS then issues the specifications to vendors.
- Competing vendors and integrators assemble configurations that represent the best compromise among acquisition price, performance, expandability, and conversion/implementation costs.
- The committee that drew up the specifications decides which proposed configuration satisfies the performance requirements at the lowest long-term cost and risk.

In the final analysis, the role of hardware configuration expert is too varied to be filled by any one person for all cases. The systems programmer or PC expert can usually handle decisions within an already selected architecture. So many factors come into play in major architectural decisions that it usually pays to assemble a committee of experts.

Computer operations

Computer operations is a profession in decline. Oracle and other modern systems have eliminated most of what they used to do:

- Key input is now done interactively by users instead of keypunch operators.
- Job scheduling is done by users via their own menu screens.
- There are few tape jobs anymore, except backup.
- The demand for reports is down because information is available online.
- Users can have the reports they do need printed on local printers.

The question is how to handle the jobs that remain. This is not an issue in traditional mainframe shops. They usually have enough older systems, and enough volume in backup and printing, to support some sort of operations unit. In Oracle shops the major tasks remaining for operations are tape backup and high volume printing. No user department typically wants a noisy impact printer. In any case, it takes a skilled operator to load and align multipart forms, mount serially numbered check stock, and anticipate when the printer will need more paper. Tape backup is more automated. It involves mindlessly mounting one cartridge after another as the computer requests, and there are backup systems that switch volumes automatically to reduce or eliminate the need for an operator.

Output distribution is often an operator function. Operators get continuous forms decolated and burst, get envelopes stuffed, exchange diskettes, tape and other media with other locations, and set up to send and receive telecommunications. Operators are usually responsible for managing dial-in teleprocessing. They periodically have to reset modems and forcibly log people off the system.

Quality assurance is the operations job of checking output before it is sent to users, not to be confused with the quality control function of making sure the developers write good systems. Someone familiar with the application, usually the user who requested the job, makes sure that the run date, ink quality, registration, and so on are good enough for the purpose.

Where there is less than enough work to occupy a person in an operator job position, the role is usually handled by whoever handles data administration or system administration. If there are only a few demanding print jobs, they can be given over to the user departments.

Quality control

The ideal of maintaining a separate organization to impose quality standards is out of favor. The individuals who produce a product are the only ones who can know it intimately and ensure its quality. The traditional role of quality control (QC) has been to act as a traffic cop, holding up development or release of a product until it meets the installation standards. Given the volume and unworkability of traditional life-cycle standards, it meant that although QC didn't understand the products they were given to approve, they could find grounds for rejecting almost any of them. This role is being abandoned because it is counterproductive. What is left?

Quality has to be built in. It is impossible to have a quality design without quality analysis, and it is impossible to have quality programs without a quality design. It is hard, and inappropriate, for an outsider to judge the technical merit of these work products. If QC has a role to play, it is to ensure that the development teams follow the procedures. They can confirm that the development team and users have walked through and accepted the work products. They can see that there is a test plan, a project schedule, and user documentation. QC can aid the process by serving as advisors to the development team rather than policemen for management.

Although the ultimate test of quality is user satisfaction, the best that can be achieved before a product is turned over to users is a thorough simulation of live operations. That takes test data. One of the major responsibilities of a person in the QC role is to see that individual projects and the development staff as a group have well-defined test plans and comprehensive test data. It is fairly easy for an outsider to check: "So this is the form. Please point out the test database and the transaction scripts you use to test it."

Configuration management

Application teams have internal configuration management (CM) functions to manage functional baselines. The need is echoed at the installation level because individual applications must share data and an operating environment with one another.

The installation baseline includes configuration items that are broader than a single system. A change in the chart of accounts structure or part numbering scheme generally has rather far-reaching implications. A decision to use Microsoft Windows on every PC in the shop would raise questions: would the terminal emulators still work? Would any keymap functionality be lost? Which applications would be affected?

Very few installations are so organized that they keep installation baselines on paper, especially for smaller machines. However, there needs to be someone who can assess the effects of any proposed global change or at least knows who to convene for a discussion. Most of the time the CM role is shared with the person who does systems programming or handles the DBA role.

Librarian

The librarian is responsible for managing reference materials. References rank with training and tools among the significant resources people need to be productive. There are a number of different types of documentation a shop might need. Though more and more documentation is available through online help systems, there is no substitute for a hard-copy document to sit down and learn a topic. Library material usually needed includes:

- Oracle reference materials for common use. Every developer needs a handful of books at their desk such as SQL, PL/SQL, and SQL*Forms references. The ones they use less frequently would only be clutter to them and an expense to the company. If a developer can be confident the books will be available in the library when they are needed, that is where they belong.
- Operating system reference materials. A programmer needs a few common references such as job control at his or her desk. The rest should be available in the library.
- Licensed software references. The responsible analyst and designer customarily keep a full set of vendor documentation and users have the pieces relevant to them. Other people with occasional needs to see the documentation should be able to check it out from the library.
- Reference books by independent authors. Many of the most useful references on Oracle, Unix, and other operating systems, PC software, and many other computer topics are not written by the vendors but by outsiders. The lead technicians in the shop, the systems programmer, DBA, and expert programmers all have their own libraries. Making them available to everyone else through the library encourages the rank and file to develop their own expertise.
- Production system documentation. The library should be the place to go for authoritative information on production systems. It does not need to be in hard-copy format. In fact, machine-readable material is much more likely to be up to date. The librarian should be in a position to grant access to anyone who needs to know. As a footnote, the librarian should make it a rule to accept full suites of documentation for a given baseline or nothing at all. Inconsistent documentation is frequently worse than useless to a library user.
- Periodicals. The professional staff needs to keep up with the industry. They also spend a fair amount of time in the shopper role defined in chapter 9. There are some standards, like *ComputerWorld, Oracle Integrator, Oracle User Resource,* and *PC Magazine* or *PC World* that ought to be available to serve both ends.
- Glossy Brochures. Product literature arrives in the mail and people pick it up at conferences. They usually lose it unless they act on it immediately. An alternative is to give it to the librarian to keep in a loose file.
- Standard reference materials such as a dictionary, ZIP directory, white- and yellow-page phone books, *Oracle Business Alliance Program Products and Services Catalog,* and product catalogs.

A library needs shelf space. Access has to be controlled if the librarian is going to enforce check-out procedures, otherwise it should generally be open for the convenience of after-hours workers. The check-out issue is a classic trade-off between convenience and control. An honor system is the only practical approach where there is not enough of library function in the organization to support a full-time librarian. Even when the library can be staffed, the inconvenience of a formal check-out procedure has to be weighed against the integrity of the library and the cost of lost books. To keep any control at all, a library needs:

- Posted rules to cover checkout and return procedures and to indicate which references must stay in the library.
- Clear markings on library copies of books.
- A catalog of everything that is available for checkout and of documentation that is available online.
- A checkout sheet for every item available for borrowing.

The need for reference books extends beyond the library itself. Every professional keeps the books they use frequently readily at hand. It helps if the librarian knows who has what, so the shop can order the appropriate references with a new release of Oracle or the catalog can include reference books that an individual keeps at their desk. Buying books is sometimes an involved process in a corporate bureaucracy. The librarian can be the one to deal with bookstores.

The management requirements for PC software licenses are similar to those for books. If the company has bought them, someone needs to know where they are. The librarian role can include ordering new packages and upgrades.

The librarian role is usually handled by an administrative person. Some professional who makes heavy use of the library, like the systems programmer or DBA, can be assigned to oversee the operation and help with technical issues.

Software process coordinator

Watts Humphrey (1989) defines the need for a software engineering process group (SEPG). His premises are simple. First, if nobody is in charge of defining procedures for standard tasks, people will all do them differently. Quality and productivity will be highly variable and certainly less than optimal. Therefore there must be standards and procedures suited to the tools at hand. Secondly, if nobody is charged with improving the procedures, they probably will not improve. Creative people's innovations will amount to ways around the system instead of becoming improvements to the system. Therefore the creative people have to contribute to continually improving the way things are done.

The development environment consists of computer hardware and software tools. In a broader sense it includes cultural givens like organization and accounting practices, externally imposed givens like government documentation standards, and shop practices that apply to other environments besides Oracle. It might include a commitment to store-bought methodologies like those from Ed Yourdin and James Martin. Standards and procedures such as those described in chapters 14 and 15 describe how the installation accomplishes its work within the given environment.

The SEPG's charge is to continually improve the way things get done. This equates to improving quality and productivity. The SEPG should be a driving force in the selection of development hardware and software tools. Management needs input from the developers themselves to make optimal cost versus function trade-offs in buying tools. Optimizing the return on the investment once the tools are bought is even more a matter for the technicians.

The SEPG, a sort of committee of the whole of the professional staff, has to be the organization in charge of maintaining standards and procedures. They are the chief users and beneficiaries, and certainly the ones whose commitment is needed to make them work. The SEPG needs management. A lean-running Oracle shop will probably find it expedient to assign the role to a single software process coordinator (SPC).

The SPC is the ultimate consensus role. Input comes from the whole professional staff, and at least the senior members have to buy into any changes to the process. They not only have to agree with them in principle, but they have to commit to using them. The SPC's function is to solicit and assemble suggestions for change, organize whatever discussions are needed, and get software tools ordered, and get standards and procedures updated as appropriate.

CASE technologies define major elements of the software process. In a CASE environment, the SPC and the CASE expert or coordinator will usually be one and the same. Their major issue is how to integrate called subroutines, programmed modifications, non-Oracle and non-CASE systems and other external factors with the CASE methodology and tools. Project managers are good candidates for the role of SPC because they deal with every phase of the development cycle. Humphrey points out that rotating the SPC role makes a lot of sense. The mission is to examine potential changes, and changing the people results in changing points of view.

CASE expert

There are experts in using CASE as well as experts in managing it. Since CASE is the ultimate software process management tool, the expert in charge should have a broad vision of what CASE means to the business and the development process. That person is the software process coordinator.

The experts in the mechanical aspects of CASE, such as importing metadata or re-engineering triggers, are generalists who should stay busy with project work but have time available to help their peers as needed.

Summary

There are usually more specialist roles within a shop than people filling them. Each shop has to establish job titles, position descriptions and salaries that make sense within the organization. Table 10-1 shows the typical combinations of roles that go into job descriptions.

Specialists' career paths do not as frequently lead into management as they do for generalists. They tend to acquire more skills and responsibilities as they grow within an organization, then move to another when they run out of headroom.

Depending on the size of the shop, a number of the specialist roles can be filled by outsiders. They need to be available on call, although there is not enough work to keep them occupied full time. Not costing money when they are not needed is only one advantage of using outside consultants. Serving multiple clients gives them the kind of broad experience that is difficult to develop within a single organization. It allows them the opportunity to become true experts. Outside consultants do not have to change jobs to broaden their expertise. They simply broaden their client base.

Educating the masses is always an issue with specialists. Some of the things they do are not of interest to the people who use their services but others should be passed along. It is a management task to structure expert support in such a way that expertise rubs off where appropriate.

11
Training for Oracle professionals

The pace with which Oracle introduces products sustains a sizable training industry. Oracle's tools are so rich that it is an ongoing challenge for an Oracle person just to learn the tools with which they work.

Computer professionals, to increase their value in this rapidly changing industry, need a broader education than mere technical training. A career-development program should include education in the business and provide for continuing education outside the workplace.

An employer pays for training two ways. Courses cost money and cost hours that employees would otherwise spend on their jobs. The alternative of not training people is more expensive, but the costs are hidden. They include the time spent in on-the-job training, decreased productivity, increased rework, and a lower level of dedication. The questions are how much training does a person need, and how to get a maximum of training value for the investment. A comprehensive training plan takes into account who needs training, what they need, and how it will be delivered.

Career training requirements

Product knowledge is such a perishable commodity it is a shame to depend so much on it in hiring. A classified ad will stipulate that a candidate know SQL*Forms 3.0, rejecting any candidate who does not, when the programmer will be around years after those products have faded from memory and will probably need to learn a number of other tools in any case. The topmost objective in hiring should be to get a person who is trainable, who will be able to learn the tools at hand whatever they are. Not too incidentally, that person will have to master a large number of topics that are not on the list to make him or herself valuable to the company.

In the course of a career, an employee needs to become educated in a number of areas. He or she will pick up a lot by osmosis—doing the job and being around other people. Their learning covers professional education in Oracle and other data processing topics, business education, and personal improvement. The MIS department must be concerned with training staff and users in the following:

- Using specific Oracle and third-party development tools.
- Relational systems concepts.
- Analysis and development methodologies.
- Installation standards and procedures.
- End-user tools.
- Business functions and applications.
- Use of applications software packages.
- Management and communications skills.

Formal aspects of the training belong in the employee's career plan. The MIS director might dictate that everybody take courses in relational concepts and the installation standard development methodologies.

Companies that make a long-term investment in their employees—this correlates very closely with successful companies—usually put together an education plan for each employee. Table 11-1 shows typical training requirements for Oracle professionals.

Training in the business can be immensely helpful to new employees. Most data processing people are only familiar with business areas for which they have had responsibility. Some know little about what the users they do support actually do, besides using their software. It is hard for users to have confidence in data processing people who don't know how orders come in, products get made, and the bills get paid.

It is not usually feasible for the MIS department to provide in-depth courses in application areas. MIS should take advantage of courses that the departments themselves offer. What better way to introduce a new analyst to the shipment scheduling application than to have him or her attend an orientation course with new hires in the shipping department? When there are no classes, the MIS employees have to teach themselves whatever business area they will support. The most help that MIS can provide is a methodology for self study.

More than half the effect of a technical course is lost unless the students get to use it within a few months. A career training plan establishes the objective of developing a well-trained professional within the first few years of a person's employment. It helps to leave the actual schedule quite loose, sending people to class as they start on projects where they will use what they learn. Standing contracts with training organizations are an easy way to implement this just-in-time training. Oracle and other major trainers offer popular classes frequently enough to meet requirements as they come up.

Training sources

There are lots of ways to pick up education and training. A manager must keep in mind what makes training effective as he or she selects training sources for each requirement. Here, in no particular order, are factors that make training work:

Table 11-1   Typical training requirements.

Class \ Career Path	Analyst/Developer	DBA	Data Administrator	Quality Control	Configuration Management	Systems Programmer / Network / Hardware
Relational Concepts	X	X	X	X	X	X
Relational Design	X	X	X	X	X	
Introduction to the Business	X		X	X		
SQL and SQL*Plus	X	X				X
CASE Design	X	X		X	X	
CASE Generation	X					
Oracle Tools: SQL*Forms ReportWriter Oracle Card	As applicable	As needed to provide support				
Oracle Internals		X				
Oracle Tuning	As applicable	X				
SQL*Net		X				
Operating System Commands	X	X	X	X	X	X
Operating System Shell Programming	X	X				X
Compiled Languages	As Required	C				Those in the shop
PRO*Language interfaces	As Required	At least Pro*C				

- *Focus*. The student must be dedicated to the process of learning.
- *Preparation*. The student has to have the prerequisite courses or knowledge.
- *Relevance*. The student will pay attention if the topic is meaningful.
- *Hands on*. Training is more effective if it is reinforced by class problems.
- *Applicability*. Training will stick if the student can put it to immediate use.
- *Organization*. The course syllabus or study plan must approach topics in a logical order.

- *Expert instruction*. The teacher or instruction leader has to know enough to handle questions as they arise.
- *Materials*. Most students take handouts back for use as references. Strong graphic presentations and examples make the instruction stick.
- *Discussion*. It is human nature that students take instruction more seriously if they can participate in it. They also benefit by asking questions that relate directly to problems at hand.

Table 11-2 outlines the relative advantages of a number of training alternatives. The expense of the more costly ones pays for the labor involved in preparing and delivering the course. The less costly ones depend more on the students' motivation and native learning abilities. Because the biggest cost in training is usually the student's salary for the time he or she spends studying, it is good business to put quality before price in choosing the delivery method.

The acquisition methods described in chapter 16 work well for training services. It doesn't cost much to compile an RFP including a list of courses, indication of any customization that might be needed, the estimated numbers of students, and a training schedule. It is easy to locate potential vendors because training firms are very good at locating

Table 11-2   Alternative means of delivering training.

Method	Characteristics
Stand-up Training	
In-house instruction	*Economical for high-volume training requirements. Count in the cost of setting up and running student problems on in-house computer.*
Using an employee from professional staff	Requires an expert on staff. Either purchase training materials or figure on making a multi-week investment putting them together.
Using an outside instructor	
From Oracle	High cost, high quality instructor and training materials.
From a third party	Costs less than Oracle, but the buyer has to confirm the quality of instruction. May require different firms to handle different requirements. Can be very flexible tailoring a course to local needs.
Off-site instruction	*Economical for low volume requirements. Can schedule training "Just in Time" to prepare a person for an assignment.*
At Oracle	High cost and high quality instructor and training materials. Courses on almost every Oracle topic. Frequent schedules.
At a 3rd party location	Lower price, often less travel, and at times more experienced instructors than Oracle. Requires careful evaluation of the trainer's qualifications, methods and materials. Many to choose from.
Self study	*Economical, but requires discipline to separate work environment from study. Requires either highly motivated students or supervision by a trainer.*

Table 11-2. Continued.

Method	Characteristics
Tutorials	Packaged software comes with more and increasingly excellent tutorial programs. Usually well tied in with examples and the help system. Better for teaching details than broad concepts.
Computer Aided Instruction	Excellent even for non-ADP topics. Most packages track student progress with class problems and tests. Requires motivated students.
Reading and experimentation	The hacker's choice for learning software. There is somebody in almost every shop who can figure out a new piece of software just by playing with it. Usually expensive fun compared with the cost of taking a course. Encourage doing it outside working hours.
On the Job Training	Takes superior motivation and learning skills. Requires supervision by an expert to avoid expenses in terms of training time and reworking the first work products. The best source is someone on site. Consider using in an outside consultant to fill this role. If on-site help is too expensive, have a vendor or an outside consultant on tap for hotline support.
Continuing education in a university or night school setting	*Requires an investment of time and money on the part of the student. Excellent for developing general skills such as systems design, relational systems design or C programming, but unlikely to be a source of training to satisfy immediate requirements.*

Oracle shops. Any but a brand-new user probably receives mail and sales calls on a regular basis. Trainers advertise regularly in local users group magazines.

Bids received in response to an RFP provide the basis for a course of action. The MIS director can let training contracts to one or more of the respondents or use their price quotations to justify using an in-house instructor or self study.

Training schedule

A career training plan that meets the requirements in the career training requirements section above takes several years to realize. The employee cannot absorb it all, and the company cannot afford to deliver it all in one year. The MIS department should keep a training database or spreadsheet to show what courses each person has completed and what they have planned. Figure 11-1 shows a preliminary data design for such a system.

With a spreadsheet, it seems to work best when employee names go down and course titles go across. Employees are more numerous. The subtleties of who should attend which class, and when, must be handled manually because spreadsheets are weaker than an RDBMS in handling relationships.

The objective of the scheduling system is to make sure people get trained and to do it economically. When the whole year's requirements are laid out in advance it makes it

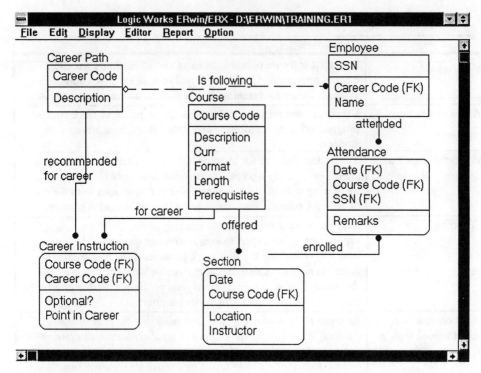

11-1 LogicWorks diagram of a training database.

easy to see which courses should be taught in house, and when it would make sense to buy self-study materials. It also provides input for the budget process.

Automated project management systems maintain calendars for individual staff members. A person's training schedule belongs with vacations and holidays among the things that will take time away from the work schedule. A project management system can help with scheduling by displaying the start date of tasks for which training is required. The system can also show the effect that taking time out for training has on the completion dates of projects to which students are assigned.

Continuing education

An employee with the desire and ability to learn is more valuable than one with mere technical knowledge. Any enterprise will benefit by encouraging their employees to continue their education through university extension and continuing education programs. Studying anything keeps their learning skills sharp and demonstrates a commitment to self-improvement. It is simply good policy to accommodate outside studies through flexible scheduling of work hours and vacation time.

Computer science and business courses teach skills of practical value in the workplace. Computer science can help technicians deepen their understanding of tools such as database theory, Unix, and computer languages. Business courses broaden a person's understanding of the information requirements within a company. An MIS organization benefits from company policies to reimburse employees for taking career-related coursework.

Training and turnover

Some companies build employees, others simply use them. Oracle and IBM are classic builders. Their philosophy is that employees will be with them over the long haul, and they want to make those employees as capable as possible. They spend a lot on training. User companies on the other hand do not spend much on their employees because they do not expect them to stick around over the long haul. Both philosophies tend to be self-fulfilling. The question is, which makes for a more productive company?

The cost of training is relatively easy to figure. If a company were to send an employee to two weeks of Oracle training every year, the cost might come to 10 percent of salary, including tuition, travel, and time off from work. How much difference does it make? Does knowing how to use a tool make a programmer 10 percent more efficient? Of course it does. Does knowing the right way to design a database make a designer 10 percent more effective? Yes it does—not to mention increased effectiveness of the programmers who have to implement the design. Does bungled design and implementation result in systems that simply have to be written off? Yes, more than 10 percent of them. A maximum annual cost of training, 10 percent of salary expense, is usually worth a minimum of 10 percent improvement in efficiency.

Using the argument above, a company can expect to recoup the cost of training a person in the following year. It would make sense anywhere there were less than 100 percent turnover. Training is certainly a less expensive way to develop needed skills than hiring; the cost of acquiring a person is on the order of three- to six-months' pay.

Teamwork is vital to successful projects, and stability and esprit de corps are essential to a team. A team that understands and is dedicated to their employer and has been together before will be more successful than an ad-hoc group with the same technical skills. A company that is willing to invest in its people builds loyalty, and training people as new needs arise makes it possible to keep teams in place.

Summary

People like to do a job right. Being prepared gives them confidence and enthusiasm. They respect and are loyal to an employer who uses their time well, preparing them for their assignments. Management's responsibility is to create an environment conducive to quality, recognizing that quality itself originates with the people who do the work. Training and education are essential components of the equation. ADP professionals must learn what makes a quality product and how to use their tools to produce them.

12
Security and integrity

It pays to be paranoid. So many misadventures can destroy or compromise data in an automated system. The DP manager must establish backup and security policies for the whole installation. Analysts and designers must evaluate the needs of an individual application to determine whether there is a need for additional measures.

What are the threats? The security concern is that unauthorized people can steal data or corrupt it through unauthorized updates. The integrity concern is that a software malfunction can render a set of data internally inconsistent and therefore unreliable or even worthless. Outright loss of data through human error, mechanical failure or destruction of the computer itself is a third concern. A fourth concern is an unacceptable loss of function during the time data operations are restored after a catastrophe.

Precautionary measures against the three threats overlap one another, as Table 12-1 shows. The measures involve controlling access to data to protect it and duplicating it so that a lost copy can be replaced. The precautions must be coordinated with one another, and the costs of protection must be weighed against the risks. The elements of protection must be balanced; a defense is only as strong as its weakest link.

Archiving

There is some expense involved in storing any kind of data. The more accessible it is, the greater the cost. The major types of machine-readable storage media, in descending order of cost and accessibility, are:

- Main memory
- Flash memory
- Magnetic disk storage
- Optical disk storage
- Removable magnetic media:
    ~Bernouilli drives and other removable disks
    ~Diskettes

Table 12-1 Data security, integrity,
and protection threats and countermeasures.

Threat	Countermeasure or Correction
Disk crash destroys the database	Restore the database from backup tapes. Bring it up to date by applying transactions from the redo file.
Fire, flood or civil disturbance destroys the installation.	Switch over to a previously identified backup machine at an alternative site, rapidly install another machine, or invoke a continuity of operations arrangement with another site.
	Use a backup copy of the data stored at an alternate location to bring the database as current as possible. Identify missing transactions using external data sources and reenter them.
Program error renders database inconsistent	Restore from backup or archive tapes that antedate the problem or write one-time programs to repair the damage.
User error inadvertently deletes or corrupts records.	Retrieve records from archive tapes that pre-date the accident and reapply them to the system.
Unauthorized users log into the system	Make frequent changes to the passwords
	Use random passwords long enough frustrate hackers
	Implement monitors that alert the operator to attempts to hack the system.
	Restrict users to certain physical terminal devices
	Augment passwords with other physical recognition devices such as passcards, voice recognition or signature.
Authorized users access unauthorized data and processes	Impose tight controls on use of "superuser" state.
	Conscientiously administer user privileges
	Use monitors that alert the operator to attempts to access password protected processes and data.
	Use operating system software that prevents one user from reading another user's area of memory.
	Use Menu system such as SQL*Menu to restrict accesses to processes.
	Use DBA devices such as views to restrict access to data.
Authorized users perform unauthorized adds deletes and updates to the data base	Use DBA devices to restrict the type of access each person has to given data types.

~Tape cartridges
~Nine-track tapes

Installations move less-frequently used data from immediate access to removable media to save money, or rather, to recover immediate-access capacity for other uses.

Data are often stored on more than one machine as a matter of course. Programmers make extensive use of PCs. They automatically protect their source programs and test data as they develop them on PCs and upload them to larger machines for test and production.

Oracle only supports one echelon of data storage—online—in the database. Data

Table 12-1. Continued.

Threat	Countermeasure or Correction
	Define processes that restrict the functions a user can perform.
	Program audit logs to record all activity by user.
Systems programmers, DBAs and other insiders access unauthorized data.	Use Trusted Oracle and secure operating systems to compartmentalize users.
	Use data encryption at the application level and keep the keys within the applications group.
Confidential reports are read or copied by unauthorized persons	Use administrative procedures to control distribution. Confine printouts to specific print devices. Number the copies. Provide shredders. Print in non-reproducing ink.
Authorized people verbally disclose confidential information	Limit the number of authorized people.
Somebody steals the computer	Encrypt the data on the hard disk.
Somebody steals media such as tape, disk, or diskettes.	Encrypt the data on the media
The wires are tapped.	Encrypt transmission. Use fiber optics.
Electromagnetic listening devices	Shield cable and worksites. Use fiber optics.

archiving must be designed into Oracle applications. This means writing processes to remove expired data from the online database and put it into another medium. The first question is, what data is expired? This is usually a judgment call. A customer might be expired if they have not placed an order in three years. A sales transaction might be considered expired three months after the date of sale if there have been no queries and the bill was paid. The application designer has to make the decision. Some of the major archiving issues are:

- How often does the archiving process need to take place, and what period should each individual archive cover? It is easiest if they match, such as having an annual backup process that extracts records that became obsolete during the prior year.
- How will the data be restored to the system if it is ever needed? Will it be restored all together or only selected records? Do related records from more than one file need to be recovered?
- What format should the archive take? Oracle or system backup formats are fast, but a character format archive is accessible to custom programs.
- What data integrity constraints apply to the archived data should it be restored? What needs to be done to ensure that foreign key requirements will be met as data is restored?
- How deep must the archive be? Is there a point at which the data can be discarded outright?
- What kind of backup protection does the archival data need? Can it be kept in a single copy?
- How does the archiving plan fit with the continuity-of-operations plan? Are archives and backups part of a single, coherent scheme?

The backup/restore procedures described below offer a bulletproof mechanism to guard against losing the whole database. It can put the entire database back exactly as it was when the lights went out. An ability to address data at the record level would be absolutely inconsistent with the mission of backup/restore. It is up to archiving processes to provide whatever is needed in the way of logical backup.

Tables of data must be exported to other systems from time to time. Database backups don't do the trick. They tend to be device dependent, they work at the table-space level, and they interact with control file data which is almost certain to be different at the target site. Oracle's export and import utilities are designed to handle requirements like this. The data can be moved anywhere.

Even export and import have their limitations. Export writes control information into the file to protect it against data errors and meddling. It is difficult to pull logical records from an export file. If there is any sort of a need to process archival data without putting it back into Oracle, it must be written to an operating system file. The best general-purpose Oracle tool for the job is SQL*Plus. The data can be selected and spooled to an operating system file. SQL*Plus has a number of limitations, the most significant being the 500-byte maximum size of an output record and its inability to work with long data types. It often takes custom programming to create archive files that are accessible to other processes.

Backup

A backup plan must allow for the many ways data can be destroyed or compromised. It must allow for the eventuality that some backup files can themselves be destroyed or turn out to be unreadable. It must also deal with the way data changes over time. The most insidious data problems are the subtle ones induced by program errors that might go a long time before being detected.

Backup frequencies for flat-file data

Everything on the system must be backed up one way or another. The simplest approach is to use the operating system backup utility to take an image copy on a periodic basis, perhaps nightly. Most shops however need a more sophisticated plan. A total system backup takes a lot of time. Moreover, it is sometimes difficult to selectively restore individual files from a total system backup, and of course impossible to selectively restore records within a database.

A plan to back up data according to its volatility will save time. Operating system software and other licensed programs do not have to be backed up; they can be reinstalled from the distribution media. The production versions of custom-written software is not very volatile. The baseline versions need to be backed up. Maintenance actions can be backed up individually; it might be that the programmers' hard copy or diskette versions of the programs will suffice.

Oracle shops often have only a few flat operating system data files. Work files, such as print spool areas, do not need to be backed up at all. The backup planner can stipulate that developers back up their own test data. They usually create it on PCs in the first place. It might be possible to put together a utility job to copy all the essential flat files by name as an alternative to backing up all operating system files.

Oracle backups

Oracle is written to ensure that the database remains consistent despite whatever catastrophe befalls it. Its interlocks guarantee that either all the database updates that make up a transaction get posted, or none do. The rollback segments handle this requirement; updates are written to a scratch area until the user commits them. With Version 7, this guarantee is extended over distributed databases using the two-phase commit process.

Oracle recovers smoothly from a power outage. The disk files that make up an Oracle instance contain all the information needed to roll back incomplete transactions and start over. No more than the transactions that were underway at the time of the crash are lost. A disk failure is the only type of problem in which significant amounts of work stand to be lost, and Oracle supports a variety of backup schemes rich enough to handle any requirement.

Operating system utilities are the only way to back up a complete Oracle instance. Exports and imports are satisfactory for reorganizing and for use with individual tables, but they cannot capture the state of an entire database.

The simplest approach is a cold backup. The Oracle instance is shut down and an operating system copy utility is used to copy all the database files. Closing the database ensures that the data remains internally consistent as it is copied. The backup has to include all of the operating system files that make up the instance and its control files. Restoring, then, is a matter of copying those files back as they were and restarting Oracle. In this form of backup, all the transactions between the time of the backup and the crash are lost. They have to be rekeyed. This basic approach is acceptable for many small applications, and it avoids the operations problem of transaction logging.

Major applications cannot tolerate losing all of the transactions between backups. Oracle's approach has been to implement transaction logs, called *redo files,* that contain a time-stamped copy of every transaction. The recovery process then involves restoring the database and control files, as above, and then using Oracle's recovery utility to apply transactions from the redo log for the period between the backup and the crash.

Using redo logs takes some planning. To be of any use at all, they must be on a separate disk drive from the database files. The RDBMS takes logging seriously; it locks up when the redo log files are filled. Either the redo logs must be big enough to handle all the transactions between backups, or the redo log files have be spilled to secondary files, either on tape or disk, before they get full. Oracle's SQLDBA utility has an archiving function to handle the job.

Oracle's archive writer works either manually or automatically. In manual mode an operator has to intervene to tell the system when to archive the redo log files. In automatic mode the archiver is on duty full-time in background mode, emptying redo log files to flat files (disk or tape) in operating system format. The automatic process is suited to bigger installations, where it makes sense to keep the transactions rolling off the system in a continuous stream.

One weakness in the redo log file system in Version 6 was the fact that the system locked up when it could not write to the redo log file. Version 7 overcomes the problem by permitting duplexed redo files. The kernel writes to both as long as they work, but keeps going with the survivor if one goes down.

Some mission-critical databases have to be online around the clock. Others, even though they can be taken down, are so large that there is not enough time to back them up off line. Oracle is among the first vendors to adequately solve this problem. The user makes an operating system copy of the Oracle database files while the database is open. It is, of course, inconsistent. The various records within a given transaction might well straddle the portions of the database file already copied and yet to go.

The database restored from these fuzzy backups must be made consistent before it is of any use. Oracle's SQLDBA recovery procedure uses the time stamps in the database and redo log records to apply the appropriate updates and bring the database current as of the time of failure. Figure 12-1 shows how the backup works, and Fig. 12-2 shows recovery.

The process uses one more device to insulate itself from operator and medium failure. The redo logs are archived to a disk file rather than tape. This step eliminates the need

ORACLE VERSION 7 HOT BACKUP SCHEME

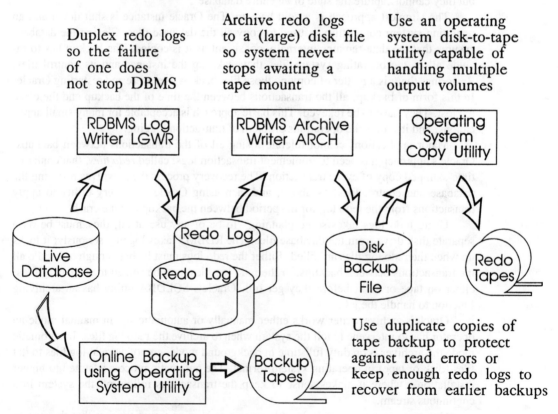

Duplex redo logs so the failure of one does not stop DBMS

Archive redo logs to a (large) disk file so system never stops awaiting a tape mount

Use an operating system disk-to-tape utility capable of handling multiple output volumes

Use duplicate copies of tape backup to protect against read errors or keep enough redo logs to recover from earlier backups

12-1 Flow of the most extensive Oracle backup process.

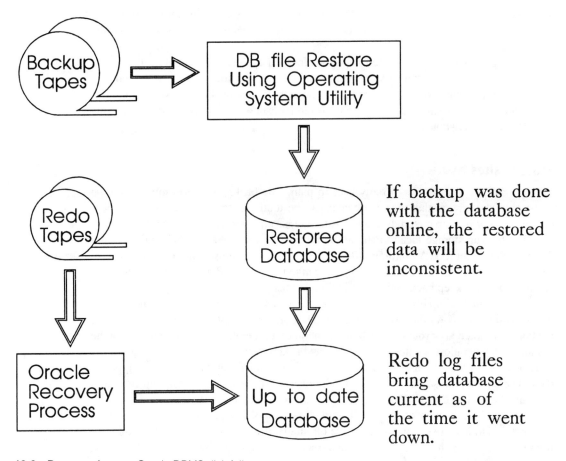

If backup was done with the database online, the restored data will be inconsistent.

Redo log files bring database current as of the time it went down.

12-2 Recovery from an Oracle DBMS disk failure.

for an operator to mount the device and substantially decreases the risk of a device failure. That disk file is in turn archived to tape using an operating system utility. The utility, rather than any Oracle process, can then deal with the issues of multivolume files and tape labels. The file can be copied twice if desired to provide the highest level of confidence.

Backup versions

Whatever method is used to create backup volumes, the installation needs to keep several generations of them on hand. The most recent is the one to use under normal circumstances. If the most recent copy cannot be read, it might be necessary to use the next most recent. If the purpose of a restore is to correct a human error, such as the accidental deletion of a mass of records, it might be necessary to go back to a time before the error.

Redo log files are cumulative. Whereas one backup completely supersedes the previous one, the redo log files must be saved for as far back as the oldest generation of backup in order to ensure that the database can be brought current. The impact of read errors is more significant. If one version of a backup cannot be read, the previous one will do. However, one missing or unreadable redo log file can make all generations of backup worthless. As Fig. 12-1 shows, it is good practice to make duplicate tape copies of the redo log files.

Some library systems use different periods for their cycles. They might keep a week's worth of daily backups but also store month-end backups for the previous year, and perhaps year-end backups for a few years back. The more distant backups are only of interest if they are in a flat-file format. It can be useful to recover a few records from a long time back but seldom a whole database.

Storage sites

Multiple storage sites are key to any backup plan. The backup scenario must make the worst-case assumption that the data center can be totally destroyed. There has to be a complete set of backup materials at an off-site safe haven to recreate the system.

The backup storage location should be far enough removed that the same calamity doesn't wipe it out too. A building at the far end of a plant site will not do if it could be swept by the same fire or flood that gets the computer room. DP managers and DBAs of small shops often keep backup libraries in their homes.

The off-site backup library must be complete, recent, and consistent. The most recent backup copies are by far the most often used. They are kept on site. Figure 12-3 illustrates the common practice of rotating the father generation to the off-site backup and return the grandfather generation on site each time a new backup is created. The cycle frequency is usually different for software and data backups and is often different for different types of data. The data administrator and system administrator need to set the plan up in such a way that the backup date will work together to create a complete system.

"What if the backup copies don't work?" is always a nagging question. A simple alternative is to keep two generations at the off-site facility. No backup system is fail safe; it helps to have the phone number of a data-recovery specialist when an unreadable tape absolutely must be read.

Security

Doing the simple things right will provide enough security for most installations. Oracle and the operating system vendors provide tools that are adequate to protect data against casual compromise or destruction of data. Counterespionage measures against dedicated agents is a topic for another book. Each application takes a different mixture of technologies and techniques to provide the necessary level of protection.

Operating systems and Oracle both provide password-protection schemes. The passwords are stored within the system in an encrypted form. In commercial-level implementations, the systems programmers, systems administrators, DBAs, and data administrators can get at the encrypted password data and access the material it protects without too much difficulty. It takes more elaborate mechanisms such as Trusted Oracle to compartmentalize data in such a way that the systems experts cannot see user data or encrypted passwords.

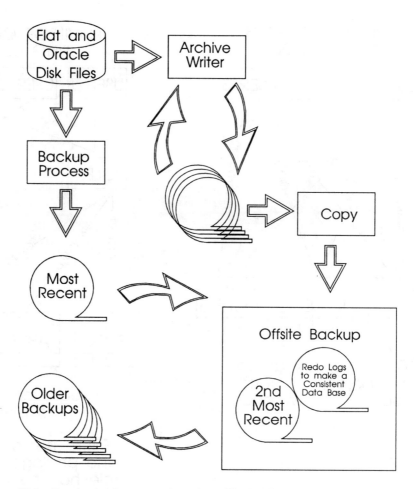

12-3 Rotating backup tapes through an off-site safe haven.

Oracle is simplifying security by expanding their use of the roles concept introduced in SQL*Menu 5.0. In that system, each user is assigned a role. Only the menu options that have been granted to the user's role are presented. Version 7 of the database expands the concept to data access. The data administrator, instead of granting each individual user access to every object they need, defines and grants access to roles. The DBA then assigns one or more role to each user. Figure 12-4 shows the process. Because human error is the major cause of security lapses, this mechanism must improve security by making it easier to administer. The disciplines required to make vendor-provided password schemes effective are:

- Use passwords that are not easy to guess. Somebody with a bit of patience can guess enough combinations of short passwords and personal names to eventually gain access to a system. They can also pick them up by watching someone key the

PRIVILEGE GRANTS WITHOUT ROLES

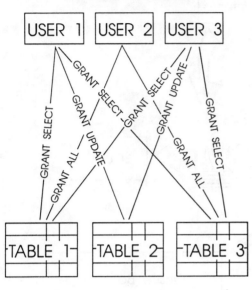

Each user is granted permissions on each object one by one

PRIVILEGE GRANTS USING ROLES

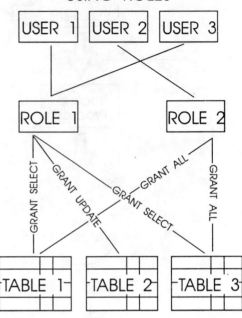

Privileges are assigned to roles.

Each user assumes all the privileges of each role he or she is given.

12-4 Simplifying access control through the use of roles.

password in. The process is more difficult when passwords are longer and less obvious.

- Force users to change passwords periodically, perhaps once a month. Some operating systems do this as a matter of course. This reduces the exposure whenever a password is compromised. It also demonstrates that management takes password protection seriously.
- Make sure that the system administrator and data administrator give objects an appropriate level of protection. Password protection does not mean much if all the data in a system is open to anyone who logs in. The system has to control access by application and role.
- Design applications to take advantage of available security features such as user views and roles.
- Write administrative procedures to support system security. More data is compro-

mised by carelessness than any other way. Control the circulation of sensitive reports. Don't let programmers test with live personnel or contract data.

It costs very little to use the features that vendors provide. The major expense is for personnel to administer security. There is some expense in additional overhead, primarily in the use of views to restrict access to Oracle data.

Summary

Security, integrity, and continuity of operations are generally unexciting issues. They are to your business life what insurance is to your personal life, a necessary evil.

Hardware and software vendors provide most of the tools needed to protect the data. Management's first job is to make sure that analysts and designers plan for data protection in their designs. Once the needs are expressed, the system and data administrators can compile a combination of application and shop level procedures to handle them.

13

Quality control

The terms *quality control* and *total quality* management are so ubiquitous that the acronyms QC and TQM have become recognized throughout American industry. The business press contends TQM is a Japanese graft that has taken unevenly on American rootstock. However it is doing generally, what is called TQM brings a number of concepts that are highly applicable to data processing.

The first task for an Oracle shop is to define quality. That being done, the next question is how to achieve it. Real quality takes common sense mixed with the precepts of quality control and total quality management.

The best summary of the trade-offs involving quality was the note on a manager's door shown in Fig. 13-1. The things that ensure a quality product, like testing and adherence to standards, take time and cost money. The tendency is to substitute wishful thinking for the practice of quality when money gets tight; that is, there was a commitment to quality in the first place.

The philosophical difference between quality control and total quality management is in whom the responsibility for quality is vested. QC assumes that an external agency, management aided by the QC department, is responsible for quality. TQM states that quality is built in. The people who design and build a product are fundamentally responsible for its quality. Data processing needs some of both. The system developers as a group establish and maintain their own standards and procedures. They routinely review each other's work over the course of a project. There might also be a formal test and acceptance process upon system completion.

Quality is a relative good. The absolute is customer satisfaction—getting the company's business done. The MIS director has to balance the costs of quality control against the returns. It depends on the application. The Service Employees International Union (SEIU) uses Oracle to maintain a mailing list. They get name and address data from their locals. If they make a mistake, some member misses a newsletter or gets two. A certain margin of error is tolerable. The Central Pension Fund of the Operating Engineers (CPF) keeps detailed history of union members' lifetime contributions and issues the monthly checks on which retirees live. They hear about it if a check is wrong. Their margin for

> *I can give it to you fast.*
>
> *I can give it to you cheap.*
>
> *I can give it to you right.*
>
> *Which two do you want?*

13-1 Quality trade-offs in a nutshell.

error is zero. They have never failed, and never intend to fail, to get the checks out. The developers of these two systems have concepts of quality that differ, but each is totally appropriate to their application.

The objectives of quality control

Quality must serve the ultimate objects of an enterprise. Corporations want to maximize profits, schools to offer the best possible education, CPF to pay people right, and SEIU to satisfy members and minimize postage. Quality data systems do what the enterprise needs done.

The most universal benefit of quality is getting the job done at a minimum overall cost. Life-cycle cost, the most frequently applied measure, means the cost to conceive, write, operate, and maintain a system until it is replaced. The MIS department sees direct costs for design and development, training, maintenance, and hardware utilization. The major cost in user departments is staffing—the people it takes to run the application.

Quality has strategic benefits as well. Federal Express proved that in the freight-forwarding business, a well-designed and implemented distribution system that guarantees rapid delivery is a competitive advantage. But for the quality of the Word for Windows and Corel Draw software, this book would contain fewer and less ambitious graphics—and might not sell as well.

An enterprise needs quality control to the extent that it brings the benefits of quality, cost reduction and a better ability to achieve their ends. Quality costs money. A company has to implement QC to optimize the balances between costs and benefits. This chapter explores means of doing that in an Oracle environment.

Elements of quality in an Oracle environment

Both Dr. Deming (Aguayo, 1991) and Humphrey (1989) equate quality with predictability. A data processing organization is producing quality work when it can accurately predict how long it will take to develop a module and how many errors will be found at each phase. The only way to achieve predictability is through a standard process, and if the standard process is flawed it can be fixed.

The corollary is that quality starts with using as well as having standards and procedures. Shops that have exhaustive standards often observe them in the breach, like the national speed limit. They are too onerous to bother with. An MIS director needs to be honest with him or herself and set up procedures consistent with the organization's will to enforce them and the shop's needs for quality. A thesis of this book is that traditional standards and procedures can be simplified for an Oracle environment, especially Oracle CASE, and that the developers are in the best position to rewrite them.

Figure 13-2 divides quality issues into environment and practice: preaching it and doing it. Preaching comes first. Standards and procedures must be written and worked into the culture before they will be observed. Standards must evolve from within the organization. ADP professionals have to respect them enough to use them and change them when they stop making sense.

Oracle is faster moving than traditional development and generally needs less documentation. Chapter 1 describes the differences. Chapter 14 covers how a shop specifies standards for the documentation required, and chapter 15 covers the procedures for producing that documentation.

Auditing quality

The axiom that quality cannot be added on but has to be built in certainly applies to data processing. An effective auditor focuses on how the data-processing professionals produce their products more than the products themselves. Compliance with procedures is at least as significant as compliance to standards.

Checking the quality of every component of a system is almost always an unjustifiable expense. The auditor would have to become thoroughly conversant with the requirement, read and critique the analysis and design documentation, read the code, and test the executable system. Then there would be a question of what to do with the findings. Correcting the individual problems an auditor happens to uncover is a patchwork solution. The developers themselves could do it less expensively if given time. Only a total disaster justifies rewriting the system. The bottom line is that auditing the data-processing product is not a very satisfactory tool for quality control.

Processes can be audited, and the assumption is that quality processes produce quality products. An auditor can review how an ADP shop's standards and procedures are used within a development project. Processes are far less numerous than the products; they are repeated for each subsystem and each module. An auditor can do a reasonable job of following a handful of interviews, reconstructing how the users and analysts agreed on a data design, or watching a programmer develop a form. The auditor can judge how well

The Environment of Quality
   in Standards
      Standards apply to all major tools used in the shop
      Standards apply to all aspects of quality: accuracy, performance, completeness, usability
      Standards for user interfaces address:
         Look and Feel
         Response Time
      Standards specify help support
      Standards apply to user documentation and training
   Quality in Procedures
      Define processes for project management
      Define processes for configuration management
      Define processes for peer review
      Define formal quality control processes
The practice of quality
   Quality in Analysis
      The scope of an analysis effort is appropriate to the user's requirement.
      Analysis products accurately represent business data and processes, current and planned
      Analysts earn users trust and confidence
   Quality in Design
      Automated and manual elements in the design work together to handle the business
         requirement.
      The automated solution delivers information where it is needed, when it is needed
      The design is easily understood by all parties: analysts, designers, users, implementers
         and general management
      The design is integrated with installation standards.
      The design can be modified and expanded to incorporate future needs.
      The design speaks for itself, without need of authors to interpret it.
      The design defines testing procedures to measure its success.
   Quality in Code
      Code is written in conformance with installation standards
      Code presents a uniform interface to the user
      Code is written to be easily maintained
      Code is efficient
      Code is reliable
   Quality in Testing
      Testing done in accordance with installation procedures
      Test criteria in the design document are satisfied
      Test data covers all cases
      Testing predicts live environment performance
   Quality in User Support
      Documentation, training and help support make it possible to use system easily
      MIS is responsive to user questions and problems
   Quality in Operations
      Computers deliver applications systems when and where needed
      Response time is fast enough that users do not lose productivity
      Access and data security protects users from each other and outsiders
      Backup plans allow the company continue in business through a worst-case disaster.

13-2 The elements of quality.

the job is done in each instance and to what extent the task follows established standards and procedures. Consistency is the key. The auditor seeks to confirm that people have been trained in the methodologies they use and participate in maintaining them.

Chapter 15 on procedures discusses the kinds of quality control procedures associated with each life-cycle phase. The paragraphs below address the meaning of quality in each step.

Quality in analysis

Successful analysis is understanding the problem and developing working relationships with the users. Written deliverables are a byproduct. Interview notes and process descriptions are necessary to confirm the understanding of the requirement. The data design is a model of reality, shared by analysts and users, in a format the developers can use. The product to which quality applies is the shared understanding of the problem, not just the deliverables which facilitate it.

Line management or the QC staff can monitor quality by assaying the chemistry of meetings. Quality is there if there is an active exchange of information and the meetings conclude in consensus.

QC should ensure that the scope of every system is written down. The users need to know what they are getting, and MIS needs to know the outer limits of a prototype project. The data model should always be documented in hard copy. Beyond that, the QC staff must judge the extent to which communications depend on written documents. A geographically dispersed development effort or one that uses a large team must depend more on written communications than a small-team prototype effort. A two-person design team might be able to carry process requirements in their heads and share them; a 10-person team cannot.

Quality in design

The first measure of a design is whether it will satisfy the requirement. The characteristics of a great design are that it solves the problem with economy, consistency, ease of use, and anticipation of the future growth of the application.

The best indications of a good design are that the user and the project team understand it and are enthusiastic about it. An outside auditor has a hard time evaluating the applicability of a design by looking only at the requirements statement and the design documents. Enthusiasm and a willingness to work with the designer are both an endorsement of the technical merits of an architecture and a sign that the project team has enough goodwill in reserve to see it through their inevitable problems.

An auditor can approach the technical merit of a design several ways. The design has to be well enough expressed on paper or through a CASE tool that project members can understand their assignments and how the pieces of a system relate. The important documents such as the entity-relationship diagram must follow conventions. The auditor can judge whether those that do not take an intimate knowledge of the application, such as the entity/relationship diagrams and the test plan, make sense.

Quality in testing

Regardless of the quality of a design, there is no substitute for debugging. A piece of software works when a series of tests indicate that it does what it needs to do. Testing is an intrinsic part of the development process. Test data and testing procedures are part of the design. Performing the tests is part of development.

The quality issue is whether the tests are well conceived and well executed. An auditor can compare the test data and scripts against the data design and business rules to see how well different data scenarios are represented. On the development side, the auditor confirms that the tests are regularly done as a matter of both procedures and practice.

Quality in programming

In programming, process is almost everything. If the programmers (including those who will maintain the system) are happy with the way programs are developed, then how is an outsider to quibble? By ensuring that the project team has followed the procedures for code walk-throughs and testing, the auditor has confirmed that the software is satisfactory in the eyes of its most interested and expert critics.

Quality in selection and procurement

Company watchdogs usually oversee the procurement process. MIS doesn't have to specify how to get the lowest cost. The key issue is getting the right hardware, software and communications.

MIS is usually responsible for specifying hardware and network requirements. Management or the QC staff can ask quality control questions such as:

- Does the hardware and network plan map to the strategic plan?
- Was the specification left open late to admit developments in technology?
- Is the procurement timed to coincide with the need?
- Are the size and volume projections that drive the procurement accurate?

User involvement is the key to quality in buying applications software. Users pick it because they use it. The person in charge of quality control must look at the selection process more than whatever paper it may generate.

MIS is usually responsible for building its own development environment. The first few quality control questions in buying systems software such as Oracle tools are similar to those for hardware:

- Is the software consistent with the strategic MIS plan?
- Was the specification left open late to admit the most recent developments in technology?
- Is the procurement timed to coincide with the need?

MIS must shoulder more of the selection load for systems software, if only to tell procurement how packages compare with one another. A quality selection includes most of the processes above for applications software, except that the user is MIS itself.

Summary

Quality must be built in, and quality control has to come from within. A manager or outside auditor cannot assess the quality of a product nearly as well as those who built it.

An audit that focuses on process more than products exploits the only expert critics available—the authors of a system. If they have been allowed the time to follow internal quality-control procedures such as design and code walk-throughs, their professional pride will have led them to create a solid product. They can be expected to be proficient with their tools if they have had training and access to expert help as it is needed. They can be expected to respect standards and procedures if they are responsible for maintaining them and for holding each other to observing them.

14

Documentation requirements and standards

Sun Yat-sen wrote "In the construction of a country, it is not the practical workers but the idealists and planners that are difficult to find." Often data processing is short on plans; programmers make plans up on the fly. The gulf between ideals and practice is best seen in documentation. Almost every shop has fairly rigorous development standards, but most shops dispense with them on a project-by-project basis in the name of expediency. Users get the systems that programmers write.

What standards apply in an Oracle environment

The fatal flaw in traditional documentation is that it is not on the critical path to producing code. It takes time to write thorough analysis and design documents. The supposed return on the investment is realized in the form of a better and more maintainable system. Most shops' experience is mixed. No matter how much they invest in writing requirements and design specifications, the users seem unable to conceive their requirement except in reaction to an implemented system that does not do the job. In addition, most developers are more interested in and better at writing systems than writing specifications. Experience has taught developers that "doing it right" with full documentation is not the most practical way to solve a problem.

This chapter seeks a middle ground. Documentation represents planning, and foregoing planning invariably leads to disaster. On the other extreme, the work represented by elaborate design specifications goes down the drain as the programmers cobble up new features to satisfy the user as the system is being written. The specs rapidly become useless as they fall out of sync with the code. The question is, what documentation remains essential to success in a development environment such as Oracle's that accommodates and encourages the programmers doing design?

The magic of CASE tools is that through them documentation produces code. Figure 14-1 shows that the metadata that are used to produce data models and function definitions at the analysis level go on to generate the basis of module design and data design in the

CASE PLACES SPECIFICATIONS IN THE SHORTEST PATH TO WORKING CODE

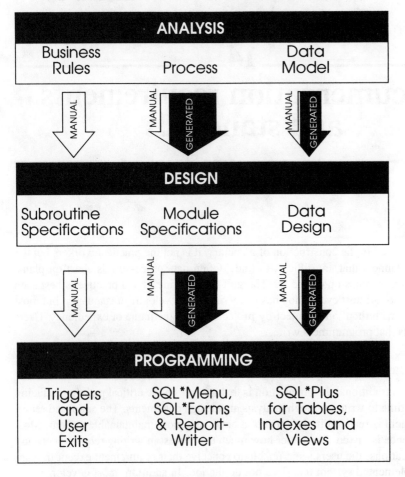

ANALYSIS		
Business Rules	Process	Data Model

MANUAL — MANUAL / GENERATED — MANUAL / GENERATED

DESIGN		
Subroutine Specifications	Module Specifications	Data Design

MANUAL — MANUAL / GENERATED — MANUAL / GENERATED

PROGRAMMING		
Triggers and User Exits	SQL*Menu, SQL*Forms & Report-Writer	SQL*Plus for Tables, Indexes and Views

Black portions of arrows indicate where CASE generates one life cycle stage from the previous. The white portion indicates manual effort to create the next stage product.

14-1 In CASE, documentation that produces code remains consistent with that code.

next life-cycle phase. They, in turn, are the source for generating the code of which the system is made. Up to the last phases of polishing the programs, the documentation reflects the current state of the code because it is used to generate the code.

An Oracle development project without CASE must rely more on traditional forms of documentation. Still, the productivity and self-documenting nature of Oracle's 4GL tools obsolete traditional standards. In the final analysis, each shop must make its own decision based on its applications, culture, and the influence of tradition and other languages and DBMS. This chapter lists the types of documentation commonly associated with each development stage and offers a comment as to how they apply for Oracle developments.

Implementing standards within an organization

This chapter provides a quick reference of the most common elements of documentation. Several firms offer exhaustive documentation methodologies, among them Ernst and Young and Price, Waterhouse. An all-embracing methodology, which takes two to four feet of shelf space, is so comprehensive as to be oppressive if implemented in the whole. Each shop has to decide what it needs to specify across the board and for individual projects.

Projects define the process. A shop needs to decide what types of documentation a project needs and codify them in installation procedures. There is usually a standard to specify the format of each document type. The ultimate product is machine-readable source and executable code, which is also subject to standards.

Projects of any magnitude require some sort of project management, which itself should be subject to written procedures. Figure 15-1 shows the relationships among standards and procedures, tasks and deliverables, and project management.

This chapter is organized in standard development sequence. It addresses the utility of the deliverable products that development procedures customarily specify. It's not intended to serve as an installation standard. That would be inappropriate; the premise of the book is that developers need to establish their own standards. This chapter identifies work products that can be specified in a shop's procedures and for which standards might be necessary.

There are a number of excellent references to use in setting up standards and procedures once a shop decides what is needed. Richard Barker's *Case*Method Tasks and Deliverables* fits Oracle extremely well. James Martin's *Information Engineering* series is a standard reference.

The purposes of documentation

Documentation is written communication; written communication in turn is no less than the cornerstone of civilization, allowing as it does the accurate transmission of thought across time and distance. In data processing, the distance factor can be conceptual, as between user and analyst or designer and programmer. The time dimension recognizes that no person or team can carry a complete system around in their minds.

That being said, Oracle can decrease the need for written communications for the following reasons:

- Oracle's nonprocedural representation of module logic provides greater abstraction than traditional code. A person can carry more of an SQL*Forms design than a CICS transaction design around in their head because Oracle takes care of such details as database reads, screen mapping, and master-detail relationships.

- There are fewer people involved. Communications among the analyst, designer, and programmer improve vastly when they are one and the same person. Informal communications work much better among three people than among twelve.
- Oracle development takes less time. People remember the work they did two months ago much better than that done two years ago. It is realistic to expect prototyping developers to keep relatively large elements of a design in their minds as they go.
- Oracle code is more concise and self-documenting. Nonprocedural code by its nature says what it wants to accomplish rather than how to do so.

When a project shrinks to a critical size, it's as though an afterburner kicks in. Eliminating the most voluminous documentation lightens it up to go even faster. However, the lure of speed can be fatal. A lightly documented project dies when it loses momentum. The project might have to be abandoned or restarted if it turns out to be larger than anticipated and people cannot carry it in their heads or if a critical person leaves. The remainder of this chapter addresses commonly used standards and the risks involved in not using them.

Strategic planning documentation

Strategic planning is independent of any implementation methodology. Organizations that need to integrate their data systems at the enterprise level should set strategies and priorities at the executive management level. Table 14-1 shows the typical documentation associated with a strategic plan.

Whether or not an organization formalizes the strategic planning process, general

Table 14-1   Strategic-plan documentation.

Document Name	Contents and Usage	Example
Goals Statement	The items which define long term success for the enterprise	1. Sustained growth, 2. Competitive Advantage 3. High Quality Goods
Objectives	Short-term ends which are specific, measurable, and to be attained within a given timeframe	1. 60% gross margins by FY 1993 2. 99.8% accurate invoices by June 1992
Critical Success Factors	Things to do to achieve the objectives	1. Define new chart of accounts 2. Install Oracle General Ledger 3. Develop Order Entry System
Organization Chart	Who's who, by title	The reporting organization. Some titles may be charged with multiple responsibilities.
Chart of Functions	Hierarchical diagram showing major functions performed by the enterprise	Major functions performed by organization. Some, such as sales and order entry, may be spread across many elements of the organization chart.
Function/ Organization matrix	Cross reference the above two documents.	

Table 14-1.   Continued.

Document Name	Contents and Usage	Example
Enterprise Model	Chart showing work flow among organizations. An example would be how an orders flow thorough a manufacturing plant or patients flow through a hospital.	
Current Information Architecture	High-level data flow and E/R diagrams showing how major systems support business areas and relate to one another.	See data flow diagram example, Figure 14.7 and E/R Diagram example in Figure 14.6
Future Information Architecture	High-level chart showing how major information systems will support business areas and relate to one another in the future.	See data flow diagram example, Figure 14.7 and E/R Diagram example in Figure 14.6
High-Level Process Definitions	Descriptions of major information processes in the strategic information plan.	
Strategic Information Plan	List of actions to take in realizing the future information architecture.	1. Bring up Oracle on Netware 386 2. Link Oracle DBMS on Netware 386 and VAX platforms for distributed query. 3. Migrate Customer Inquiry function to Netware
Major Entity Definitions	Descriptions of major data groupings and the key fields used to manage them. These seed the data element definitions to be developed in the analysis step.	See Figure 3
Cost Justification	Spreadsheet analyses of the line items in the strategic information plan, showing estimates of the return on investment as a function of the cost to implement them and benefits of doing so. Also includes a list of non-quantifiable benefits. This is essential supporting material in setting priorities among items in the Strategic Information Plan. It can be expanded in the design phase to select among alternative designs and rejustify the project.	See Chapter 19 for an example

management usually initiates or at least okays the development of major systems. Unless they work through the strategic planning process and produce the above documents, there is a good chance of embarking on projects that have not been adequately thought out. The MIS department takes on a lot of risk accepting a job without a clear understanding of its objectives or without providing a clear estimate of what it will cost. MIS protects itself by encouraging strategic planning.

Failure to develop long-term plans for the enterprise and data processing is the worst of false economies. There should be no scenario in which enterprise-wide systems do not figure in a strategic plan. Applications-level strategies are essential for the corporate and MIS strategic planning described in chapter 5.

Analysis documentation

A problem must be understood before it can be solved. Analysis is the discipline of studying and documenting requirements. End users and existing data systems provide most of the information used in analysis. The analysis process is successful when the users concur that its work products define the requirement and the data processors find the definition sufficiently complete that they can design a system to satisfy it.

When there is one, the strategic plan is the cornerstone of systems analysis. It includes preliminary versions of the data design, functional decomposition and data flow diagrams for the system. The Oracle CASE product does not distinguish between the two, treating analysis as an extension of the strategic planning process. Other CASE products address the strategy phase by defining goals, objectives, and critical success factors into the metadata. A CASE tool brings the advantage of a standard format, but word processing works as well. Strategy-phase metadata does not generally carry forward into successive life-cycle phases.

Analysis documentation in Oracle usually centers around data: the entity-relationship diagram and the supporting data dictionary entries. Too often that is the only analysis documentation. Although the other pieces might not apply to every system, they are hard to do without when they are needed.

An installation standard for analysis must give the analyst credit for judgment. The data design and a functional decomposition are always mandatory. Beyond that it doesn't work to dictate that every analysis project will include one each of a prescribed list of documents. The analyst has to document whatever is not self-evident, the exceptions.

Analysis is not pure and detached. It must be cognizant of the information strategy that precedes it and the design that will follow. Most analysts go about their work with an image of a solution forming in their minds. Although the analyst needs to keep an open mind with regard to the design, it is proper to allow external considerations to affect their definition of the requirement. A project cannot succeed unless its scope fits within budgetary constraints. It is highly beneficial if the requirements are seen in such a way that they can be implemented on existing hardware, or happen to coincide with what a package can offer.

Documentation reflects the analyst's role as a broker. The decision as to which entities and processes will be included fully, partially, and not at all within the scope of the requirement is to a certain extent political. Recording the compromises struck along the way helps the designer and implementers stay with the scope and spirit of the system. Standard analysis deliverables include:

- Analysis plan.
- Interview guides.
- Interview notes.
- Attribute (data element) definitions.
- Entity definitions.
- Entity-relationship diagrams.
- Data flow diagrams.
- Functional decomposition diagrams.
- Process descriptions.

- External interfaces.
- Packaged software compliance analysis.
- Cross-reference tables.

The following subsections describe the contents of each type of deliverable.

Information gathering plan

The scope of a prospective system determines the breadth of analysis. A plan for gathering information usually includes:

- Planned interviews with representatives of the people who will use the system.
- Planned interviews with users of other systems with which the proposed system will interact.
- Analysis and at times reverse engineering of the existing software systems that now do the job and with which the new system will interface.
- Reading whatever documentation is available about the process to be automated, including procedures for the existing system.
- Reading about and seeing demonstrations of implemented solutions to the requirement, including textbooks and packaged software.

The analysis plan usually includes a schedule of activities and a staff that will work on analysis.

The thrust of all Oracle's productivity tools is toward improving implementation productivity once analysis is complete. It is never appropriate to shortchange analysis in the interests of expediency. A poorly analyzed system is usually a dead loss in that it is cheaper to discard design, code and all, and start from the beginning than to amend it. The worst mistake an MIS director can make is to pour good money after bad in an attempt to salvage an ill-conceived system.

Interview guides

An interview guide provides structure to the exchange of information between user and analyst. It helps the interviewee prepare for the interview by identifying the prospective topics. The contents are:

- An introduction, which states the reason for the interview and the nature of the project. Most people are more willing and able to help when they can see the bigger picture.
- The interviewee's name and telephone number.
- Questions about the interviewee's job and use of the system being analyzed.
- Questions about the organization: reporting structure and job titles of the interviewee's organization and the other organizations with which he or she exchanges information.
- Questions about how the job is currently being done and shortcomings in the process.
- Questions to identify the things with which the interviewee works, including tangible objects, services, labor, and information entities that support them.
- Questions about organization as they relate to the system: who does what; where

does information come from and where does it go? What is the flow of other work objects, such as products in manufacturing, information in a network system, or parcels in a delivery system?

- Questions about volume and workload. How many of each type of work object and data entity are there? How big are they? How much time does it take to handle one?
- Questions about business rules. Some typical ones are how does the person decide which carrier to use in shipping a parcel, compute the reimbursement amount in an insurance claim, or determine pension eligibility.
- Questions about what the interview missed. The interviewee should always be prompted for information which they think is relevant but does not figure in the interview guide.
- Name and phone number of the interviewer, and an invitation to stay in contact as things change and new ideas come to mind.

Interview guides work best if there is enough white space in them that interviewees can fill out answers in advance. Some will and some won't. The questions should be in a logical sequence because they provide structure to the interview process. The final question should almost always be the one that invites the interviewee to go into topics which he or she feels were overlooked in the interview guide.

The whole interview process is hard work. Doing it well sets the stage for success over the whole life cycle. A properly conducted cycle of interviews gathers not only data, but a cadre of inside salespeople who will support the system because they have a personal stake in it and believe in the MIS professionals charged with making it happen.

Interview notes

Interviews result in raw data with little inherent organization. There is no substitute for the brute force approach of writing down pretty much what the interviewee said, bringing together related observations to the extent possible. Accuracy and completeness count more than style.

An interviewer's notes serve as a primary reference in piecing together the elements of analysis. They also confirm to the interviewee what was heard and understood. It is essential that the interviewer commit the results to a word processor shortly after the interview, before memory goes stale. The notes should mention any further research suggested by the interviewee, such as books to read or people to talk to. Interviewees are especially impressive when the interview notes also include notes on the other sources they recommended.

Most analysts use an interview note format to summarize their findings from written sources such as books and system documentation. It is usually not necessary to prepare anything analogous to an interview guide before conducting such research; a penciled list of points to research will suffice.

Attribute (data element) definitions

The data element definition (DED) captures information needed in design as it becomes available. The definition includes:

- A data element name, when possible in a format which will later serve as an Oracle column name. The section below titled "Naming Conventions" discusses conventions for choosing names.
- A description of how the data element is used within the system.
- The format and length of the data element (if available).
- Description of edits and computations which involve the data element.

CASE automatically captures attribute definitions. Shops that do not use CASE usually have a home-grown data dictionary in Oracle or, at a minimum, a DED in word processing. Figure 14-2 shows the description of a typical attribute. This reference is used from strategy through implementation and grows along the way. It does not have to be completed during the analysis phase.

Name: SSN

Definition: Social Security Number. Used as the key field for identifying people. The system generates artificial SSNs for foreign nationals and people who could not be expected to provide their SSNs.

Format: 11 Characters. Alphameric for generated SSNs: leading alpha followed by 10 numeric. May require a separate attribute to indicate the SSN type: real or generated.

Edits: Real SSNs must be 11 characters long, all numeric with dashes in the 4th and 7th positions. Generated SSNs must have a leading letter followed by 10 digits.

Computation: Business rules will be written to search appropriate data bases and return confirmed duplicate people and suspected duplicate people to prevent their insertion into the database. An Oracle sequence will create the numeric portion of generated SSNs. Processes that access the sequence will be responsible for invoking the standard subroutines that search for potential duplicates.

There will be US. Citizens and residents within the system such as grandparents of students who have SSNs that cannot reasonably be requested. There must be a process to change the key when such an SSN does becomes available.

14-2 Data-element description of a typical attribute.

Definitions of entities

CASE tools handle entity definitions automatically. Shops that do not use CASE need to create their own system for tracking entity definitions and relating them to the attributes (data elements) which make them up. The entity definition usually includes the following items.

- Entity name, usually in a format that can be used as an Oracle table definition.
- Description, telling what the entity is. The description includes who creates it and where it is used. Subtypes should be covered in the description.
- Unique key attributes, those that will serve as a primary key for the table.
- Foreign key attributes, those that will determine how the entity relates to other entities.
- Volumes if available: number of records anticipated, the frequency with which they are created, updated and deleted, and percentage of nulls.
- Subtype indicators. Identification of the things that act similarly within the system but that must be recognized as distinct, such as individual and corporate parties to a contract.

Figure 14-3 shows a typical entity description.

Entity-relationship diagrams

ER diagrams are the most universal piece of documentation in a relational system. They show how entities are related to one another by shared attributes. CASE produces ER diagrams automatically. Non-CASE users do them by hand, with freehand drawing packages, and with ER diagrammers such as LogicWorks' ERwin.

The act of creating and reviewing ER diagrams resolves inconsistencies. Because the user community is the ultimate source of knowledge about the records they must keep, they have to participate. One of the analyst's tasks is to teach diagramming conventions, which are fortunately rather simple to learn, to the users. The most common difficulty is in normalizing the users' view of their world. People are inclined to see data in light of their current restraints. If the clients file currently provides for two contacts, they think of a client as having two contacts instead of two entities, client and contact.

A system designer uses the analyst's ER diagrams as the foundation for the database design. Figure 14-4 shows the elaboration of the simple entity-relationship diagram in Fig. 11-1 into tables and columns. It is mostly a matter of defining the column formats.

All installations, including those that use CASE need standards for ER diagrams. The automated tools provide users with enough flexibility that a uniform style is important. Among the conventions that CASE experts such as Ulka Rogers and David Hay propose are:

- Resolve many-to-many relationships as early as possible. Although they are permissible for the sake of simplicity during strategy, they cannot be implemented, and resolving them often surfaces the fact that there is a valid entity hidden in the middle of a many-to-many relationship.
- Put organizations and people to the right of ER diagrams.
- Put records of physical things such as packages and inventory items on the bottom of ER diagrams.
- Follow the *dead-crow* rule by placing the entity with multiple occurrences above or to the left in diagramming a many-to-one relationship.
- Do not bend the lines linking two entities, because it makes the relationship hard to read.
- Include two verb phrases that relate the entities both ways and identify the cardi-

Entity Name: Person

Description: A person associated in some way with the school. Staff are associated in the capacity of an employee or contractor employee. Other persons include applicants, alumni, parents, students, trustees and benefactors. A single person may be associated with the school in multiple roles; see role entity for more detail.

Aliases and name changes are not normalized through the use of multiple records. There is one attribute for "also known as". Other attributes that may occur multiple times per person, such as address, are normalized in the design.

Unique Identifier: SSN is primary key. As indicated, it may be real or generated.

Volume: 1500 records, with approximately 10 adds and 50 updates per month except during application period (Oct-Dec) when there are approximately 100 records added per month, and admissions (March) when there are approximately 200 updates.   Records of terminated employees will be archived by an annual batch process three years after their date of separation. Records of ex-students and applicants will be kept online for one year.

Entity Name: Role

Description: One role that a person plays within the life of the school. The same person may be active in many roles, which is why roles cannot be treated as subtypes of person. Subtypes and sub-subtypes of roles are:
- Employee
    - Administration
    - Teaching staff
    - Custodial staff
- Parent or Guardian
- Student
- Alumnus
- Trustee
- Benefactor

Employment attributes are carried in the employee subtype.

Unique Identifier: SSN (foreign key) and role code

Volume: Approximately 20% more than person entity, with the same volatility.

14-3 Two entity descriptions.

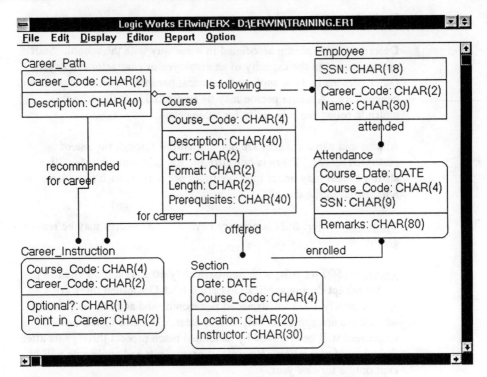

14-4 Data design derived from entity-relationship diagram in Fig. 11-1.

nality of the relationship. The sentences "A customer can place many orders." and "An order is placed by one and only one customer." describe the relationship between the customer and order entities from both ends.

Figure 14-5 illustrates these principles in the entity-relationship model for a private elementary school. As usual the most complex relationships involve people. This example resolves the problem through a roles table that recognizes the fact that a person can play many roles.

Analysts must be free to use their judgment when the two-dimensional constraints of paper set the rules in conflict with one another. Diagram complexity is a problem in every system of any magnitude. There is no single or simple solution. Experts offer the following suggestions:

- Do not show attributes in ER diagrams.
- Use oversize paper.
- Split the diagrams along functional or subsystem boundaries, simplifying entities on the periphery of the subsystem being shown.
- Simplify by not showing subtypes.
- Omit obvious validation tables (that is, state code, area code) from ER diagrams.
- Simplify relationships (that is, allow many-to-many) for purposes of diagramming.
- Simplify time relationships. If a relationship can be many-to-one over time, but only one-to-one at one point in time, show it to the user at one point in time.

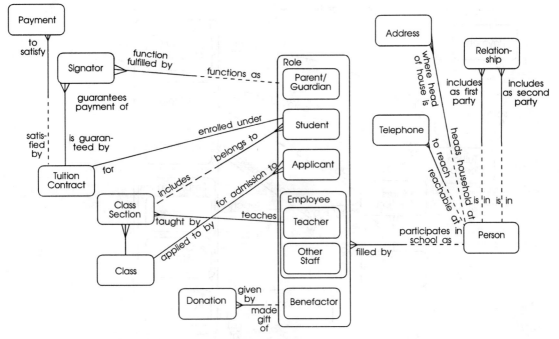

14-5 Private elementary school entity-relationship diagram.

Figure 14-5 above contains details that are not relevant to the financial side of the organization. The business people are interested in sources of revenue, primarily tuition payments and donations. The diagram in Fig. 14-6 is a simplification which omits the concept of roles and shows a many-to-many relationship between contracts and signatories. The simplification will work well enough for the money managers. It shows that parents are responsible for paying the bills. The diagram implies that information about the student, such as address and telephone number, will be available in the student record. The fact that it is distributed to other entities as shown in Fig. 14-5 is not really of concern, so long as it is available.

The beauty of a simplified diagram is that the intended users can relate to it and correct any misconceptions. The analyst can later apply the corrections to the master ER diagram.

The factor of time enters into almost every data model. In the example in Figs. 14-5 and 14-6, students and teachers work by school year. Over the years teachers will teach and students will belong to many classes. In standard form of simplification, the ER diagram in Fig. 14-6 represents relationships at one point in time. Only after the point-in-time relationships are fully worked out should the users be presented with a full data model including the time dimension. ER diagrams can be overwhelming; the analyst must lead the user along one step at a time.

Simplification is a presentation technique to facilitate communications with users. The analysis should be based on a fully normalized representation of the entities within an application. The analyst should note how borderline cases in normalization are

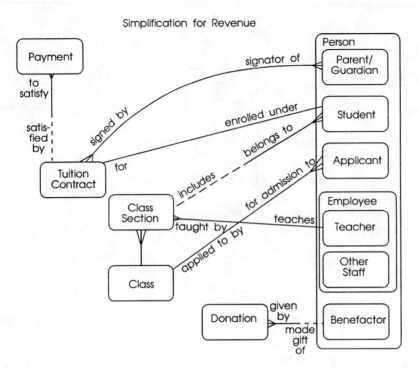

Simplification for Revenue

14-6 Simplified ER diagram.

resolved. In the example above, it could be satisfactory to carry primary and summer address attributes in a person's record rather than normalize them into an address entity. The attribute definitions should contain a sentence to describe and justify the decision.

Paper diagrams are vastly better than words to convey the relationship among data entities. A CASE tool is an order of magnitude better than paper. It adds the dimensions of context and detail zooming. The context dimension allows a user to flip among different ways of looking at the same thing, such as entity attributes, narrative description of the entity, processes that use the entity. Detail zooming allows a user to take a macro view of the whole data model, then zoom into any portion of it to whatever level of detail they desire.

CASE's *"electronic kaleidoscope"* enables the analyst to sit down with users and talk through every angle of a data model simply and quickly, and even amend it on the fly. It makes good use of the analyst's time not having to draw and redraw pictures, and it makes good use of the users' time as they work with the analyst to develop a complete and mutually agreed model.

A data flow diagram shows how data flows through a sequence of procedures in a business function. Figure 14-7 illustrates how paperwork and records flow through the various processes in the admissions office of a private school.

Whereas entity-relationship and functional decomposition diagrams are static, data flow diagrams emphasize action: who does what with which data and in what order. High-level data flow diagrams are a useful way to visually depict the operation of a whole division or department. At the lowest level they can represent the function within a module of code.

Oracle's CASE tools support data flow diagrams, but they are not along the critical path. It can generate code without them. This is consistent with Oracle's nonprocedural approach.

Process descriptions

Analysis describes the business. The entities, attributes, and relationships describe the data that it keeps. Process descriptions describe how that data is used. Information is not an end in itself but exists to support business functions. For that reason, the process descriptions have more the flavor of business than data processing.

Decomposition diagrams such as that in Fig. 1-3 show how processes are subordinate to one another in a hierarchy. Flow diagrams such as Fig. 14-7 show how information passes among them. Process descriptions tell what they do. The tables and data elements they operate on, and whether they create, update, delete, or simply reference those data

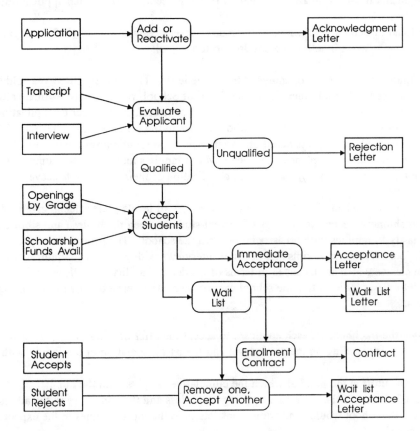

14-7   Data flow diagram of a private school admissions process.

elements, describes a large portion of their function. The data integrity rules associated with the data elements imply more function. Business rules that will be enforced through subroutine calls merely have to be mentioned. Any functions beyond these represent logic unique to the process. They need to be described in some procedural fashion, either text or some form of pseudocode.

Businesses are usually organized by areas of responsibility each of which accomplished its mission through a unique set of functions. Figure 14-8 describes such a function within a private school. These unique processes usually map well into an organization chart and a functional decomposition diagram. In the example, sending out letters of admission is part of the admissions process, which is in turn part of administration.

Most businesses involve elementary processes which are repeated with variations. Formulas and algorithms belong in the process descriptions. Figure 14-9 is a typical al-

Process: Send out Admissions Letters

Description: Admissions are done in February of each year. Each applicant will have submitted an application sometime after October 15 of the preceding year, which applications open.

The Head of School who handles the grade (Nursery, Lower School (K-3) or Upper School (4-6) follows these steps in admitting children to the school:

Determine the number of openings at the grade level. The Nursery three-year-old class is all new each year. For all other classes the Head of School reviews must estimate attrition by the number of deposits received with re-enrollment contracts, the number of applications out, that is, transcripts requested by students who will rise to the grade level in question. The estimate has to be an educated guess based on experience. The Head knows the historical ratio of applications out to acceptances. Students whose families move over the summer and those who leave for public schools typically give no indication of their intention to leave.

Create an ordered admissions list for the class. At all levels preference is given first to children of parishioners, second to siblings of current students, then to children and siblings of alumni, and lastly to families with no association with the school. The process is subjective. The Head of School reviews transcripts and notes of interviews with parents and applicants in an attempt to form classes which are balanced in terms of gender and ability. Applicants whose transcripts and interviews indicate that the school cannot adequately serve them will be sent rejection letters.

Weight the likelihood of each applicant to accept the offer of admission. The estimate is very subjective, depending on the grade level and the past association of the family with the school.

Create a cutoff at the point at which the cumulative weights total the number of positions open at the grade level. If there are four openings in a class and the names are in the admissions priority shown, the school would send admissions letters to the top six names in the expectation that two will not accept.

14-8 A mainline business process.

162 *Documentation requirements and standards*

Name	Weight (likelihood of acceptance)	Cumulative Weight
Ishihara	80%	.8
Gaither	40%	1.2
Ethan	50%	1.7
Daschner	90%	2.6
Adams	80%	3.4
Franklin	80%	4.2
Carothers	60%	4.8
Harkin	50%	5.3
Bellknapp	80%	6.1

Send letters of admission to those who make the cut. Send wait-list letters to others who are qualified but fall below the cut.

Update the status of the applications to show the action taken.

Data References

This process updates the Role entity to change an applicant's status from Applicant to Admitted. It refers to the Class entity for class size and for statistical data on historical acceptance rates. It uses the Student Mailing process to compose form letters.

Process: Mailing List Creation

Description: A standard process to assemble mailing lists for form letters. The process accepts as input the role for which the mailing list is to be created, the criteria for choosing names within that role, and additional attributes to select for inclusion in the body of a mailing. Its output is a file of names, addresses and variable text to include in the body.

Data References: This process selects from the Role, Person, Relationship and Address tables. It makes use of the fact that by the constraints of the data base that every person is either a head-of-household and has an address, or has a member-of-household relationship with one and only one person who is a head-of-household. The rules for finding an address are:
1. Use the person's summer address if the person is a head of household and it is summer, otherwise,
2. Use the person's primary address if the person is a head of household, otherwise,
3. Locate the single relationship which indicates the head of the household in which the person lives. Use that person's address as determined by rules 1) and 2).

Invoked by: Mailings to students, mailings to employees, mailings to potential donors.

14-9 A business algorithm/repeated process.

gorithm—the procedure for creating a mailing list. An algorithm is, by definition, a common rule that applies to more than one instance of a requirement. This one describes how to pull together names and addresses for a mailing list.

As Oracle is practiced today, the prototype process often takes the place of process descriptions (analysis) and program specifications (design). Prototyping is nothing more than rapid-turnaround rework. The premise is that once the analyst and user working together have defined the data, the process logic is almost self-explanatory. This might be an illusion.

The nuances of data relationships often do not emerge until the analyst examines how the data are used. If the analyst were content with mere data design in the example here, it might not be evident that head-of-household is an important attribute. It is needed to determine whose address to use in a mailing. An analyst (who might well turn out to be the programmer) makes development more efficient by thinking a process out and writing it down in advance. Thinking about processes at several stages of system evolution—analysis, design, and programming—improves the quality of the product. It sets more minds to the task of figuring how things must work and what can go wrong.

Data administration considerations

An analyst can normally take data administration for granted. Exceptional requirements require some thinking. The data administration document is a free-form compilation listing exceptionally large tables, tables with high add-change-delete activity, tables that require exceptional precautions for accuracy or backup, and tables with exceptional security requirements. It amounts to a note to the designer about potential pitfalls in planning the implementation. Figure 14-10 provides an example of data administration considerations.

External interfaces

The external interfaces document identifies other systems that will provide data to the system or use data from it. The topics it covers include:

- What data elements (attributes) need to be exchanged with other systems?
- What is the data element format in the other system?
- On what schedule is the data available for input, or must it be available for output?
- What volumes are involved?
- In what medium and format does the other system use the data? That is, what conversion is involved?
- Does the other system make demands for accuracy or timeliness which exceed those inherent in the one being analyzed?

Figure 14-11 shows an example of an external interfaces document.

Oracle's CASE tools allow one application to refer to entities which belong to other applications. Unless there are notes to the contrary, the assumption is that access to the foreign entity is unrestricted.

Role and Person Entities:

Backup: The daily backup and continuity-of-operations requirements are the same as for the entire database, that is, daily backup. The backup plan requires that the three most recent days' backups be available for recovery purposes; that the previous month-end's backup be kept in off-site storage (the business manager's house) to protect against destruction of the school; and that one year's month-end backup tapes be kept as a deep backup.

Archiving: The roles entity controls archiving requirements of itself and the persons entity. Records for a person can be deleted when that person no longer has any role in the life of the school. Each subtype of the role entity has different archiving characteristics

Applicant subtype records have the following characteristics: 1) they are numerous; 2) they are of no interest once the school year for which they were made is over; and 3) they contain bulky scanned images of transcripts from other schools. For this reason they can be deleted without archive at the end of each school year.

By state law employment records must remain available for five years after termination. Person and role records of employees will be left on the system for that period, then archived to paper or microfiche. An entry in the finder entity, indexed by SSN and last name, will provide a quick online reference to the archived records.

Student and parent records are numerous and of little interest once a student has left the school. The role and person records of departing students and their families will be archived to paper or microfiche at the end of each school year, providing those people do not continue in other roles. A row will be added to the finder entity for each person whose records are archived.

14-10 Example of data administration considerations.

Interface: Payroll Service Payee Information Update

Entities/Attributes Required:
The following attributes are required in a fixed length record the format of which is specified by the payroll service:

> Employee Name
> Employee Address
> Monthly salary
> Number of Dependents
> Direct Deposit Bank Name
> Direct Deposit Account Number
> Payroll Deduction data: type and amount

Volume: 50 changes per pay period, except during June hiring season when it is 200.

Medium: Modem transmission to ABC payroll service.

Timing and Frequency: Transmissions made evening of 12th day of month and 3 days before end of month. PC placed in auto-answer mode to respond to auto-dial by payroll service.

14-11 Example of an external interface description.

Packaged software compliance analysis

It makes sense to investigate package offerings before doing any custom development. When to start looking at packages is a chicken-and-egg question. Do you define the requirements then look at potential solutions, or see what other designers have conceived as solutions before examining the problem at hand?

There are decided benefits to looking at packages early. It educates the analyst and users alike about problems and features they might not even think of. It also brings price into the equation. Almost every implementation involves trade-offs between cost and function. Packaged software, with its published prices, brings them into clear focus.

A compliance matrix shows how well each individual package meets the needs that the analyst has identified. Every analysis includes notes for subjective evaluations: nice-to-have features, partial fits, and strengths and weaknesses of the company. Table 14-2 shows a few lines from a compliance matrix for project management systems.

Cross-reference tables

There are as many ways to design a system as to build a building. Just as a superior architect studies how a building will be used before designing it, a superior analyst looks at how the data will be used. Cross-reference tables show which functions use which entities and attributes and how they use them: create, read, update, and delete. They are often called *CRUD* matrices, the acronym formed from the first letters of the four named functions. What falls out of a CRUD matrix can be interesting.

Functions that affect no attributes and attributes that are not used in any functions are candidates for elimination from the system. Either they are not needed or they call attention to an oversight by the analyst.

Table 14-2   Packaged software compliance analysis example.

Oracle Project Management System Evaluation Matrix	Eval. Weight	Vendor A Pct/Points		Vendor B Pct/Points		Vendor C Pct/Points		Vendor D Pct/Points	
Able to enter & display wrapped 40-character task descriptions on both Gantt and PERT	40	100%	40	60%	24	0%	0	0%	0
Graphics output from both Gantt and PERT	30	100%	30	100%	30	100%	30	100%	30
Ability to rearrange elements in PERT charts	20	0%	0	100%	20	0%	0	0%	0
Accepts actual expenses fed from Accounts Payable	30	100%	30	100%	30	40%	12	100%	30
Accepts actual labor hours from Time Accounting System	50	100%	50	100%	50	40%	20	100%	50
Feeds departmental / corporate budgeting system	20	0%	0	0%	0	50%	10	0%	0
COMPOSITE SCORE			150		154		72		110

When multiple processes update the same tables, it begs the question as to why they are not combined. The analyst should examine whether it would be reasonable for one user to collect all of the update data at one point in time. Controlling updates is a great help in ensuring the integrity of a database.

The affinity of processes with tables and the transaction volume going through online processes suggest how to organize the system. Frequently referenced tables are high-priority targets for denormalization. Is it possible to mash tables together to reduce I/O operations? Table usage also indicates whether a distributed database philosophy is workable. Knowing how processes and tables are aligned will help determine how the menu system is structured, whether by user roles or system tables.

Valuable as they are, cross-reference tables are tedious to develop. Furthermore every change anywhere in the analysis affects them. One of the great virtues of CASE is that it does them automatically.

Design documentation

Analysis describes the problem to be solved and design outlines the solution. The two are very closely related, especially where rigorous methodologies and tools such as CASE are used. Oracle's CASE tools automatically generate default design-level objects from the corresponding analysis objects. There are two fundamental levels of design documentation for processes:

- Processes within the functional decomposition, called mainline processes.
- Library subroutines called by mainline processes (and each other).

One of the great economies of Oracle, especially with CASE, is that processes within the functional decomposition of the system are usually highly predictable. Coders can write or CASE can generate most of them without a design specification. Users often write the specifications in effect through the trial-and-error process of a prototyping implementation.

Subroutines provide processing support of other modules. They need specifications because the many coders who use them must have a common understanding of how to invoke them, what data to pass, and what to expect in return. Specifications for subroutines usually follow the standards that a shop will have established for third-generation language implementations.

The deliverable products in system design include:

- Data design.
- Data implementation plan.
- Menu structure and global parameters.
- Process specifications.
- Test plan.
- Cost justification.

Figure 14-12 shows how analysis products relate to design products on the data and process sides.

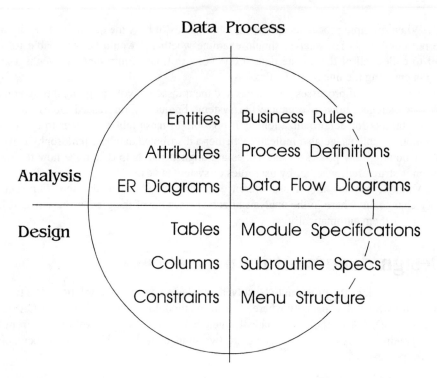

14-12 Relationships among analysis and design, data, and process documentation.

Data design

The data design establishes the database structure of tables, views, and indexes to be used by the application. These are the denormalized, real-world implementation of the entities, attributes, and relationships documented in the analysis phase. The data design consists of the following documentation:

- Column definitions, derived from attribute definitions in the analysis phase, with lengths and data types established for all the fields. The column definition also might include validity criteria for the column contents (to be entered as constraints) and formulas for computing derived columns.
- Table definitions, derived from entity definitions in the analysis phase, which define the columns within each table. The table definitions are often made in SQL START files, which create tables and indexes. The table definitions include foreign key constraints.
- Index definitions.
- Diagrams of the relationships among tables only if they differ significantly from the ER diagrams. The same entity-relationship diagramming conventions used in analysis work to represent actual tables.

Data implementation plan

The data design has implications for a DBA: which user IDs will own the tables, how will tables be distributed into tablespaces, and what views will be used for convenience and to restrict access.

A system of any magnitude needs a written data plan which lays out instances, tablespaces, user IDs and views and provides a rationale for the way they are set up. It starts by listing the anticipated problem areas in managing data for the system, which can include:

- Performance
- Data volumes
- Access security
- Data integrity and backup
- User administration

The data implementation plan can include actual or prototype SQL to set things up. It is usually combined with the data design SQL, which creates tables and indexes. The SQL should carry comments that echo the implementation plan or refer to it.

Menu structure and global parameters

Oracle systems tend to be close to the user. Users almost always have the ability to choose from a menu of functions; in a system of any complexity, the structure is two to four menus deep.

One of the designer's first tasks is to work out how functions will be presented to the user. It starts with a straightforward transformation of the functional decomposition developed in the analysis phase. A useful menu structure is more involved than the functional decomposition for several reasons:

- Menus group functions by their users rather than according to the decomposition logic of the application.
- Menu structures have to keep user privileges in mind. Users with different privileges need different menus.
- A given process might appear multiple times in a menu structure for use by different users or simply to make it close at hand wherever a user might need it.
- A menu process organizes functions by the order in which they are used and the frequency with which they are needed. The designer might group infrequently used processes into low-level menus without regard to how they fit within a functional decomposition.
- It is often convenient to group like functions together, such as updates on one menu and reports on another, to make it easy to find them.

The designer should refer to the discussion of SQL*Menu layout considerations in "Working with Oracle Development Tools." The design considerations are similar for systems which use SQL*Forms or operating system shell scripts to implement menuing.

The designer must specify the interaction among processes below the menu level. SQL*Forms processes can invoke subordinate forms. A batch process invoked from the menu might execute several batch programs. The discussion should also address batch processes that do not go through the menu structure, those that a system operator initiates from the operating system command line or which the system itself initiates on a periodic basis.

Although menu structures can be shown graphically, they change so often during the development of a system that an indented word processing representation is often most convenient. Outliners are excellent for the purpose. Figure 14-13 shows an example. Note that the list of applicants by grade level appears twice—for the people doing admissions and for those making up classes. The archive and delete option of the applications menu will only be displayed and available for the head of admissions.

The menu design includes defining parameters used by programs to communicate with one another. In an Oracle system, these include the substitution parameters/global variables used by SQL*Menu and SQL*Forms to communicate with each other and processes that they invoke. Many systems also use operating system shell variables and temporary files to communicate among programs and processes.

In contrast to object-oriented environments, Oracle systems usually make a clear distinction in character and usage between execution-time variables and database values. Execution time variables must be rigorously defined only to the extent that the programs

Applications
    Enter and Update Applications
    Enter transcript data
    Admissions
    List Applicants/Acceptances/Wait List by Grade Level
    List Applicants/Acceptances/Wait List Alphabetically
    Archive and delete prior year applications (Head of Admissions only)
Student Administration
    Student and family personal data maintenance
    Classroom assignment menu
        Assign students to classes
        List Applicants/Acceptances/Wait List by Grade Level
        Student list by gender
        Student list by academic performance
        Student list by zip code
    Report cards
        Report card data maintenance
        List report cards by class, with statistical summary
        Grading curve graphs
            Historical at a given grade level
            Current year at all grade levels
    Transcripts
        Create a transcript
        List applications out by school and grade
        Maintain address / admissions personnel data for other schools

14-13 Example of menu structure.

which create and use them share a common interpretation of their format and meaning. Table 14-3 shows typical entries. The designer makes the initial list; programmers invariably modify it during the course of writing a system.

Process specifications

A process is a procedure or module. A module in Oracle can be any of the following:

- In SQL*Forms, one entire form or a block within a form.
- In SQL*Menu, one page of the menu or the whole menu system.
- A PL/SQL code block such as an SQL*Forms trigger or Version 7 stored procedure.
- An SQL*ReportWriter report.
- An Oracle*Card Process.

Table 14-3   Example of a list of global parameters.

Substitution Parameter/Global Variable Name	Description	Set by	Used by	Format
&UN	User Name	SQL*Menu logon	All Oracle processes	CHAR(30)
&PW	Password	SQL*Menu logon	All Oracle processes	CHAR(30)
&TT	Terminal Type	SQL*Menu logon	All Oracle processes	CHAR(30)
&RM RPT_MONTH	Current month for reporting purposes; defaults to current calendar month	Operating system shell which invokes SQL*Menu for application	All application processes	CHAR(6) Format YYYYMM
&FY FISCAL_YEAR	Current fiscal year	Operating system shell which invokes SQL*Menu for application	All application processes	CHAR(4) Format YYYY
&CLASS	School class (grade level)	User within an SQL*Forms process	get_subj routine, report processes	CHAR(2) Upper Case N3, N4, K or 1-6
&LOV_CLASS_SUBJ	List of values class. A list of abbreviations of the subjects appropriate to a given grade level. get_subj(4) might return the value "LangArts SocStud Math French Spanish PE Music Art Science"	get_subj() subroutine	Prompt & error messages within SQL*Forms	CHAR(240) upper & lower

- A top-level batch program in any third- or fourth-generation language invoked from SQL*Menu or the operating system.
- A subroutine called by any of the above, such as a user exit.
- An operating system shell script.

Oracle 4GL developers working in a prototyping environment almost always work without program specs. As analyst/designer/programmers, they know what the user needs and feel no need to write it down in advance.

The user will correct them if they get it wrong. Programmers also know that traditional process specifications are not much use in 4GL program maintenance. Documentation is superfluous because the code speaks for itself.

CASE designers handle most mainline process specifications at the CASE tool level. The CASE generator knows how to construct data editing logic from the metadata definitions of tables, attributes and relationships. Some non-Oracle CASE products provide coding language that allows designers (acting like programmers) to use to write procedural logic.

Written process specifications are almost the exception in many Oracle shops. The developers feel, correctly, that for simple one and two table SQL*Forms and SQL*ReportWriter processes, the data imply the process. They are in danger of overlooking the fact that specifications are very useful, often indispensable in situations, such as:

- Involved processing logic within mainline procedures. In the school example used throughout this chapter, the SQL*Forms process to update data on people would be such a process. The form would have to be written to make sure that no applicant or student has an address record, but that each one is linked through a row in the relationship table with one and only one person who does. That much might be accomplished through Version 7 constraints. The form, however, would have to be designed to help the user find a relative who is already in the file and to present friendly and informative error messages when there is a problem. Even a genius programmer could not write the process without planning it in advance—in other words, writing a specification.
- Library objects, pieces of code that will be used several places within the system. The written specifications ensure that the coder who writes the routine and other coders who call it agree on the number, format, and sequence of the parameters to be passed back and forth.
- System-wide procedures, such as error conditions to check and error message presentation. Even when there is only one developer it makes sense to give some advance thought to functions that will recur throughout the system.
- Complex program logic. Whatever decision table or flow chart a programmer needs to write a module belongs in a specification document, even if the programmer himself writes it. If it has not been preserved, anyone who maintains the code will have to recreate the logic. Table 14-4 shows a decision table for file matching within a C language program. Decision tables are a technique dating back to card machines of the 1950s. They have advantages over flow charts and other types of diagrams in that their concise format can easily be copied directly into program comments. They retain their original virtue, which is that their format

Table 14-4   Decision table example—
merge files sequenced by SSN (major)
and address (minor), eliminating duplicates.

Conditions	Cases							
Old < New (thru Addr)	Y							
Old > New (thru Addr)		Y						
Old = New (thru Addr)			Y	Y	Y	Y	Y	
Old < New (SSN)			Y		Y			
Old > New (SSN)				Y		Y		
Old = New (SSN)							Y	
Both SSNs phony					N	N	Y	Y
Actions								
DUP SOURCE=D		X	X					
DUP SOURCE=A			X	X				
Write out Old				X	X			
Write out New				X	X			
Perform Read Old Rtn	X	X		X	X	X		
Perform Read New Rtn		X		X	X	X	X	

forces a program designer to consider all the alternatives that a program has to handle.

Almost every data processing shop has standards for writing program specifications. There would be no benefit in proposing one here. A shop fortunate enough not to be saddled with something inherited from the 1970s can fall back on common sense. A program spec should:

- Give an overview of what the process does.
- Define the inputs, with appropriate references to the data design and menu system parameters.
- Define the outputs, again with references to the data design and menu system parameters.
- Describe the process in enough detail that the programmer can write it, using narrative supported by decision tables, pseudo-code, and references to analysis documentation such as business rules.
- Include or reference test data and a plan to test the module.

Designers abjure writing program specifications because writing them is a tedious exercise. The MIS director needs to recognize that it is possible to encourage planning without imposing a requirement for formal specs. The program manager can schedule design walk-throughs in which the designer, programmer, and user work the kinks out of the designers' scribbled notes and diagrams before they start developing a prototype of a program.

Test plan

A prototype is code that can be made to work. In contrast, a production system should be code that can hardly be made to fail. Though the prototype process is a great way to develop mainline program logic, it takes planning to handle the exception situations. A developer cannot rely on the users to figure out everything that can go wrong.

A test plan starts with a list of what can go wrong. A major area of concern is the part of the system that end users see. It needs to ensure that the users cannot get lost and confused. It absolutely must guarantee data integrity and go into the elements of a system that a user never sees such as backup, recovery, and reorganization. Obvious problems to check for are:

- The user can destroy relational integrity.
  ~By deleting records with foreign key references.
  ~By changing key fields.
  ~By adding records without validating foreign keys.
  ~By adding duplicate records.
- The user can enter invalid data.
- The user can hang the system.
- The user can get system error messages that don't provide a clue as to how to recover.
- Programs present incorrect results.
- The user can get incorrect results or lock the system by starting processes out of sequence.
- The system will not perform adequately with a production work load.
- Users can lock the system by going after the same data or get inconsistent results by not locking data.
- Users can access data that is supposed to be restricted.
- The system compromises passwords.

Testing is an organizational issue. Chapter 9 describes the roles of the test designer and test data developer and chapter 15 covers testing procedures. Most designers and developers hate developing test data; a vast number don't do it. They test with live data or copies of live files just because it is easy. One of the many problems with this approach is that testing can take far too long because of the volumes involved. Another more significant shortcoming is that the developers have no way to know what parts of their logic never get used. Results are inconsistent because the testing of update programs changes the database. Lastly, live data often contains sensitive data. The test plan for an Oracle system needs the following elements:

- A separate user ID containing master versions of test data with SELECT access granted to the public.
- Utility routines to copy tables from the test user ID into developers' own user IDs.
- A small test version of every table that will be updated by the system. Developers can easily copy a small table to their user IDs, test the update program and examine the results.
- A small version of every table that will be reported. This is often the same as the

version for testing updates. There should be enough data to force test reports to about three pages.

- Larger versions of test files as appropriate for volume testing.
- Test scripts for online update processes, with data matched to the test tables.
- Test data files for import processes.
- Test scripts for integration testing, running data through multiple modules or the whole system.

The test plan should specify the conditions that exist in each test table and the conditions to be tested by the test scripts. The designer might leave the actual creation of test data and scripts to the developers.

Systems that are developed under contract typically require a formal acceptance test. The contractor gets paid when all the documentation is in order and the system passes the test. The whole system needs to be tested and approved at once, after which any changes tend to cost money.

Test plans belong in even the most abbreviated system documentation. The rapid prototype developments depend especially on well-chosen test data. Giving thought to the data a system must handle is tantamount to designing the system itself. Without a test plan, it isn't designed.

Cost justification

The cost estimate for implementing a system can be much more accurate once it is designed than during the analysis phase. The design specifies what the implementation involves. It is prudent management to reassess the advisability of a project at major milestones in its development. Figure 14-14 shows two review points. Barry Boehm, from whom the spiral concept is borrowed, uses a four-level spiral with as many review points.

Almost every justification document contains a cost/benefit element—how much will the project cost and how much will it yield in increased revenue and reduced expenses. A complete analysis projects risk as well as cost. It evaluates what can go wrong, the likelihood of it happening, and the possible costs. Chapter 19 describes the process in detail and provides examples. The format is almost identical for deciding among alternatives and making the final go/no go decision.

It is often hard to fit approvals into the Oracle development cycle. One of the things that has made Oracle popular in the first place is that a system can mushroom into place before management has time to prevent it.

Development and maintenance documentation

Every piece of documentation communicates to people later in the life cycle of a system. Programmers write for themselves in their next incarnation as maintainers of a system and for their users.

In smaller systems where the members of the same compact team serve as analysts, designers, and implementers, there is a strong tendency to dispense with formal documen-

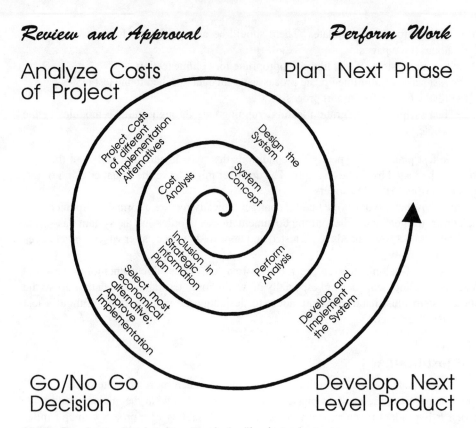

Analyze Costs
of Project

Plan Next Phase

Project Costs
of different
Implementation
Alternatives

Design the
System

Cost
Analysis

System
Concept

Inclusion in
Strategic
Information
Plan

Perform
Analysis

Select most
economical
alternative;
Approve
Implementation

Develop and
Implement
the System

Go/No Go
Decision

Develop Next
Level Product

14-14 Development and review steps in the life of a project.

tation. Comments are it. When these teams also lack a commenting ethic they can find
themselves going in circles a few months into a project trying to remember what they did
why they did it.

A strong text editor is a vital ingredient in any development environment, especially
in prototype development. A shop that does not enforce formal documentation absolutely
must make it easy for developers to comment their code. It helps to use the standard
quality control mechanisms described in chapter 13, such as having programmers read
one another's completed code. The development deliverables are:

- Source code
- Maintenance documentation
- Executable code
- User documentation

Source code, comments, and maintenance documentation

Well-written source code, rich with comments is the most useful form of maintenance
documentation except when the code comes from a CASE generator. The standard style

and commenting protect a shop's investment in code. Stated another way, programmers find it easier to scrap and rewrite an unstructured or uncommented module than to figure out what it does.

A one- or two-page coding standard for each programming tool within the shop will provide programmers the reference they need. The outline for typical standards is:

- Visual format standards: how to handle blocks, indentation, and page breaks. Whether or not each statement goes on a new line; how many lines per module.
- Comments:
  ~How comments fit into the visual format.
  ~Mandatory entries, such as name, date, and purpose for maintenance comments.
  ~Style, such as complete sentences in a paragraph format.
- Logic structure
  ~Use of case statements and branching statements
  ~Use of subroutines and library modules

Because maintenance documentation is written for the developers and by the developers, standards should be set by committees of developers who work with the tools in question. Most programmers take pride in the appearance of their code. Quality control serves as a reminder of the standards that apply in individual instances.

User documentation

This is the video age. Users don't like to turn from their tubes to look up how to use a system. An application should deliver everything a user needs to know via the screen. The installation standards discussed above will describe how documentation is delivered in a specific environment. It is useful to have a separate standard to cover the content of user documentation.

Writing user documentation should be a collaborative effort. The analyst and designer provide process overviews, the data dictionary provides reference information for individual tables and fields, and the programmer writes whatever is needed to describe how the process works as implemented. The system looks much more professional when a talented wordsmith integrates the documentation. A sizable shop might have a documentation specialist on staff. Otherwise there are numbers of freelance specialists available in most areas. The elements of user documentation are:

- Online help text, delivered through tool-specific mechanisms. SQL*Menu and SQL*Forms have limited built-in help facilities, but have the hooks to support very sophisticated user-written help systems. A comprehensive system has the following features:
  ~Help text is maintained in a database of its own, where it can be readily updated without affecting the application system it supports.
  ~Help is available in different contexts, usually the field, block and form levels for SQL*Forms.
  ~The help system is indexed so that users can select a reference topic.
  ~The help reference files can be customized by user, to support foreign languages or different departments with different requirements.

- Online error messages, each of which either provides the problem resolution or tells where to find it.
- A paper document keyed to the online help and error messages. The hard copy format is easier than online help for doing extended reading.
- Training materials. Depending on the system these can include a syllabus for stand-up training, class problems, a tutorial, and self-study courses. Training and reference materials should be coordinated.

Naming conventions

People need names for data processing objects like entities and key fields as early as the strategic planning phase. It is immensely helpful if everyone in the development process uses the same names consistently. The most convenient way to handle the requirement is through standards and procedures. The procedures identify tasks in which people assign names to things and reference an installation standard that tells how to do it.

People assign names to provide a unique handle for an object within the context in which it is defined. The context of a field is the record in which it appears. The context of a program variable is the program. The context of a login ID is the network or computer to which it applies. The major requirements for a name within a context are:

- It must be unique.
- It must be easy to use.

The major factors that make a name easy to use are that it is short (if it has to be typed frequently) and that the exact spelling is easy to remember.

Name qualifications and naming hierarchies

Names must be qualified when their context is not evident. *SSN* uniquely identifies a social security number column within a single table. When a context such as a program or SQL statement includes two tables with SSN columns, a reference must indicate which table in order to make the reference unambiguous.

There are any number of hierarchies that can provide context. Some of them are shown in Table 14-5.

Hierarchies overlap. An SQL*Forms .inp file belongs to an object type hierarchy (.inp file within SQL*Forms) as well as an application hierarchy. An SQL*Forms program might have the name EMP_UPD. Another application could have a form called EMP_UPD. Another branch of the company could have an application with the same name. There could be a report called EMP_UPD. There might well be several versions of the form in question. There will exist an .inp, an .frm, and a database version of the form. All of the hierarchies have to be named to completely identify an object.

Programmers often like to be able to deduce the nature of a thing and to whom it belongs from its name alone. The generic term for naming schemes which makes this possible is intelligent keys. Representative names with built-in intelligence about their owner might be:

Table 14-5   Hierarchies within Oracle systems.

Hierarchy Type	Elements within the hierarchy			
Database	Instance	User ID	Table	Column
Application	Organization	Application	Module (multiple layers)	Variable Name
Geography	Company Location	Building	Room	Computer
Object Type	Tool	Flat or data base	File extension	
Version	Design Level	Release Level		

ACCTS_REC_CUSTOMER_MASTER_TBL,

AR3050F (an SQL Form .frm file belonging to accounts receivable),

or

AR_CUSTOMER_NO.

Such names used to be useful because COBOL, to name one language, had an awkward scheme of qualifying variables. Giving the same variable a different prefix each time it appeared (as in input, work, and output) was much easier than using qualified names.

Oracle is different. It expects duplicate names and has powerful and easy-to-use features for handling them. More to the point, there are so many possible qualifiers for any type of object that it is impossible to build all such qualifiers into a naming scheme. Therefore the given name of an object should serve only one purpose: to conveniently identify the object. Oracle provides the facilities needed to qualify that name with the names of other objects when it is not unique within a given context.

Assigning unique names

A name has to be unique and easy to use. Uniqueness is a two-way street. Each object should have one and only one name, and each name should apply to one and only one object.

In a well-defined system objects are either identical, in which case they carry the same name, or different. An application should not, for instance, define one field as CUST_NO CHAR(12) and another CLIENT_NUM CHAR(10) . Shades of gray lead to poor systems. In database design, they indicate that the database is not fully thought out or normalized. A major responsibility of whoever assigns names is to make sure that no substantially identical object exists within the system before assigning a name to a new object.

A common repository ensures that names are unique within its domain. The data dictionary that supports Oracle should usually be broad enough to handle systems written for other computer environments within the installation. It is hard to anticipate when systems will be consolidated. The data dictionary should ideally span all the parts of a business entity which have to interact. Each shop has to decide which types of names belong in the repository. Oracle entities and attributes, columns and tables generally do. Program variables do not, and program modules may or may not.

Choosing names that are easy to use

Spelling is easy in the Spanish, Arabic, and Vietnamese languages because the rules are so precise that a person can spell what they hear. The same should be true for data processing objects. A programmer who knows that the month-to-date accumulated accounts payable field must appear in a report should not have to spend time figuring out whether it was MON_TO_DT_ACCUM_AP or MTD_ACCUMULATED_PAYABLES. A shop needs generic rules for forming all types of names.

There need to be different rules for different types of names. Oracle names are 30 characters long and MS-DOS names only eight. The difference is that there are a quintillion quintillion quintillion more unique names possible in Oracle. Put another way, it is much easier to choose meaningful Oracle names. Common rules for forming names for objects in an Oracle environment are:

- Every name is broken into segments.
- Segments are separated by underscores.
- Each segment is either a complete word or an agreed abbreviation.
- Synonymous segment names (like FIRM and CORP) are avoided.

The scheme has to be supported by a dictionary of segment names that is easy enough to implement in Oracle. The data administrator is a logical referee with regard to acceptable abbreviations and what constitutes synonyms.

Short names in MS-DOS and older IBM and HP environments are a problem in two ways. They have to identify their own context unless their file system or directory does so, and there are not enough characters to create a meaningful name. Most shops use intelligent key type names like:

- Application ID: two characters.
- Identifying name or unique number: five characters.
- Object type: one character.

People who work on the system have to either remember or look up the fact that PL50032R is the monthly payroll summary. The name doesn't say.

Oracle naming conventions

Oracle developers have shared some common sense standards that are worth noting here.

- Table names are plural, such as EMPLOYEES or VOUCHER_PAYMENTS. Views follow the same rules as tables.
- Column names are singular, such as EMPLOYEE_NAME.
- Whenever possible, the same name is used for the same column in every table in which it appears. ORDER_NUMBER in the orders table equates to ORDER_NUMBER in the picking slip table.
- A common set of segments with unique suffixes are used to distinguish between different uses of the same data type. Assume the employee's and the manager's social security numbers both appear as columns in a personnel table in order to establish the reporting relationship. The column SSN cannot appear twice. Instead

they are named SSN#EMPLOYEE and SSN#MANAGER. This indicates that both will use the format specified for SSN in the data dictionary.

- Whether or not a field is used as a key has nothing to do with the field name. The usage (primary key, foreign key, or not a key) will depend on the table in which a column appears.
- In a violation of the intelligent-key rule, index names are formed by adding the suffix _Xnn to table names to which they apply. No systematic attempt can be made to add intelligence to indicate which set of keys is used—it can get very complex. Furthermore, it never matters once a key is established. The RDBMS alone decides which to use.
- By standard, four-character shorthand synonyms are defined for major tables. These are especially useful in Pro language coding. Continually repeating fully qualified column names can be very tedious.
- User IDs and database links are not coded into applications code. The table names compiled into code must be synonyms. It is up to the DBA to establish the appropriate public and private synonyms to provide users access to the indicated tables. This rule ensures that applications code is portable among users and database instances. It also means it will not be affected by changes in SQL*Net's scheme for addressing objects within a network.

Oracle installation standards

Every Oracle installation, and every application within those installations, deals with keymaps and issues of screen and report appearance. A shop avoids considerable grief by dealing with the issues authoritatively the first time they come up.

Key usage

Oracle Corporation provides different keymaps for each version of each product on each terminal type. Emulator packages add their own mapping. It drives users crazy. The MIS director must have the systems programmer set standards. The steps are:

- Determine what terminal types are in use by developers and which by users.
- Determine which Oracle tools are in use by developers and which by users.
- Write down all the function key functions that end users need. Include the ten user-defined keys available for runtime SQL*Forms and SQL*Menu.
- Create a map for each combination of tool and terminal type showing what key the user has to press to invoke each function. Try to make the maps as consistent as possible with one another. The ideal is that any function, SHOW KEYS for example, in SQL*Forms is the same as SHOW_KEYs in SQL*ReportWriter, and SHOW_KEYS on a VT220 is the same as SHOW_KEYS on a PC. The tolerable minimum is that every function is available in every environment.

There are ten function keys in SQL*Menu and SQL*Forms available for functions to be defined by the installation or application. An installation standard HELP facility might need to reserve one or two of those for its use. Installation standards should set aside other keys for any other common usage such as invoking operating system functions.

The keymap issue can be effectively defused by using SQL*Menu under SQL*Forms. Users can then pick a function from a menu instead of invoking it with a function key. They use the function keys for what they remember and fall back on the menu for the rest. Starting with Version 4 of SQL*Forms, Oracle's tools will be written primarily for use in bitmapped environments. The use of mice will greatly reduce key mapping problems for developers as well as users.

Layout standards

Oracle applications are easier to use if forms, menus, and reports follow a standard format. Installation standards must address the format of heading lines, conventions for drawing boxes around blocks, conventions for pop-up windows, page numbers, field alignment, cursor movement, use of color and use of fonts in printing. *Working with Oracle Development Tools* has detailed suggestions of what to specify.

Version 5 of Oracle's CASE dictionary product carries screen and report formatting preferences at the application and module levels. The designer can enter master design standards directly into the CASE tool, after which they apply to all generated modules except where expressly overridden.

Documentation in a CASE development environment

This chapter mentions CASE development frequently because documentation requirements are different in CASE. System documentation without CASE usually consists of narrative documents supported by tables and diagrams. With CASE the CASE outputs become primary and narrative supports the exceptions. Table 14-6 shows the major differences between the two. Significantly it reveals how much documentation remains even in an environment using CASE prototypes.

Table 14-6   Comparison of documentation requirements in Oracle CASE and non-CASE environments.

Documentation Item	Without CASE	With CASE
Entity Definitions	Essential	Done within CASE
Attribute Definitions	Essential	Done within CASE
Entity-Relationship Diagrams	Essential	CASE designer diagrams
Functional Decomposition	Hand-drawn diagrams	CASE designer diagrams
Function Descriptions	Written in WP. Entity/attribute references must be captured by hand-made cross-reference system.	Written in CASE just as in a word processor. Captures entity/attribute references.
Data-flow diagrams	Useful, but effort to do a thorough job is often not warranted.	Much easier because CASE carries needed data and draws the diagrams.

Table 14-6. Continued.

Documentation Item	Without CASE	With CASE
Business Rules	Write them down using WP.	Write them down using WP. CASE only indicates which modules use them.
Cross reference diagrams	May not be worth the effort	Easy and always done, with considerable benefit
Data Design	Done by hand from entity and attribute definitions; laborious	Default flows directly from ER definitions. Modifications (denormalizations) easily handled.
Menu Structure Design	Develop within WP.	CASE handles decomposition, generates default menu structure.
Menu system variables / passed parameters	Develop design within WP	Develop design within WP; there is no CASE support
Program Specifications	Desirable for mainline processes. Specifications definitely needed for subroutines which implement business rules.	Mainline processes flow in large measure from CASE analysis. Specifications definitely needed for subroutines which implement business rules.
Test Plan / Test Data	Essential	Essential; not supported by CASE
Cost Justification	Depends on project and company	Depends on project and company. Except for the availability of statistics useful in sizing, not supported by CASE.
User Documentation	Essential, custom-written	Essential. CASE provides support for user prompts but does not do the whole job. Comprehensive context-sensitive help may come later.
Program Comments	Essential for maintenance in all modules.	Only needed where CASE-generated code is modified.

Summary

This chapter has addressed the utility to Oracle developers of customary development standards, and how those standards can be interpreted in an Oracle environment. Which standards make sense to use at all is a very valid question, given that small Oracle shops typically dispense with a majority of them, as do larger shops for smaller projects. Rapid prototype development, a bias for action over words, is the new paradigm.

Most developers share the insight that narrative documentation is often dispensable in Oracle projects. In non CASE developments program specifications are often unnecessary because all processes are routine and understood by the SQL*Forms or SQL* ReportWriter tool. CASE embodies most documentation; in CASE environments narrative it is needed mostly to describe exception situations. Effective standards must identify the places where written documentation remains essential. It has to embody the compromise between demanding so much documentation that it all gets ignored and so little that a system cannot be effectively developed or maintained.

Eliminating documentation steps to speed development carries risks. The installation procedures need to include quality control steps that ensure skipping documentation steps does not become a habit. The project manager should decide what can be omitted on a document-by-document, module-by-module basis. There is often little to salvage when an undocumented project goes awry because the planning steps were done in haste.

15

Procedures

Procedures define standard methods of handling recurring tasks. They cover the performance of jobs that the MIS shop is tasked by users to accomplish and functions internal to the data processing shop.

Procedures knit the elements of management together. Standards and procedures work hand in hand, standards defining the format of the products developed through the tasks specified in procedures. The tasks that a shop's procedures specify fit into a work breakdown structure, subject to control by project management for a project of any size. Figure 15-1 shows the relationship among standards, procedures, and project management.

Users and developers must buy into the concept of using standard procedures. They have historically been a matter of deferred gratification. Following prescribed procedures appears to add to the time it takes to develop a system, frustrating users who want results yesterday and will insist they could do a job faster on their PCs using dBASE than the MIS shop can do it in Oracle. MIS has to sell the long-range benefits of following procedures. They equate to the common sense of thinking ahead.

The life cycle of systems that grow without formal disciplines is fairly predictable. An end user will start with a dBASE file of customers. Pretty soon he or she adds prospective customers, then prospective orders. To make things easy, he or she bootlegs a downloaded copy of the catalog to pick up pricing information from the mainframe. Soon the user has a full-blown system with the following characteristics:

- It works, and the department depends on it.
- It does about 40 percent of the job that really needs doing.
- It includes several upload and download bridges with formal automated systems.
- The user department is out of resources to expand the system.
- The user will assure anyone that data in the system is 99 percent compatible with other automated systems.
- MIS, which has known about the system in a roundabout way, gets stuck with it when their integration plans take in the business sector.
- Users want any new system to work just like the dBASE one they wrote and know.

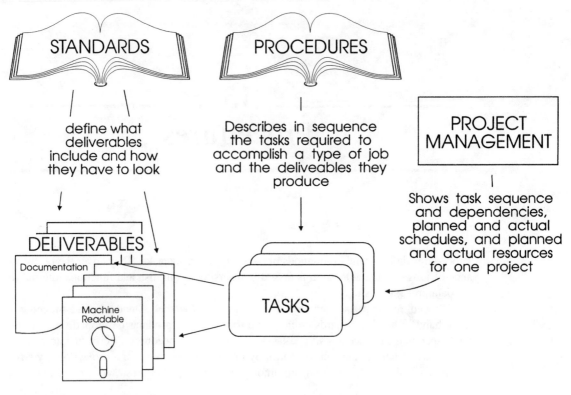

15-1 Relationship of standards, procedures, and project management.

Taking over these systems is a thankless job for MIS. A formal set of procedures that applies to all development, within user departments as well as MIS, can help prevent them. Stated positively, the payoff from sticking with procedures is:

- They make sure that data systems can all work together and share data as they need to.
- They make sure management has examined the costs associated with a project.
- They force users and the MIS staff to agree on a definition of the problem and the proposed solution before rushing into implementation.
- They help ensure that projects are selected rationally instead of politically.
- They guide analysts to the alternative that offers the best overall return on investment.
- The standards they specify minimize the overall cost of systems, before and after they are implemented.

The MIS department cannot go it alone with a long-term view. It needs top management support in demanding that users allow time to follow procedures and do the job right. The way to secure and retain that support is to build credibility by producing good results and being rather dogmatic about adhering to the procedures that bring them.

A shop's procedures must address the major repetitive activities they perform in carrying out their mission. Standard topics cover the system life cycle:

- Strategic planning.
- Analysis.
- Design.
- Programming.
- Testing.

and processes that might fall into several life-cycle phases:

- Initiating data processing projects.
- Configuration management.
- Project management.
- Licensed software evaluation and acquisition.
- Interview process.

This chapter addresses topics in the sequence shown. The individual sections refer to chapter 14 on standards for a description of what is in the deliverable products which the procedures say are required.

Strategic planning

Data systems are essential to the operation of almost all modern enterprises. They also cost a lot of money, often 25 to 50 percent of an enterprise's capital investment. Information systems belong in the enterprise-wide strategic planning process alongside every other major investment.

Top management usually requests, or at least approves, major data processing projects. An application-level strategic planning process closely related to the corporate strategic planning described in chapter 5 establishes which ones to do and the order in which MIS will do them. The majority of user requests are too small to warrant top management attention. MIS department management, perhaps assisted by a user board of trustees, decides which projects it can accept and what priority to give them. They initiate projects as the right kinds of resources, usually people, become available.

Top management needs to borrow on MIS department expertise to estimate the costs of new information systems. The benefits of the systems they can usually estimate themselves. On their end, MIS usually needs to put projects in context before they can estimate the costs: what other systems can it build on, when is it needed, and what functions will it do?

MIS and corporate strategic plans are interdependent. Table 5-1 shows how MIS readies for strategic planning; then when top management suggests a direction, MIS develops feasibility, cost and risk projections, and top management decides what they can live with. When the dust settles, the MIS department has a few years' backlog of major projects with which they can flesh out their own strategic plan. The cycle never ends. The executives have to let MIS know when they change direction, and MIS has to let top management know when their estimates of cost, timeframes, and feasibility change substantially.

MIS can introduce its own agenda into strategic planning. They can frequently argue that there is money to be saved by replacing current hardware and software systems. Economies come in the form of reduced machine costs, reduced maintenance costs, reducing the cost of developing new systems, and positioning the company to take advantage of new ADP technologies.

The data processors usually provides experts to lead strategic information planning. It is customarily a fairly intense, short duration effort involving user management and MIS. As its leaders, MIS people have to :

- Plan the goals of the study.
- Staff the study with capable MIS people and make sure that users contribute top-level talent.
- Organize the participants into appropriate work groups.
- Motivate the participants by reiterating the importance of the goal.
- Control the process, keeping the ball rolling.

The process must accommodate the well-known dynamics of people:

- Committees debate and ratify decisions.
- Two- and threesomes craft decisions.
- An effective communication involves one effective speaker and at least one effective listener.
- Individuals create work products and develop new ideas.

In other words, MIS people are the scriveners who create most of the deliverable products. Users describe the requirement and ratify the work products. The MIS study leader must get close to the opinion molders on the user side and work with them to strike the decisions that the committee will subsequently ratify.

The corporation is the author of the model. Data processing, the owner of the modeling tools, becomes the custodian. Top management has a tendency to assume that data processing, which usually instigates development of the model and will make the most use of the result, is its primary beneficiary. This is wrong on two counts. Data processing supports the mission of the whole company and must understand that mission to do its job. Far more important, you find that rational data systems support rational organizations and conversely, that tangled data systems are a strong indication of organizational problems. Top management has a deep interest in delineating clean and logical boundaries between departments and between data systems. It prevents them from working at cross purposes.

Corporate strategic planning's first task is to identify the whole universe of corporate activities, show how they relate to one another and map them to functional groups within the corporation. A second task shadows the first. The corporation must keep information records which reflect its activities. A strategic plan shows, at a high level, what information the corporation needs and which groups create, maintain, use, and ultimately own the data to create it data. Versions of the plan show data flows as they exist in the present and future. A strategic plan is a plan of action. It establishes:

- What projects or activities the corporation will take on?
- Which parts of the company are responsible for each project?
- When the projects will be done?

Executives choose which projects to undertake on factors much more broadly based than data processing, among them return on investment and competitive considerations. They need estimates from data processing for scheduling and for the cost side of return-on-investment calculations.

Data processing uses the process and data maps developed as the initial planning tasks to associate automated processes and records with line items in the strategic plan. They are the basis for estimating the cost of automated support. Processes more or less follow the data in business applications. The most significant factor in sizing a relational system is the number and complexity of the data entities it manages.

Estimating the cost and duration of a data processing project is difficult even when the requirements are available and resource are known. The dependencies among systems make it even tougher at the strategic planning phase. The MIS department's contributions to the process include assessments of the relative cost of one implementation sequence over another and the cost of doing a project with current staff versus expanding or using contractors.

The strategic plan takes a high level view of data and processes. It focuses on major entities such as parts, orders, and employees without getting into detail. The purely informational attributes (data fields) are not important but the key fields that link entities together are. At the strategic level, processes are important primarily as an indicator of who owns the data. Most companies purchase software to handle really complex processes such as analysis of seismographic data or image processing. The local issue remains collecting data to feed the process and using the information which comes out.

Laying the groundwork for strategic planning

Data processing texts often have an info-centric view of strategy, as if MIS drives the process. That view is wrong. Top management sets strategy, and the information people have to work to get invited to the party. Depictions of strategic planning as a one-time, linear operation are also inaccurate. Top management is more or less continually concerned with strategy, and the MIS department must remain ready to participate.

The best form of preparation is to think about strategy before being asked. Figure 15-2 shows the sequence of events. The MIS department can and should budget resources to develop an enterprise data model based on current systems. MIS department analysts surely know the major data entities and business functions within the organization. They can use informal contacts with the user community to clarify points of confusion. The information model includes:

- Data element definitions
- Entity definitions
- Entity-relationship diagrams
- Process flows

STRATEGY PROCEDURE FLOW

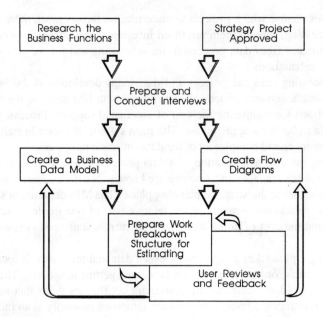

15-2 Sequence of events in strategic planning.

A CASE data dictionary or repository of any stripe will handle these very satisfactorily, but they can as well be handled with small databases or even word processing files and hand-drawn diagrams.

A common problem in compiling an enterprise-wide data model from existing data processing systems is that they don't fit together. The same data element might have different names and different characteristics in different applications. Tables that are more or less the same might appear in different places.

Although it is not possible to integrate existing systems when their incompatibilities remain hardened in existing code, the modelers can diagram relationships as the ought to exist at the logical level. They must include comments in the data model noting the synonyms, redundancies and ambiguities that exist in the systems as implemented. A major goal then of applications redesign is to reconcile the physical data model with the logical model.

Many of the best business strategies depend on new data processing technologies. A smart MIS department keeps up with technology and shares interesting developments with user departments. Their homework pays dividends when the users include them in developing strategies to exploit the technology.

Start the strategic planning process with interviews

Once top management and the user department have asked what it will take to do the system, MIS has a green light to spend some resources for research, also known as strategic planning. It starts by asking questions. The interview process for strategic planning, which is substantially the same as for analysis, is described in the section below entitled "The interview process in strategic planning and analysis."

First impressions are lasting impressions. The confidence that interviewers instill in their prospective users and the contacts they establish are just as important to the eventual success of a project as what they may learn. It is very important to organize and execute strategic interviews well. Chapter 14 shows the contents of an interview guide and notes.

Creating a modified business model

The business model organizes the findings of the interviews into a single document. It states the charter of the study in the introduction and cover management's goals and objectives, the shortcomings of current systems, and the user's view of what they need.

New business strategies usually change what the business does and who does it. They require an extension of whatever business model the MIS department has—or creating a new one if there is none. Analysts enter the entity and data elements definitions into the data dictionary as soon as they are agreed. They sketch high-level entity-relationship diagrams on blackboards or paper until there is some concurrence, then modify the entity and attribute definitions in the automated data model to produce nice-looking diagrams. This warrants a caveat. Richard Barker, Oracle's top manager for CASE, recommends caution in rushing to have CASE draw diagrams. Computer-generated images may suggest an accuracy that is not yet present. The problem doesn't arise with hand-drawn diagrams.

Creating a flow diagram

The major work in systems development is in developing processes. A work or data flow diagram shows the processes that capture data where it is available, distill it into information and deliver it where it is needed. To provide a complete picture the flow should include processes that are not, or not necessarily, automated. Figure 14-7 shows a typical flow diagram.

Creating a work-breakdown structure

Decisions cost money. Not just the money committed by the decision, but money to make the right decision. The MIS director must be ready to tell top executive management what it costs to predict the cost of implementing a system. Figure 15-3 shows how the range of estimated costs for a system narrows the more money is invested in producing the estimate.

Project costs consist of purchases such as software and hardware from outside vendors and labor to develop the system. Labor is usually the hardest to estimate. The standard approach to costing is to identify the tasks involved in executing the project, estimate

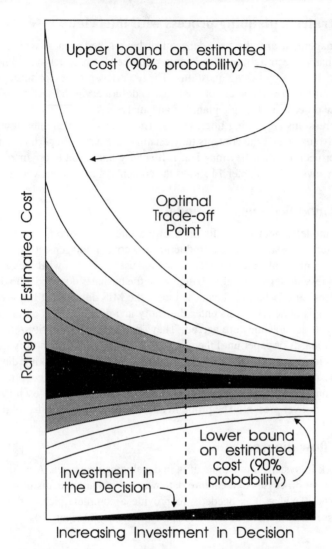

15-3 Trade-off between investment in a decision and quality of the decision.

the labor in each, and extend the cost. Chapter 18 describes estimating techniques and chapter 17 covers putting together a work breakdown structure.

The MIS strategic planning process

The two essential data points that MIS provides back to the enterprise strategy session are the projected cost of a project and their level of confidence in the estimate. Is it a wild guess or a sophisticated wild guess (WAG or SWAG)?

MIS internal deliverables include the questionnaires and responses, preliminary data design work and estimates for producing the system. The set of approved (and likely to be approved) projects represents the MIS department's project backlog and is the foundation for their own strategic planning.

The MIS department's strategic plan derives from the enterprise plan. It translates the backlog of individual system requirements into aggregate staffing, hardware, software and network requirements for the department. The deliverables include:

- Goals statement
- Objectives
- Critical success factors
- Organization chart
- Chart of functions
- Function/organization matrix
- Enterprise model
- Current information architecture
- Future information architecture
- High-level process definitions
- Strategic information plan
- Major entity definitions
- Cost justification

Analysis procedures

Analysis echos strategic planning. It is the second iteration of the same process, in more depth. Like strategic planning it begins with research. The analyst must prepare for the role of the MIS department envoy and applications expert.

The MIS department is the place to start learning about a requirement. A newly assigned analyst needs to study strategic plan documentation about the application and talk to the MIS staff who have been involved in existing systems and the new strategy. It is useful to compile a high-level data model using existing system documentation and perhaps even frame out a data model and system decomposition in CASE to provide a context for the information to be gathered through interviews. The analyst is thus prepared to learn from the users and gain their confidence in their initial meetings.

Define the scope

The users who live with the problem they want solved are the primary source of information about it. The second step of analysis is to conduct interviews according to the process described in the section entitled "The interview process in planning and analysis" below.

Users' descriptions of what they need in a system are like the fabled blind men's views of an elephant. They each see it from a different perspective and their views often conflict with one another. Taken together, the scope of what the users envision is usually more than the budget will support. The analyst's genius is to lead the users in synthesizing a common statement of the overall requirement. The scoping procedure usually involves the following steps:

1. The analyst assembles process descriptions offered by individual users into a statement of what the whole system has to do. Users must be available to answer questions and they might help sorting out the processes.
2. Working intimately with users, the analyst identifies major entities and key attributes in the system and which processes create and use them. These go into the CASE system or the data dictionary. The analyst prepares entity and attribute definitions for the major data elements within the system.
3. The whole team, analyst, key users and user management, meet to define the system scope. The issues are:
   • Process definition: ratify or change the analyst's definition of the processes within the system.
   • Scoping: decide which processes will be done, which will not, and which can wait until after the initial phase of the system.
   The analyst is an expert advisor rather than an advocate in this process. The users decide what they want. The analyst provides cost and feasibility estimates and points out tradeoffs. Some of the sharpest trade-offs come in packaged software. The analyst should know which features can be handled by licensed software and which ones will dictate a custom development.
4. The analyst captures the group's decisions with regard to the scope, organizes them into a summary document and distributes them.

Scoping is an iterative affair. The more the analyst learns about the requirement in the course of developing analysis documentation, the better he can decide what belongs within the scope of the project. Phasing goes hand in hand with scoping. The analyst might specify core functionality that is needed immediately as phase I of a project, to be followed by additional phases that expand the scope of the system. The analyst's phasing scheme trades off the users' requirements over time with the risks involved in building too much at once and then proceeds to estimate the costs of development and the resources available to do the job.

Compose the analysis products

Once the scope is defined the analyst and key users meet to complete a data model. An analyst must compose the team with care, choosing user counterparts who are both representative and have enough interest to learn. Entity-relationship modeling is the one aspect of data processing that the users have to understand. The best way to teach the concepts is usually in the context of their own application. The whole team thrashes out the relational design issues of entity definitions, types and subtypes, key definitions and the like. The final round of doodles is the agreed data model.

The analyst serves as a facilitator in the data modeling process, using chalk, pencil diagrams, CASE, and drawing tools to illustrate the concepts under discussion. He or she also represents the interests of outside systems. New systems cannot blindly redefine entities and attributes that already exist within the enterprise or in software packages that may be bought to support the application. The analyst helps find trade-offs between a conceptually pure data model and one adapted to meet existing real-world designs. The analysis deliverables usually include:

- Analysis plan
- Interview guides
- Interview notes
- Attribute (data element) definitions
- Entity definitions
- Entity-relationship diagrams
- Data flow diagrams
- Functional decomposition diagrams
- Business rule/algorithm logic descriptions

The procedures of an installation specify the conditions under which each type of documentation is required. Chapter 14 addresses the utility of each type of document and suggests the format and contents to be specified for each.

Quality control

The procedures of an installation should outline steps to ensure the quality of an analysis. The first question is who is responsible for quality control. It is usually the project manager, with participation by the project team and oversight from their management. Sometimes it is an outside QC group.

The QC checkoff list covers procedures and deliverables. A major question on the procedural side is whether the required interactions with the user have taken place and were fruitful. How many interviews did they do? Who was interviewed? Did they complete design walk throughs with the user? Do the users understand the requirements statement? Do they concur in the compromises in scope and phasing expressed there?

Deliverable products are easy to examine in that a reviewer can collect them for comparison against the installation standards. As standards writers are usually more ambitious than actual analysts, they usually come up short in such a review. The more difficult question is whether the products are adequate to the job and whether the labor to make them more complete will be offset by future savings. The weakness of independent QC groups is that they are not usually in a position to make such broad judgements. They will force adherence to the standard whether or not it makes sense.

Design procedures

Classical Oracle design divides into data and processes. Data design is the adaptation of the data model established in the analysis phase to real-world constraints of performance, hardware constraints, and the actuality of existing systems. Process design describes the programs. Design usually includes an element of integration planning, as processes and especially data are adapted to mesh with existing systems.

Sequence of activity

Data precedes process in the Oracle world. The designer's first step is to complete the analysis by adding any remaining nonkey attributes to the entities. The analysis process often glosses over purely informational fields that play no part in entity-relationship modeling. In the design process the designer completes data element definitions by assigning data types and lengths. A typical step would be breaking the ADDRESS attribute into the ADDRESS_LINE_1, ADDRESS_LINE 2, CITY, STATE and ZIP columns.

Next the designer lays out tables. Most tables and columns correspond one to one with entities and attributes. The designer often has to denormalize major tables for the sake of performance. Typical steps include:

- Adding summary a column to a master table so the RDBMS does not have to constantly summarize across detail records.
- Defining fields that can occur only a few times multiply within one table (that is, CHILD_NAME1, CHILD_NAME2 . . . CHILD_NAME10 in an employee table, or a long column called CHILD_NAMES to hold multiple names separated by spaces, instead of using a separate CHILD table).
- Creating duplicate copies of master tables, one optimized via its indexes for update and the other for queries.

Table layouts are all the programmers need. They can go to work while the DBA and the designer work out tablespaces, indices, free space, extent sizes, and other factors that will affect performance.

Oracle systems cannot do without a conscientious data design, but the utility of process designs depends on circumstances. The waterfall paradigm (Fig. 1-1) required specifications for each module within the system that had to be coded. The prototyping paradigm holds that it is more efficient to write code than specs. By its reasoning developers can get by without written specifications because:

- Oracle coders are the analyst/designers who know in their heads what they want.
- With Oracle 4GL tools, it is quicker to write code than write about it.
- CASE, the RDBMS, and Oracle's 4GL tools automatically handle a major portion of editing and relational integrity logic.
- Users are better at critiquing code they can actually use than dry specifications.

Application of standards

Oracle Programmers devise elaborate ways to circumvent standards that demand rigorous design specifications. One quasi-government user interviewed for this book has developers prototype to the 95 percent level and then write a thin specification using the prototype code as exhibits. Each Oracle management team has to develop its own procedures for designing processes. Here are some points to consider in defining the process:

- Any design needs a menu structure to give it form. Designers and programmers need a concept of how the finished system will appear to users.
- The design needs to specify any system-wide conventions not covered by installation standards (see chapter 14 for a discussion of them).
- Reusable modules, so called black boxes, need written specifications that describe their function to programmers who will use them. In Oracle these include copyable trigger code, user exits, and compiled language modules which are available to be called into other modules at compile, link or object time.
- Any module complex enough to require napkin doodling in the design process

should have a specification, even if it ends up only as comments embedded in the source program. The maintenance programmer will need a doodle to get started on fixing the code.

Programmers will waste a lot of time reworking code unless system-wide objects are specified up front. It makes sense to put them in writing even on one- and two-person jobs, simply because programmers forget from one week to another exactly how a process worked or the format of a variable. A fundamental limitation to prototyping is that it applies only to unique processes. Any function or data that is used more than once within a system needs to be specified.

Oracle's CASE is entirely consistent with the concept that multiple-use items need to be specified. Unique functions and processes in Oracle's CASE are organized in a top-down decomposition. The standard subroutines they call, usually embodying business rules, are referenced only by name. The CASE generator creates code within the mainline processes to link them with independently specified and coded procedures for business rules.

Process design specifications, like all design documentation, should be subject to configuration management. This is a strong argument for requiring specifications for standard subroutines. How often does a programmer change a called subroutine and ask "Where else did I use that?" A configuration management system is able to extrapolate the effects of a design change throughout the system. Chapter 14 describes standard design deliverables, which include:

- Data design
- Data implementation plan
- Menu structure and global parameters
- Process specifications
- Test plan
- Cost justification

Quality control

Procedures should define the measures to take to ensure the quality of a design. As with analysis, the first issue is who is responsible for quality control. Most shops follow the precept that the development team is responsible for the quality of its own work and give primary responsibility to the project manager. If there is an independent QC group, they usually review all phases of development, including design.

A reviewer examines a combination of form and substance. Form is easy. The reviewer matches deliverables against the templates established by the installation standards. It is also easy to misjudge what is actually needed. Substance is harder, almost impossible for an outsider to assess independently. Quality deliverables has to be the result of a quality process. The reviewer has to probe the design process to make sure that the designers asked the relevant questions.

Both the form and substance are fairly easy to check for test plans and test data. Do they exist? How extensive are they? What sort of mapping is there between the test data and the functional specifications?

Programming procedures

Programmers need firm standards, but usually not procedures. Conventions are a better means of encouraging programmers to work efficiently. Most shops might have skeleton COBOL programs or standard trigger code that people routinely use as a baseline, but who is to question a programmer who writes every program from scratch, so long as they get results? It helps to recommend ways for programmers to be more efficient but it is usually counterproductive to try to enforce them.

Conventions for developing code

Several conventions to consider for an Oracle development environment are mentioned in "Working with Oracle Development Tools," among them:

- Keep model PL/SQL trigger routines in a common library. Copy and adapt them as required for individual forms.
- Use .inp files, a full-screen editor, and the SQL*Forms generator instead of the Forms designer to debug trigger code in versions prior to SQL*Forms Version 4.
- Debug queries in SQL*Plus, then read them into SQL*ReportWriter.

Code development conventions must mesh with design procedures and the standards that apply to deliverable products. The Software Engineering Institute and total quality management philosophies recommend that standards, procedures and conventions be established and maintained by the people who use them. It is important to give the development staff an opportunity to discuss their conventions. How formal they are, or whether they are even written down, should be largely up to them.

Updating design documentation

Reality is the best teacher. Depending on the skill of the analyst and designer and the clarity of the users' vision of the requirement, code runs between 75 and 95 percent true to the documentation. A programmer must always deal with cases and make interpretations that are not precisely covered in the design. A programmer often fiddles with the tough sections of code off and on up to the point the module must be delivered.

This is the compelling logic behind the use of prototypes. A specification takes time to write and is never 100 percent complete to start with. There is no way to keep the specs in sync with changes in the code. The question is, why bother with a specification?

The answer is that design specifications are worth updating only if the installation has been judicious in selecting which specs get written in the first place. They need to be kept current if they apply to objects that will be called by other programs or logic too complicated for comments to satisfactorily describe. It is worth changing documentation if these fundamentals are altered. Conversely, there should not be any specs in the first place for trivial programs.

A CASE generation environment changes the whole scenario. The design becomes the source. It remains totally consistent with the generated 4GL source code until the point at which the latter is modified. The programming process deliverables described in chapter 14 include:

- Source code.
- Maintenance documentation.
- Executable code.
- Updated design documentation.

Quality control

Code reviews, in which the programmers on a team review one another's work, are the standard means of quality control. They are far less important in Oracle's 4GLs than in 3GLs because the tools themselves provide so much of the structure and because so much of the substance of a program is evident in using it. Code reviews apply primarily to procedural code.

Testing procedures

Testing is a time-consuming process and often frustrating task that reminds programmers all to clearly of their own fallibility. It is also indispensable in producing quality systems.

Unpleasant but essential? That calls for management! The developers have to be led by management to establish quality assurance and testing procedures that apply to all phases of the life cycle.

- Analysis: establish test criteria associated with data integrity constraints, edits, and business rules.
- Design: develop a system test plan.
- Development: execute the test plan.
- Maintenance: perform regression testing after maintenance.

Test data

Certain testing principles apply to almost every Oracle development. There must be at least one test database with the following characteristics:

- It contains all the tables within the system.
- It belongs to a User ID associated with the application and not with any individual developer.
- All developers have SELECT permission on the tables. Only the test designer has update permission.
- Every table that will be used for updating or reporting must be populated.
- Each populated table must contain enough rows to represent every case to be tested and to force every report into multiple pages.
- Each populated table must contain few enough rows that a programmer can easily find differences by comparing dumps of the table before and after any process to be tested.

There might be additional test databases. It is often useful to have a full-size test database to use for volume and stress testing. Figure 15-4 shows the ownership and distribution of test data.

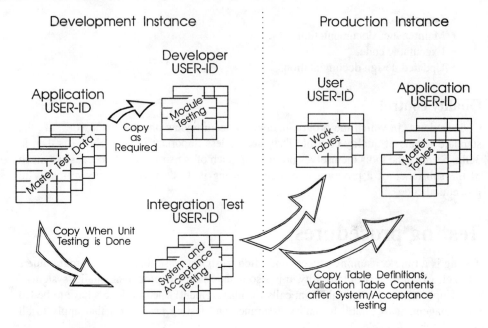

15-4 Typical Oracle setup for test and production.

The tools and procedures for using the test database(s) are always similar:

- Developers copy test tables they need from the master database into their own user IDs as required.
- There is a standard utility function to perform the copy function. Note to implementers: CREATE . . . AS SELECT does not work with tables containing LONG data types. Use COPY instead. A common approach is to write a shell script that accepts the names of tables to copy as parameters, creates an SQL start file containing the appropriate COPY statements, and then invokes SQL*Plus to execute the start file.
- There is a standard utility function to find the differences between the master copy of any table and the copy in the developer's user ID. This shows the results from testing an update process.

Every online process (read: SQL*Forms program) requires a test script of transactions to process. Needless to say they have to be coordinated with the test database so they apply to records that exist there. The SQL*Forms edit keystroke facility is useful for capturing and replaying exact sequences of keystrokes in regression testing. The most workable approach for testing forms under development is usually to have the tester key in an entire transaction from scratch during each testing session.

Starting each test from the beginning of a transaction can be a real labor in large forms. Creating test script files with an editor would be an alternative, except that Oracle's format is exacting and difficult to work with. Designers might find it worthwhile to have test data generators written to create key script files for the major processes.

Test libraries

A test environment needs administrative controls to ensure that each module is properly tested and integrated before being released to production. There are several version control systems available to handle this function, Intersolv's PVCS being the best known. Smaller shops might want to implement informal systems on their own.

Three is the minimum number of library systems that affords any sort of control. That provides one for development, one for integration and acceptance testing, and one for production. Individual programmers keep work in progress as files under their own accounts and database objects under their own user IDs. Figure 15-5 shows how libraries are distributed in a small development environment.

Whether or not formal access control is implemented using operating system accounts and passwords, there must be an agreement as to who updates the libraries. A classic problem in Oracle development environments is that developers keep meddling with the data structure by altering table definitions. Each time the test tables are regenerated, forms and reports that used to work no longer do. The solution is to make one person responsible for maintaining the table definitions, master PL/SQL library and other shared resources, and have that person make sure every developer knows when a change is coming.

Accepting and initiating development jobs

The backlog of major MIS projects in organizations that use strategic planning is generated by that planning process. Most requests, however, are not for major systems. Users

Test

Developer Account	Application Account
Code under Development	Master Module Libraries - test version
	Test Data Libraries
	Master SQL to Create Tables

Integration/ Acceptance Test Account
Modules to be Integrated
Tested Subsystems

Production

Production Account	User Account
Production Versions of Executable	Work Files
	Login Procedures
Production Versions of Source Code	
Production Files	

15-5 Typical operating system accounts for test and production.

ask for them directly. MIS needs procedures for accepting work, figuring out what it entails, and assigning people to do it.

Good procedures support the diplomacy needed to keep users happy and at the same time protect DP resources. Labor to handle small requests usually comes out of overhead. They must be kept small. Large ones, even when they will pay their own way, usually go through strategic planning or some other process that assigns them a priority. In any case the MIS department must keep the backlog visible. Figure 15-6 shows a typical process for accepting work into the MIS shop.

It was never desirable and it is no longer possible to let users cool their heels waiting for the MIS department to spring some people loose to handle a project. Users will go off

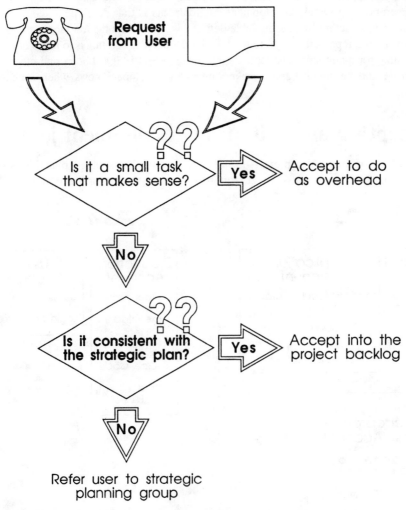

Request from User

Is it a small task that makes sense? — **Yes** → Accept to do as overhead

No

Is it consistent with the strategic plan? — **Yes** → Accept into the project backlog

No

Refer user to strategic planning group

15-6 The process of accepting a job.

and develop what they need on PCs. They later lay the system on MIS' doorstep, when it has become too big to handle. MIS needs an internal procedure to review the backlog periodically and take measures to keep it from growing out of hand. They need to know when to hire or reassign staff, engage consultants or contract out to get the support their users need.

The MIS shop accepts jobs on their merits. They do them when they have people available. The procedure for assigning jobs out of the backlog as people become available, shown in Fig. 15-7, makes sure that priorities are respected in initiating jobs and sets up appropriate job accounting numbers.

The interview process in strategic planning and analysis

An interview process is appropriate for information gathering in the strategic planning and analysis phases of a project. Interviews are the first contact many users have with MIS, and as such are very important. They set the tone for an entire development. MIS

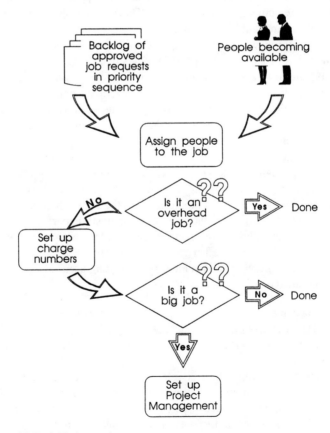

15-7 Initiating tasks.

department procedures ensure that they are methodical and complete. The steps the analysts need to follow are:

- Learn the application. Talk to analysts who have been working with the users. Read the user-level documentation for whatever system is currently being used. Read standard industry reference works and software company literature to learn nomenclature and common issues. Prepare a preliminary list of questions to ask. The analyst's objectives are to understand as much as possible of what the users say, and to impress them that MIS and the analyst know what they are doing.
- Confer with user management to set up a slate of interviewees. Discuss what they expect each interviewee to contribute, making sure that both the user's and the analyst's agendas are covered. The analyst's objective is to cover everything the user considers important and ferret out issues they may have overlooked.
- Set up an interview schedule. Brief the interviewees on the purpose of the interview. Provide them with a letter or fax stating the overall purpose of the interview and major issues on which their help is needed. A hard copy serves the interviewee as a memory aid, reminding them of the purpose of the interview as well as the date and time. Provide them in advance with a comprehensive interview guide if there are a large number of topics to cover. The analyst's objective is to impress the users that their time will be well used.
- Conduct the interview. Cover every point that the user was requested to prepare, but allow the conversation to expand to topics that the user feels are relevant. Be especially careful to nail down nomenclature and word usages peculiar to the application. Listen keenly to shortcomings of current systems. Gather materials and references that the interviewee might provide. The objectives are to learn as much as possible about the process and to establish a long-term information source and ally in implementing a solution.
- Write up the interview, including a review of the materials and sources provided by the interviewee. Call the interviewee to clarify points that are not fully understood. Give a copy of the write-up to the interviewee for review and correction. The objectives are to be factually accurate, to impress the user of his or her importance to the process, and to further sell the user on the analyst's expertise.
- Incorporate major findings from each interview into subsequent interview guides. Probe the areas that need further investigation. The objective remains to get the most out of each interview, and to identify competing user interests which the analyst will be called on to reconcile.

User confidence and user involvement are as fundamental to success as anything to do with design. The interview process gathers as much information as possible and opens the lines of communication to collect more as needed. It establishes the users as allies in the development process.

The analyst brokers competing user interests and also represents the MIS department's interests in dealing with users. Getting the full scope of user needs and opinions at the outset is vital. Prototyping projects especially tend to be shaped by a few loud voices on the user side. The analyst bears responsibility for making sure that an automated system addresses the whole problem.

Packaged software selection

Though classical data processing references do not acknowledge it, packaged software considerations color every phase of a system life cycle. The premise of packaged software is overwhelmingly logical: economies of scale. It is cheaper for one company, the vendor, to write a piece of common code general enough for hundreds of companies to use than for hundreds of companies to write the application from scratch.

Table 15-1 shows that packaged software considerations enter the life cycle at the strategy phase and remain throughout. The strategy, analysis, and package selection phases make use of the same selection process applied with differing degrees of rigor.

Chapter 16 describes the process of selecting a vendor. The steps that are specific to licensed software are:

1. Users and analysts determine the functional requirement as well as is appropriate for the project phase.
2. The analyst establishes operating environment constraints, primarily the possible operating system and DBMS.
3. The analyst and users locate packages that appear to suit the requirement and get vendor literature.
4. Users and analysts match the functional requirements against various packages' capabilities.
5. Users and analysts see demonstrations from vendors whose packages best fit the requirements.
6. The analyst estimates dollar costs of writing functions that are not in an individual package, and assigns a dollar value to nice-to-have features that are in the package but not in the requirement.

Table 15-1   Packaged software in the system life cycle.

Phase	Action
Strategic Planning	Perform a market survey to determine if it is likely that a package can do the job. If so, estimate the cost of the package for the target platform and the cost of customizing and implementing it.
Analysis	To the extent that it does not compromise function, define the data model and process requirements to be consistent with the most attractive packaged software offerings.
Package Selection	Evaluate available packages against the requirements to identify the best one for the job. Decide if the package is more attractive than custom development.
Design	Fashion a data design that integrates the data model from the analysis phase, the data design of existing systems, and the data designs of whatever purchased packages have been selected.
Implementation	Select parameters to define how the package will be used. Build bridges between the software packages and existing systems. Write custom code to handle unique requirements.

7. The analyst computes a total price for each package, including installation, training, and the adjustments above.
8. The analyst and others negotiate with the top two or three vendors to get best offers.
9. Procurement personnel evaluate the companies behind the products.
10. The team award to the company that offers the best balance of low price and high confidence of success, or opts for in-house development if no vendor offers an adequate and competitive solution.

Software selection does not have to involve a lot of documentation. The following pieces can be appropriate depending on the cost of the package, the investment that the enterprise will make in implementing and using it, and how much competition there is:

- Specifications to provide to potential vendors.
- A request for proposal or invitation to bid.
- A compliance matrix showing how well each vendor meets the requirements.
- Financial models of the total cost of each vendor's offering and of custom development.

Project management procedures

MIS will estimate the labor and direct costs involved in every project as it is accepted into the backlog. Projects of more than a nominal size, perhaps one staff month, might be defined to require a charge number. The MIS shop loses accountability when larger efforts get charged against overhead. Every project has an assigned project manager responsible for reporting progress. The procedures might require that projects larger than one or two staff-years have their own project management system.

It takes some procedures to determine the size of the project in the first place. It is useful to provide a standard format, perhaps a spreadsheet layout such as shown in chapter 18, for initial computations of project size and schedule.

Project management systems must tie in with time and financial accounting systems. The MIS department must establish cutoff dates for time and expense reporting and establish the mechanism for getting data back and forth among the systems.

Configuration management (CM) procedures

All kinds of systems, software included, depend on the ability of their component parts to work together. A Volkswagen won't work with Cadillac tires, and an MS-DOS version of Lotus won't run under MVS. A production application is a set of programs and file and database definitions that work well enough as a unit to have passed integration and acceptance tests.

Under configuration management, the individual items of which a system is composed are called configuration items. Design documentation, programs, database definitions, terminal hardware, operating system software, network software, and Oracle products are all configuration items in a typical Oracle application. A change in any one of them is apt to disrupt the operation of the system.

A set of configuration items that have been tested and proven to work together is called a configuration baseline. CM handles the orderly transition from baseline to baseline. The only way to make sure that an entire system still works after any change is to alter the test procedures to include whatever feature was altered, then retest everything that might have been affected by the change. The amount of labor involved in this regression testing means that the only practical way to manage change is to make a number of changes at once.

The production system represents a starting baseline. The configuration manager defines a functional baseline to include all of its function plus a specified number of enhancements, additions, and corrections that have been agreed to by the analysts and users. Designers and programmers implement the changes, testing the individual modules, and then regression testing the whole system. The modified system is released as a new operational baseline after it has passed all the tests.

An MIS shop that requires comprehensive software CM almost invariably uses licensed software to do the job. The package dictates to some extent the kinds of procedures that are needed. Procedures alone offer all the control that exists in informal shops, and they have to be created from whole cloth. Among the procedures needed are:

- How users submit requests for change, and how the MIS group evaluates and approves change requests.
- How the analysts establish functional baselines.
- How test data is maintained for each baseline.
- How test data is distributed to testers.
- How baseline libraries are maintained for development, integration and acceptance testing, and production.
- How configuration elements in database format (such as SQL*Menu or SQL*ReportWriter) are converted to an operating system file format, or how CM is implemented within a database environment.
- Procedures and controls over the migration of configuration elements from development to system test libraries, and from testing to production.
- How to keep corresponding configuration elements in sync among different media, among them word processing, CASE, source files, databases, and executable code.

Other procedures

Procedures are worse than useless if nobody follows them. Their existence weakens the ones that ought to be observed. With that caveat in mind a shop should consider having procedures for the following:

- Locating vendors
- Evaluating packaged software
- The RFP process
- Use of CASE tools
- Program development in different programming languages

Some form of reference is useful even where formal procedures are not justified. It makes sense to put together a library of books that members of the staff think will be of common interest. Have the user who located the book make index entries into a reference database.

Summary

Quality and productivity are inseparable from consistency. Knowledge of the procedures is a sizable fraction of the intellectual assets a professional brings to the job. The group of people assigned to a project have to agree on how to accomplish each of the tasks that make it up, what to expect from one another.

All professionals agree with the abstract premise that procedures are necessary. They will often differ over whether a specific procedure needs to be formalized. Effective procedures cannot be so burdensome that developers ditch them in a crisis; data processing sees too many. The developers have to agree that their shop's procedures are worth the effort. The best way to achieve that end is to charge them with maintaining their own procedures.

Standards and procedures are inseparable. Standards are definitional. They dictate the form of a work product. Procedures are, well, procedural. They indicate the sequence in which work products need to be produced and which ones are needed in a given circumstance.

CASE methodologies embody standard approaches to data collection, diagramming, and data presentation. The kinds of procedures change, but the need for them is unabated. Among other things, the procedures must establish how CASE interacts with traditional development activities such as writing subroutine code and modifying generated code.

16
Sourcing

Solving problems, not writing code, is the quest of a computer professional. A good analyst finds as much delight in solutions that are begged, borrowed, and bought as those that he or she designs from scratch. Developers take a lot of pride in the environments they put together to maximize their own productivity.

The marketplace for computer products and services is overwhelming in every way. There are phenomenal numbers of products, distribution channels, advertising channels, and forms of business relationships to deal with. The MIS department needs to organize for shopping. It needs to be able to make intelligent purchases to meet well-defined needs, and it needs to be open to new ideas which develop in the marketplace.

Distribution channels

Oracle and other vendors in the Oracle market are very imaginative in their use of distribution channels. They have to be. Their products often don't cost enough to support a field sales force, but they are not so simple that they sell themselves. Table 16-1 shows the characteristics of the distribution media.

The wide variety of distribution media represents the vendors' constant search for an optimum balance between service and price. At one extreme is the briefcase-toting sales force: very effective at presenting a product and configuring a solution, but expensive to maintain. Mail order houses are at the other extreme, offering little support but highly competitive on price. Some products like PCs are available through every channel. A buyer must choose the appropriate channels based on the size of the purchase and the amount of help they need configuring a product and getting it installed.

Oracle has established several types of third-party relationships in its business alliance program. Value-added resellers (VARs) build and sell proprietary Oracle-based applications. Independent software vendors write products, typically front ends, that tie into Oracle. Preferred systems integrators (PSI) package hardware, software, and communications environments with Oracle. Members of the Independent Oracle Consultants Alliance (IOCA), are independent consultants that the company recognizes as experienced Oracle professionals. Oracle users can call 800-345-DBMS for a *Business Alliance*

Table 16-1 Computer product distribution media.

Sales Medium / Characteristic	Vendor Field Sales Force	Direct telephone sales by vendor	Distributors, representatives and integrators	Mail Order houses	Retail Stores
Typical Oracle Products	Oracle products for all platforms	Oracle Direct Marketing for shrink-wrapped desktop products; Oracle TeleSales for workstation sized systems	Oracle RDBMS and tools for small minis		
Typical third party software products	Mainframe applications software, proprietary systems software for mainframes	Minicomputer applications and utilities; systems software.	Unix systems software, Unix utilities	Shrink-wrapped PC, OS2 and small Unix system software	Shrink-wrapped PC software
Typical hardware products	Big minicomputers and multiple PCs or work stations	PCs and work stations, LANs	Minicomputers, Work Stations, PCs	Work Stations, PCs	Work Stations, PCs
Technical Sales Support	Systems engineers in the sales force	Dial-in demos; demo personnel from HQ; hotline experts for questions	Distributor product support hotline; vendor hotlines	Mail order houses have limited expertise; demos can be a problem.	In-store demo software.
Systems Integration	Major vendors are expert at integrating their own products, sell consulting support.	Usually have consultants to recommend.	Recommend integrated hardware & software solutions using products they represent.	Usually sell only components	Increasingly offer integration services, especially for LANs
Pricing	Look for orders $10,000 and up. Have to cover overhead of the sales force	Works for orders in the $100s to low $1000s	Works for orders in the $100s to low $1000s	Usually under $1000	Usually under $1000

Program Products and Services catalog. Members of the Business Alliance Program display the emblem shown in Fig. 16-1.

Finding products

Everyone is bombarded with information about Oracle-related products. The best way to go about buying one is to take a structured view of the marketplace and give yourself the best possible chance of finding all the alternatives. Information sources to consider include:

- Oracle itself.
- *Oracle Business Alliance Program Products and Services Guide* for VARs (applications), PSIs (hardware integration), ISVs (Oracle-compatible front end and add-in software) and independent consultants who belong to the IOCA.
- Advertising in business journals that apply to your industry.
- Library research.
- Conferences and trade shows: IOUW, regional OUG, COMDEX, CASE, Unix, and others.
- Consultants.
- Networking—word of mouth.
- Information services.

Oracle has a product line broad enough to require specialized sales and marketing support people in RDBMS products, CASE, and applications. The sales staff keeps major

16-1 Oracle business alliance program emblem.

customers current on Oracle's product offerings through marketing calls. Smaller clients, and those who buy Oracle through resellers like Unisys and Bull, sometimes have to ask to find out. Oracle puts out a number of periodicals designed to keep users informed about their offerings and strategies.

The Oracle VAR catalog carries listings of applications that third parties have written for Oracle environments. It is a reasonably complete catalog. Oracle avoids making any evaluations or recommendations.

The Auerbach and Datapro reports are traditional sources of information on hardware and software industry offerings. The market has become so large, and the references so general, that it can be difficult to conclude which products are suited to a particular need. They are useful supplements to use in qualifying vendors.

Subscriptions to Auerbach and Datapro cost a fair amount of money, more perhaps than their value to a small enterprise or a small department. Almost any college or university that offers a degree program in data processing will have them available in a library. Most school libraries are open to users from the business community. Some have staff knowledgeable in data processing who can be of real help in finding materials. Many large companies, especially in the technology field, maintain their own data processing libraries.

The many narrow-focus data processing periodicals are a wonderful medium for bringing buyers and sellers together. Limited circulation means reasonable advertising rates, which permit relatively small firms to address their markets with large, informative advertisements. The magazines' editorial content naturally supports their advertisers. Table 16-2 offers a list of titles to consider. The library connections recommended above are a good source for the magazines to which an installation does not subscribe.

Conferences and trade shows are a Mecca for vendors. Oracle users groups sponsor the International Oracle Users Week every year in September, European conferences, national conferences throughout the world, major regional conferences such as East Coast Oracle in the US, and local conferences. A number of vendors staff their booths with people who know their products in depth and can provide insights that don't come across in advertising. Shopping the booths gives a wonderful sense of the overall direction of the markets. Hot topics for 1992 include GUI (graphic user interface) front ends, client/server, networking, Unix, Oracle applications, database machines, and CASE.

An MIS manager can learn a lot about products by word of mouth. Interviewees and new employees are happy to share their past successes. MIS professionals share their experiences at trade shows, in outside classes, and wherever they happen to meet. Equally important, computer users meet their counterparts from other companies through their own outside activities.

There are consultants and integrators who make a business of putting together Oracle systems. They might confine themselves to hardware, networks, and systems software, or they might assemble turnkey systems, complete with applications software. It is worth talking to these firms before attempting do-it-yourself integration. They usually earn whatever premium they charge for the time and knowledge they put into an integration. At a minimum, the horror stories they have to tell about do-it-yourself integrations will alert you to potential problems.

The most consistent way to collect high-quality, comprehensive information on sources is to pay for it. Cheryl Smith of HFSI uses Information Strategies Group (703-

893-0833) to survey sources for hardware and software purchases. Information Strategies Group (ISG) searches its industry database to find products that meet the functional requirements and fit HFSI's hardware and operating system environment. The report they deliver describes the product and the number of installations. ISG contacts the vendors for sales literature to include in their report. Going further, they provide brief financial histories of the vendors to give a sense of their reliability as business partners.

Compuserve's extra-charge databases provide excellent facilities to allow an installation to do its own product research. The research/reference option under computers carried at the time of this writing descriptions of over 72,000 software and hardware products. To illustrate its depth, it included 26,326 application products, of which 1428 were in manufacturing, and 46 had Oracle in their name. It also carries articles from the media about the products. Its business information services carry Dun and Bradstreet information and media clippings about the companies. Compuserve is very cost effective compared with the travel and personnel costs involved in library research or the cost of an outside information service.

A bibliography of Oracle sources

The trade press is an inexpensive way to keep current on offerings in the marketplace. Subscription rates are relatively low—advertisers pick up most of the freight. The major cost is in the time spent in reading them if it were done at work, but usually there are people on staff who enjoy reading on their own time. Table 16-2 names some useful titles.

Table 16-2   Magazines with articles and advertisements useful to Oracle developers.

Title	Readership	Contact
Oracle User Resource	All Oracle	Adirondak Information Resources 212-518-6487
Oracle News	All Oracle	Publications & Communications, Inc. 512-250-9023
Unix World	Unix users	McGraw Hill 415-940-1500
DBMS Magazine	Small-system database users	M&T Publishing 800-456-1859
Oracle Integrator	All Oracle	Oracle Corporation 415-506-3435
ComputerWorld	Across the board	508-879-0700
Datamation	Mainframe bent	Cahners-Ziff 303-388-4511
Data Based Advisor	Small-system database users	Data Based Solutions, Inc. 800-336-6060
Oracle Users Group Magazines	All Oracle	
Oracle Support News	All Oracle	Oracle Corporation
Data Base Programming and Design	Mini and mainframe DBMS users	415-905-2200

The Unix marketplace is distributor territory—somewhat complex for mail order but too low priced for a field sales force. Some distributors will recommend dealers to contact, others are happy to do mail-order business. Table 16-3 names some distributors and mail order houses to have on your list.

Sourcing services

Products are national. Services are as local as the people who provide them. Whereas a product buyer can be somewhat disengaged, depending on third-party evaluations and literature reviews, a buyer of services must look at the people offered in each proposal.

A major question in services is whether the company is contracting for people or results. Who will manage the effort? Buyers will evaluate the selling company's record for delivering results in one case, and the qualifications of individual staff in the other.

Locating service providers

Chapter 7 addresses the relative merits of employees, consultants and contractors. The more expensive sources are easy to find. Big-6 accounting firms, large consulting firms, and Oracle itself market extensively on a national level. Local "body shops" are always in contact with prospects. The value they add is in convenience and in matching jobs with people to perform them.

Table 16-3   Distributors with products for the Oracle environment.

Distributor	Product Lines	Telephone
Transparent Technologies	"Everything for Unix 386/486" Sells and provides expertise on SCO and ISC Unix.	800-638-8486
Merisel	Mid-range software/hardware; will sell direct. Good tech support department	800-544-7977
Ingram/Micro D	Works exclusively through resellers, to whom they provide good technical support.	800-274-4800
Tech Data	Unix software	617-345-2400
Cucumber Books	Unix books. Expert advise for building your library.	800-223-UNIX
Programmers Paradise	Mail order systems software for DOS, Xenix, Unix and other small systems platforms	800-445-7899
The Programmers Shop	Mail order systems software, mostly with DOS origins but running in OS/2, Unix, Xenix, VMS and others	800-421-8006
The Black Box	Components, network solutions	412-746-5565

Independent consultants and small consulting firms usually offer more for the money than larger firms, but finding and contracting with them takes more work. Their professionals typically spend their time doing billable work rather than marketing. Their low overhead allows them to offer attractive rates—typically between $40.00 and $75.00 per hour. Independent consultants as a group have more experience than consultants working for others. Larger firms can afford to let junior people learn on the job, but independent consultants rarely have that luxury.

Many of the regional Oracle Users Groups have consultant special interest groups (SIGs). Call Oracle to get numbers for the user's group officers. The Independent Computer Consultants Association (800-GET-ICCA) maintains a nationwide directory of its members and can provide the numbers of local chapters, most of which maintain their own membership directories.

Oracle's Business Alliance Program (BAP) includes three types of companies that offer services. First, the Independent Oracle Consultant's Alliance is made up of independent consultants who have taken courses from Oracle or passed qualifying examinations in the areas of database design, tools programming, and performance. Oracle Direct Marketing (800–562–0720) can provide a directory of Business Alliance Program members.

The other types of BAP members, preferred systems integrators (PSIs) and value-added Resellers (VARs), often sell development services in support of their primary offerings. PSIs specialize in integrating Oracle with various combinations of licensed software applications, computer hardware, and networks. VARs put together turnkey systems using Oracle RDBMS software, standard hardware and their own proprietary applications software.

Evaluating service providers

A services contract is performed by some combination of company and people. When the company is large, like Oracle, Price Waterhouse or Booz and Allen, the client is buying the franchise more than individual people. These firms have a reputation for delivering top quality and are usually willing to change personnel to satisfy a client. The resumes that they provide as they bid a job are often more indicative than actual. The firm will work out actual staffing for each job as they win it and start work.

There is an implicit assumption on the part of larger firms that they will provide their own management on the jobs they work, even if it duplicates client management. A large part of the impetus comes from their management's need for billable hours. Evaluating a large firm's bid is a matter of assessing management as well as technical skills. Almost any of them is able to provide corporate qualifications for an Oracle bid. The critical questions are whether they can reference local jobs and whether the key management and technical people in the bid worked on the jobs they reference as qualifications.

The quality of individual members of the proposed team becomes more significant as hourly rates fall below $100.00. The service provider's options for bringing top-notch people to bear on a problem diminish with the money: it is important to hold them to the bid resumes. The MIS department procurement manager should check individual resumes for the project team. It is especially valuable to talk to prior clients and employers.

Service buyers have a tendency to demand too narrow of a skills match in evaluating consultants' resumes. On a job of any duration, the person's ability to learn is more important than specific knowledge. A developer who has had great success with Forms 2.3 is a better bet for an SQL*Forms 4.0 job than one who has only been to class and worked with Forms 4.0 for a couple of months. Whoever checks references must ask questions about a person's creativity, leadership, and determination in addition to verifying the specifics that appear on a resume.

The selection process

The major questions to ask of a selection process are did it choose the best product for the job, did it keep the level of risk at an acceptable level, and did it achieve these objectives at a reasonable price? The MIS Department manager needs to answer these questions to him or herself for every acquisition. Others will ask them only with regard to deals that go sour.

Getting bids is more a process of education than the sterile collection of price quotations. The process should allow the vendors an opportunity to influence the requirements to which they respond. Chapter 15 covers how to deal with software package vendors during strategy and analysis. To recapitulate, the sequence of events involves the following steps:

1. Composing a preliminary definition of the requirement.
2. Following the sourcing steps above to locate potential vendors.
3. Initiating contact with the vendor to let them know about the requirement and ask for information.
4. Informal selection of the most promising vendors.
5. Reading vendor literature, listening to presentations, seeing demos, and talking to references.
6. Reformulating the requirements based on vendor input.
7. Setting the final requirements in writing.
8. Deciding on a selection process.
9. Selecting a vendor or vendors.
10. Negotiating a contract.

The evaluation and selection process has to be proportionate to the dollars involved. Figure 15-3 shows the trade-offs between the investment in a decision and the quality of that decision. As a rule of thumb, evaluation, selection, and procurement costs should account for somewhere between 3 and 10 percent of the project budget. Applying these rough percentages across all acquisitions means there must be different procedures and different expense levels. The following paragraphs offer suggestions.

Individual evaluation and selection for small purchases

The person who needs it should be able to decide on a purchase of under some fixed amount, typically $1000.00, that has no broader ramifications. If a programmer needs an editor, or a project manager needs Timeline to manage a project, an analyst needs CrossTalk IV to front-end one application, or a CAD package user needs a graphics card to speed up his or her PC, they should be able to make the decision as long as they have the budget and get approval from management. To spend one day making the decision represents an investment of 20–40 percent of the purchase price. Taking into account that the overall investment in a piece of software includes the labor of the people who use it, that level of investment makes sense.

Empowering line-level people to make limited purchasing decisions on their own, albeit within a budget, is wonderful for morale. Most people love to shop. It also shows that the organization treats people like responsible adults. An MS-DOS or Unix environment programmer who gets to pick his or her own editor instead of using vi and EDLIN, the ones that come free, will pay back the investment many times over in increased productivity.

Informal evaluation for medium-size purchases

Purchases up to $10,000.00 or so are usually done using informal in-house evaluations. There need to be procedures: research the sources, contact more than one vendor, read their literature, and perhaps see demonstrations. A few days' to a week's time represents an appropriate rule-of-thumb level of investment based solely on cost. Investing more time in the decision makes sense if there are significant costs involved in using the product. If the efficiency of a $10,000.00 accounts payable package determines whether it will take three or five data entry clerks to run it, the selection is clearly more than a $10,000.00 decision and an RFP process might be appropriate.

Established procedures as described in chapter 15 are appropriate to guide the evaluation and selection process in medium-size procurements. The process should use a written requirement, usually produced as part of the strategy or analysis process and a written set of evaluation criteria. Both documents are usually in a form that can be given to the vendors.

The purchasing department becomes more heavily involved in buys within this range. The MIS department has to arm purchasing to negotiate with the vendor. It helps in negotiations to have more than one source. MIS should provide the purchasing department with their evaluation as well as vendor prices, so purchasing understands the trade-offs between price and function.

The RFP process for medium to large procurements

Large procurements benefit from a formal selection and evaluation processes. Even when the choice is fairly clear, a vendor might react to the appearance of price competition by offering better prices and conditions.

A formal procurement might be called a *request for proposal* (RFP) or an *invitation to bid* (ITB). The term RFQ (request for quotation) is more frequently used when multiple suppliers are asked for quotes on commodity-type items.

Some organizations find that once they get used to the RFP process, putting one on the street can be relatively little work. The investment is well rewarded by the work that vendors do in composing their responses. It makes the process of evaluating and comparing vendors much easier. HFSI, Inc. uses them routinely, sometimes for procurements of less than $10,000.00.

RFPs only work when the vendors' margins are rich enough to support proposal efforts. Don't expect Sun Microsystems or Dell Computer to answer an RFP for ten machines; they cannot afford to. It is more reasonable to expect value added resellers of those products (Oracle VARs and PSIs, for example) to bid on RFPs, because they make their money on higher-margin software and services.

The RFP process often assumes that a buyer's objective is to arrive at the lowest cost. An RFP is the first step in establishing a formal, arms-length relationship between supplier and client. It gets associated by reference into a contract which binds the vendor to the proposed terms and conditions, prices and deadlines.

It is a fiction to assume, as formal development and licensed software contracts usually do, that client and vendor both fully understand the requirement. The package implementer or development team needs to be free to flesh out requirements over the course of a job, to improve procedures, and to do away with the redundant and unnecessary. An enterprise must keep in mind throughout the RFP process that the objective is to find the best business partner, not merely a low-cost supplier, and give them enough freedom to do the job right. The usual steps in the RFP process are:

1. Perform a requirements analysis.
2. Make initial contact with vendors to solicit literature and demos.
3. Refine the requirements to incorporate points learned from the vendors.
4. Select the three to eight most promising candidates to receive the RFP.
5. Write and send the RFP.
6. Evaluate the proposals on their technical merit, narrowing the list of candidates to the top two or three.
7. Negotiate with vendors to achieve the best combination of technical merit and price.

An RFP is useful only insofar as it is credible to the bidders. Answering one takes time and money, so bidders have to be convinced it is worth the effort. It is fair to the process and the bidders to perform a reasonable analysis of the requirement beforehand, to have discussed the requirement with the bidders beforehand, and to hold the bid list to eight or so bidders. Bidders are much more enthusiastic about responding when it is clear how the response is to be organized and how it will be evaluated. They are wary when they suspect the purpose of a solicitation is to justify the previous selection of another vendor.

Table 16-4 describes the contents of a typical RFP. The cover letter is short because the recipient usually knows the RFP is coming. Giving the respondents explicit instructions as to how to organize their bids makes them easy to compare. The background and understanding of the problem come directly from analysis.

Table 16-5 is an example of a compliance matrix showing how well a respondent's product meets the requirement. Vendors are in a better position to fill out the evaluation than the analysts would be. Table 16-6 shows a present-value cost model. The government asks for cost models on large, multiyear bids. Cost models make sense for commercial bids when total project costs mount up towards the millions.

Contracting

The purchasing department typically handles contracting, but MIS can play an active role in establishing price, terms, and conditions.

Contracting for licensed software and services

It is generally wise to keep vendors on a short leash, buying only what is needed at the moment. The logic of this strategy is transparent when it comes to hardware: prices seem

Table 16-4   Outline of an RFP (request for proposal).

Item	Contents
Cover Letter	The cover letter is addressed to the bidder. It may be bound into the RFP document or loose within the envelope. It will: • Open by announcing the invitation to bid • Provide a short scope of work • State the deadline and delivery address for the proposal • Describe the RFP evaluation process • Provide points of contact
Proposal Organization	Provide the bidder with a format for their proposal. A typical format is: • Executive Summary • Background and Understanding (of your requirement). The bidder repeats what they are told in the RFP and adds what they learn in the course of the bid process. • Corporate Qualifications (mainly for services proposals) • Technical or Product Approach • Compliance matrix (matching their offering with lines in the stated requirement) • Management Plan (mainly for services proposals) This may include a Work Breakdown Structure such as those described in Chapter 18. • Performance or Delivery Schedule • Costs. Many RFP processes require costs in a separate envelope, to be considered only after the technical evaluation is complete.
Background and Introduction	This section formally introduces the bidder to your organization and convinces them that it is worth the effort to bid. It costs a fair amount of money to responding to an RFP, and the bidder needs to be convinced that the opportunity is real. This section should: • Provide a summary description of the company. An annual report is often a useful inclusion. • Describe the data processing environment
The Requirement	Specify the software, hardware or network requirement as well as possible. Try to make the specification functional rather than technical, giving the bidder freedom to use their expertise to assemble an optimum solution. Make lists of required and desirable features so the bidders do not have to pick them out of the text. Provide whatever numbers apply to the situation, such as:

Table 16-4. Continued.

Item	Contents
	• The number of users • Transaction counts • File sizes • Desired response times The system requirements document with CASE data diagrams is an appropriate attachment for software procurements.
Compliance Matrix	Provide a grid with the evaluation points listed down and compliance listed across, as shown in Figure 17.2. Some requesters provide an evaluation weight to let bidders know the relative importance of different features.
Cost Matrix	Each offeror will present costs in a different format. Most have the ability to shift costs around -- charging less for the product and more for services, for instance. Some allow payments over time. In large buys it is important to reduce each bid to a single dollar figure for comparison purposes. Figure 17.3 shows a simple cost matrix.

**Table 16-5   Example of items from a
compliance matrix for an inventory system.**

Feature	Yes	No	Partially (explain)	Evaluation Weight	Score
1. **Maintain five (5) lines of shipment information**	X			5	*5*
2. **Maintain multiple points of contact at ship-to location**		X		5	
3. **Handle foreign addresses and phone numbers**	X			10	*10*
4. **Ability to allocate stock to a given order, preventing its release to satisfy a later order.**	X			10	*10*
5. **Fill a single order from geographically separate warehouses**			Automatically splits into separate orders on	5	*2*
6. **Receive and store items by vendor part number when there is not a previously assigned stock number**	X			5	*5*
WEIGHTED TOTAL					*32*

Notes: Bold entries are provided to the vendor
           Light entries are made by the vendor
           Italic entries are made by the evaluator

Table 16-6   Example of a completed cost matrix.

	Year 1	Year 2	Year 3	Year 4	Year 5
1. **Cost of Inventory Control Software Package**	60000				
2. **Annual Maintenance Cost**	9000	9900	10800	11700	12600
3. **Cost of Customization Services**	45000	15000			
4. **Cost of 2 training classes/yr**	10000	11000	12000	13000	14000
5. **TOTAL ANNUAL COST**	124000	35900	22800	24700	26600
	x	x	x	x	x
6. **Discount Factor (at 5%)**	1.00000	0.95238	0.90703	0.86384	0.82270
7. **Discounted Annual Cost**	124000	34190	20680	21337	21884
8. **TOTAL EVALUATED COST:**					
(sum across Line 7 above):	$222,091				

Notes:
1) Bold entries in the matrix are provided to the offerors; they enter figures in light text .
2) The spreadsheet cell formulas for the 5% discount factors on line 6 above are:

$$1.05\char`^0 \qquad 1.05\char`^{-1} \qquad 1.05\char`^{-2} \qquad 1.05\char`^{-3} \qquad 1.05\char`^{-4}$$

to fall faster than any vendor is willing to anticipate. Spending a dollar next year might equate to saving 50 cents this year.

Software prices are more stable than hardware, but vendor commitment is not. If, for example, the enterprise has committed to install a full line of systems and applications software on a three-year installation cycle, it is probably wise to buy no more than one year in advance despite discount offers. There are several reasons:

- Installations often slip: there is no sense tying up money prematurely.
- Requirements might change, and it might be worth reevaluating the selection if another vendor comes up with a fantastic offering—or the first vendor's system does not materialize on the promised schedule.
- Vendors give better service to accounts which represent future revenue than mere past revenue. Otherwise stated, the salesman who thanked you last year for your million dollar order has taken his Mercedes to another prospect where the salesperson is trying to do the same. You would see him or her more if you still had a half-million dollars in your pocket.

A buyer should not accept software prices on big-ticket items as fixed. Software is a sunk-cost business. Distribution amounts to printing another copy of documentation and copying a tape. The incremental costs of a sale amount to little more than the salesman's commission. These factors give vendors a great deal of latitude in pricing and an incentive to discount.

Buyers can take advantage of the fact that software is extremely difficult to price.

Should it be licensed per processor? According to processor capacity? Per user ID? By the average number of users logged on at a time? By the total number of terminals attached to the processor? By the amount of work performed by the software? Oracle and other vendors have tried all these schemes. They often have different algorithms for different sized processors, which leads to wild discrepancies in pricing. One advantage of using an RFP process to solicit formal bids for software is that the bidders' pricing plans can be played against one another.

The less tangible the product, the wiser it is to contractually delay the final payment. It makes sense to pay for a Compaq SystemPro when it is delivered. It is expected to work, and Compaq stands behind it if it doesn't. The story is somewhat different with a full-blown minicomputer. There it makes sense to specify an acceptance test period of a month or so to find out if the vendor has properly integrated all the hardware and systems software. The argument is even stronger with applications software: make sure it works before writing a check. This applies to custom development as well. By withholding 10 percent of a services contract, which probably represents 50 percent of the vendor's profit, a buyer can ensure that the vendor completes documentation and last-minute fixes.

Acceptance tests are a formal device for delaying payment and ensuring quality. Somebody in MIS, often the analyst, writes down the criteria for judging a deliverable to be successful. They are usually closely tied to the RFP evaluation matrix. The vendor receives payment only when the MIS department and the user agree that their product meets the acceptance criteria.

Contracting with independent consultants

Off and on over the past few decades, the Internal Revenue Service (IRS) has periodically attempted to impute employee status to independent consultants. Though they have only occasionally been successful, when they are the IRS charges back withholding taxes, FICA, and penalties to the employer. Section 1706 of the Tax Reform Act of 1986 moved the liability to brokers in three-party agreements. A contract with an independent consultant needs to make the nature of the relationship explicit.

Figure 16-2 shows standard tests of an independent consultant, the so called "20 questions," some of which date back to English common law. It is not clear how many positive answers qualify a person as independent, but anything over half appears safe.

A contract with an independent consultant protects the client against the IRS, against the eventuality that the consultant might be let go for reasons of performance or a change in business plans, and against misappropriation of proprietary information. The client is in a very strong position vis-à-vis an independent. Not only does the client business usually have much greater legal resources, but an independent who must survive on reputation and references cannot afford to pick fights. A business will usually include clauses covering the following topics:

- Independence—the points in Fig. 16-2.
- Hourly rate.
- Time-reporting requirements.
- Invoicing periods.

1. Does the employer provide the worker with instructions as to the means and manner of performing services? *Independent contractors should not need instruction.*
2. Does the employer provide training? *Independent contractors come to the job with the training they need.*
3. Is the worker integrated into the employer's business operations? *Is the independent doing work an employee might otherwise handle?*
4. Are services rendered personally? *Can the independent substitute the services of someone besides himself?*
5. Who hires, supervises and pays assistants? *Does the independent staff his own team?*
6. Is there a continuing relationship? *Does the consultant leave when the job is done?*
7. Are there set hours of work? *Does the independent manage his own time?*
8. Is full time work required? *Does the independent manage his own schedule?*
9. Are services performed on the employer's premises? *Does the consultant have his own office?*
10. Who sets the order or sequence of tasks? *Independent contractors should not need instruction.*
11. Are regular oral or written reports required? *Does the client control how the work is done?*
12. Is payment made by the hour, week or month? *Fixed fee argues strongly for independent status.*
13. Does the employer reimburse business or travel expenses? *Independent businesspeople manage their own expenses.*
14. Who furnishes tools and materials? *An independent should be able to choose his own.*
15. Does the worker have a significant investment in equipment or facilities used in performing the services? *A consultant with his own Oracle machine is a plus.*
16. Can the worker realize a loss? *This applies mainly to fixed price jobs.*
17. Does the worker have multiple sources of income? *Independents serve multiple clients over time; many simultaneously is an even better sign.*
18. Does the worker make his or her services available to the public? *Does he advertise or market regularly?*
19. Can the employer freely terminate the agreement at any time, or is the employer obligated to the consultant pending the end of the task? *An employer is usually not contractually bound to employees.*
20. Similarly, can the consultant terminate the contract at will, or is the consultant obligated to complete the task undertaken? *Likewise, an employee is not bound to the employer.*

16-2 Common-law tests of an independent consultant.

- Payment terms, usually 30 to 60 days.
- Rights in software developed on the project.
- Protection of proprietary information.
- Contract termination.
- Arbitration of disputes.

Summary

Corporate MIS departments will continue to do less development and more purchasing and integration as the quality of packaged software continues to improve and as CASE and other technologies make it easier to integrate. The department needs to know what is available in the marketplace. More important, they need to know how to find sources of products and expertise.

The people who will use a product should be involved in selection. Data processing professionals especially need to participate in setting up the development environments. The amount of work they put into choosing a product should be proportionate to the cost.

Data processing projects are risky under any conditions. An enterprise might bring in packaged software and services vendors and independent consultants to minimize the risk; these are products, organizations, and people who have been successful in the past. Contracts with these vendors should forge a partnership, maximizing the probability of success rather than minimizing costs.

17

Project management

Project management is focused on accomplishing a given task. The project manager's objective is to use available resources to accomplish the stated work as quickly, well, and economically as possible and satisfy the patron. General management in contrast usually has a host of objectives, only some of which are related to the performance of specific tasks.

A project manager is equal parts leader, manager, politician, and technician. It takes technical skills to break the work up into tasks, estimate the quantity and kinds of skills needed to accomplish those tasks and to judge the trade-offs among alternative approaches to a problem. It takes leadership to give the project staff a sense of themselves as a team and to communicate an understanding of the project and a sense of mission. A project manager must always draw on political skills working with the end user, or project patron, to convince him or her to accept a realistic budget and scope of work. It takes more political skill working the MIS side to get the right people assigned to a project and adequate overhead resources such as DBA time. Also, it takes managerial talent to coordinate the people and resources available to get the job done.

Information is just as important in managing an ADP project as information systems are to the enterprise. A project manager needs information to be effective. Timing is critical:

- When do we need to hire the DBA?
- When do we need the outside consultants?
- How much staff do we need?
- When do we have to start installing Version 7?

Making the wrong calls costs money and morale. Even worse, misusing people's time shows a lack of respect for them. It erodes their willingness to give their all to the project.

A project of any size needs automated systems support. Most Oracle projects can be run with desktop software. Commonly used packages include:

- Spreadsheet software. Most projects start with a spreadsheet cost estimate based on a preliminary work breakdown structure (WBS). Small ones might never progress past the spreadsheet.
- Project-management software. The examples here use Timeline, a long-time bestseller for PCs. Other contenders include Primavera and SuperProject Expert. The most widely known top-of-the-line product is Artemis.
- Accounting software. The project manager needs to exchange budgeted and actual cost data with accounting.

Only a minority of Oracle project managers are comfortable with formal project management systems. Whether or not they are used elsewhere in the company depends on the nature of the business: construction companies use them as a matter of course. An MIS director who stipulates the use of project management disciplines must find training for the project manager and any administrative people who will work with the system.

Elements of a project management system

A work breakdown structure is at the heart of every project management task. The first place it appears is in justifying a project, in the strategy or analysis phase. How big is the job? What will it cost? A PM usually takes a first stab by making a pencil-and-paper breakout into tasks and subtasks, costing them individually and adding up the results.

The pencil and paper give way to a spreadsheet early on. Further reflection always reveals more and more tasks in the project. Estimating always involves a number of assumptions. How many modules are there? How productive will the staff be? Who will do the work and how much do they cost? It is easiest to work in a spreadsheet format, where these figures can be parametrized.

A project of any magnitude soon outstrips the power of a spreadsheet. It is hard to have the spreadsheet answer questions like "What does each task need before it can start, in terms of prerequisite tasks, project resources and resources from the outside?" or "Given the resources currently available, when will each task start?" or "What would happen if more people were available?" Automated project management systems are built to address the issue by tracking all the important variables:

- Task definitions.
  - ~Short description.
  - ~Long description in the form of notes.
  - ~Task length in terms of calendar or staff time.
  - ~Resources required to accomplish the task.
- The calendar of project workdays.
- Dependencies among tasks.
  - ~Performance sequence.
  - ~Permissible overlap.
- Resources available to the project.
  - ~Name.
  - ~Quantity available.
  - ~Calendar of availability.

~Unit cost (such as hourly cost of labor) or absolute cost (such as licensed software).

- Actual duration and costs of completed work.

Perhaps the most significant thing a project management system does is to keep the project manager honest. It will not perpetrate an untruth. Timeline, for example, does not assume that tasks start and end on the scheduled dates. It asks for positive confirmation that the prerequisite tasks have ended and the new one started before it will report a task as being in progress. Tasks that do not start on time slip, as do all the tasks that depend on them. It is a good watchdog because it assumes the worst. The project manager must tell Timeline that work has been completed and tasks started on time or else the tasks will be shown as delayed.

Work breakdown structures

Project management follows the scientific method of management: understand the whole by understanding its parts. You organize projects by distributing large bodies of work to top-level managers, who subdivide their portion into tasks and parcel it out to their subordinates, ad infinitum until it rolls down to the people who do the work. This atomistic approach is the best you have for estimating costs. Each task takes a certain amount of labor to perform. Many tasks incur direct costs.

The decomposition of a project into tasks and subtasks is called a *work breakdown structure* (WBS). The manager of a project works with its organization, schedule and management from conception to completion. The task is immeasurably easier if the WBS is set up well in the first place and allowed to adapt when the realities of implementation depart from the original plan. The WBS framework makes it possible to synthesize the constantly changing estimates for individual tasks into updated estimates for the whole project.

Constructing
a work breakdown structure

The logical way to build a WBS is working backward from the end products. There are tasks associated with each of them, whether they are bought or built. Most end products are the result of several tasks performed in phases. A software component has to go through strategy, analysis, design, programming, and transition. Figure 17-1 shows conceptually how the functional decomposition and life-cycle phases are matrixed together into a WBS.

A WBS must include overhead tasks that do not lead to deliverable products. One that is always present is administration. Figure 17-1 identifies methodology as another overhead task. Somebody must coordinate the use of standards, procedures, and tools on the project. Acquisition is another; somebody must handle the administrative side of acquisitions after the analysts decide what to buy. Paying for it is a cost associated with the task of buying computer hardware.

Figure 17-2 shows a WBS for data conversion, which would normally be a task

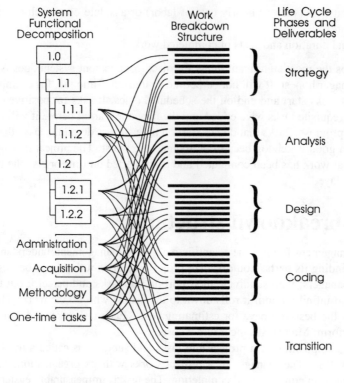

17-1 Makeup of a work breakdown structure.

within several phases of an overall project WBS. It will serve as an example; the work breakdown structure for a system of any size would be too large to use as an example.

The WBS in Fig. 17-2 corresponds to the planning phase of a project, before the details are known. It includes tasks for writing programs, without specifying exactly how many and what they have to do. The project manager cannot add that kind of detail until it is defined by earlier tasks within the WBS itself, in this case analysis and design. This is characteristic of most work breakdown structures and of project management as well. They must be updated as the project progresses, because each succeeding phase brings the following phases into clearer focus.

Managing a WBS within a project management system takes a fair amount of overhead effort. There is a point of diminishing returns in defining finer and finer tasks. How low should you go? Here are a few rules for establishing the bottom level of a WBS:

- Go to the lowest level of specialization. If each person on a project is a designated specialist, assign tasks by individual specialty. If programmers are interchangeable, go to the level of "programmers do this."
- Associate tasks with milestones and deliverables. Do not define a task unless it produces some deliverable, usually one specified in the installations standards, or completing it is a milestone on which other tasks depend.
- Create manageable work units. Tasks will be assigned to people. It is most conve-

Data Conversion Analysis

Confirm key field formats. Establish valid formats and contents for key fields, if it has not been completed in systems analysis phase.

Map old data fields to new data fields. To the extent that old and new data fields match one another, document the correspondence.

Map old records to new tables. Show the correspondence between existing records and new tables. Often data from one record is normalized into several tables.

Determine the prime source of each field. Establish which one to take when there are multiple sources for a given field. For example, if both sales and AR maintain customer data, which do we use? This step may involve translation of codes: SB (small business) in the accounts receivable file may equate to Type 2 in the customer/prospect file.

Data Conversion Design

Design a procedure to eliminate inconsistent data values. Design a routine to identify instances in which the contents of redundant data fields differ between two or more master files. Put all of the values into a suspense table. Design Forms process for users to indicate the preferred value. Design batch process (SQL*Plus or compiled) to apply preferred values to tables after conversion.

Design a data purification process. Write processes to identify existing system records with missing or invalid key field values and ensure that they are corrected prior to conversion.

Design batch conversion modules. Specify utility modules to use for conversion of files to tables.

Data Conversion Programming

Capture inconsistent data records. There will be several columns which appear in more than one data file in the present system. There will be inconsistent entries which must be rectified during the conversion. Very similar programs, probably in COBOL, will be needed to locate different values for fields which must map into a single field in Oracle. The programs will put all values into tables along with identifying key values (i.e., SSN for name) so preferred value can be applied to converted tables. Code values are a special case. Sometimes code sets overlap: certain codes can be equated one to one, and others require an user to decide the correspondence.

Load inconsistent data records. Write SQL*Loader procedures to put the selected records with inconsistent values into tables. This step will not be needed if a PRO-language specified for the capture step above.

Selection a preferred value among inconsistent fields. Very similar SQL*Forms processes to allow users to pick preferred values. Little editing is required, as these are not key values.

Apply corrections of inconsistent data. Batch processes (SQL*Plus?) apply preferred values in all tables after they have been converted.

Modules to identify inadequate key values. Oracle will use key values which are not enforced as foreign keys in the old file system. A number of batch programs (COBOL operating on old system files or SQL*Plus on those files loaded into Oracle) will examine Oracle key fields as they exist. The processes will pull records with invalid and missing keys into suspense file to be corrected. The processes will generate suggested keys if it as appropriate for individual tables.

17-2 Work breakdown structure for data conversion.

Modules to load records with inadequate keys. The SQL*Loader steps to load tables for key purification. They may be required either before or after the keys are cleaned up. SQL*Loader may not be needed if a PRO- language is used to identify inadequate keys. In any case, these modules load the bad keys, or pointers to them, into a suspense table to hold them for correction.

Online Modules to fix inadequate keys. A number of very similar SQL*Forms processes are needed to fix the bad keys held in suspense. They need full edit triggers to confirm the revised entries.

Modules to apply corrected keys. Batch processes to apply fixes. Design will determine if this is done in COBOL before load to Oracle or SQL*Plus after. The processes are not needed at all if the online fix process directly updates the master tables.

Load old-system files into Oracle tables. SQL*Loader steps are needed to put old-system files into Oracle tables.

Normalize tables. SQL*Plus processes are needed to split data from old-system tables into new normalized Oracle tables when tables and files do not correspond one to one. This process is needed in particular to take apart arrays within records (COBOL OCCURS clauses). The processes fill NON-NULL master table column for which no values are available with error codes. Users will use standard SQL*Forms update procedures to correct them prior to cutover to full production.

Program confirmation process. The converted database needs to be confirmed. SQL*Plus routines report all rows which have unsatisfied foreign key relationships. Conversion is complete when the number of report lines goes to zero.

Data Conversion.

Find inconsistent data and inadequate key values. Run the batch programs to find inconsistent values in data columns and inadequate key data. In practice this will be the last step of program testing.

Select the correct values for fields with multiple values. Use the SQL*Forms processes provided to pick correct values. Allow time for research.

Fix invalid key values: Use the SQL*Forms processes to remedy inadequate keys.

Load and normalize Oracle tables. Run the routines to load data into Oracle.

Fill in missing master table columns. Enter the essential values into non-null columns in master tables, replacing the error codes which the conversion process put there as placeholders.

Run SQL*Plus confirmation routine. Run the report processes which confirm the conversion.

nient to dole out work in one week to one month increments. It costs more to manage micro-tasks than can be saved by having them optimally executed. It makes sense to lump together small tasks such as creating the one-table forms used to maintain validation tables rather than have a series of two-hour tasks.

Figure 17-2 shows a two-level WBS that will grow to three in the design phase when individual program modules are specified. The major tasks of analysis, design, implementation and conversion are each broken into a number of subtasks. Most Oracle projects need a three- to five-level WBS.

Uses of a work breakdown structure

A WBS answers the question "What is involved in performing this project?" It is first asked as a project is being estimated. The cost of the project is the sum of the costs of WBS tasks. How long will it take? The best answer is to find a critical path through the WBS tasks, the string of tasks that have to be performed in sequence. Chapter 18 discusses spreadsheet techniques for expanding a WBS into a project estimate.

Work breakdown structures serve as the foundation for automated project management systems. These systems associate each task within the WBS with the tasks that must precede and follow it, resources required to accomplish it, external constraints such as delivery dates and external inputs such as accounting data. The automated process examines the network of constraints to compute the cost and schedule of each separate task as well as the project as a whole. It keeps the future in focus for a project manager each step along the way.

Work breakdown structures are an essential tool for estimating and managing projects. Most of the tasks in a data processing WBS fall out of a matrix drawn between a functional decomposition on one side and life-cycle phases and work products on the other. The other major tasks include management and the production of deliverables used internally within the project, such as conversion tools.

Just as you cannot fathom the mystery of a mouse by dissecting one in a lab, much of the essence of a project does not show up in the work breakdown structure. A WBS must include overhead tasks such as project management. Overhead functions sap time from other tasks as well. It is harder to account on the downside for the frictional costs of meetings, travel, unavoidable delays. It is equally hard to project the effects of genius and esprit de corps on the upside. The assumption implicit in using a WBS, that the whole equals the sum of the parts, is not totally accurate. A WBS yields the best statistical approximation available to play against a seasoned project manager's experience and intuition.

Project management with a spreadsheet

The reality of the marketplace is that while project management systems may be the best tool, people use spreadsheets. Spreadsheets do a number of things well, including (sadly) distort the facts. Nevertheless, spreadsheets are better than project management systems for early tasks, especially estimating. Figure 17-3 shows a spreadsheet GANTT chart of the conversion project shown in Fig. 17-2. Figure 17-4 shows how the cell formulas are composed.

This spreadsheet is set up with a calendar of week-ending dates across the top and tasks with starting and ending dates down the side. This one happens to use weeks. What makes this spreadsheet flexible is the cell formula, explained in the figure, that computes how many days from each task fall into each week. The spreadsheet automatically figures how much work falls into each week when the project manager updates the task start and end dates.

The spreadsheet is convenient for estimating. It is easy to add labor costs to other

		Staff Days	Start Date	End Date	Feb 21	Feb 28	Mar 06	Mar 13	Mar 20	Mar 27	Apr 03	Apr 10	Apr 17	Apr 24	May 01
4	**Data Conversion Analysis**														
5	Confirm key field formats	5	17-Feb	22-Feb	5										
6	Map old data flds/new flds	2	24-Feb	25-Feb		2									
7	Map old recs to new tables	1	26-Feb	26-Feb		1									
8	Det prime source ea. fld	2	27-Feb	28-Feb		2									
9	**Data Conversion Design**														
10	Dsgn redundant data elim proc	5	02-Mar	06-Mar			5								
11	Dsgn data purification proc.	8	09-Mar	16-Mar				5	1						
12	Design batch conver modules	2	19-Mar	20-Mar					2						
13	TOTAL ANALYST/DESIGNER				5	5	5	5	3						
14	**Data Conversion Programming**														
15	Ident Redundant Data	7	07-Mar	13-Mar				5							
16	Load Redundant Data recs	1	16-Mar	16-Mar					1						
17	Select among redundant values	5	17-Mar	23-Mar					4	1					
18	Apply selected redund. values	3	24-Mar	26-Mar						3					
19	Ident. Inadequate Key pgms	20	07-Mar	03-Apr				5	5	5	5				
20	Load Inadequate Key Recs pgms	3	06-Apr	08-Apr								3			
21	Online Fix of Inadeq. key pgms	15	09-Apr	29-Apr								2	5	5	3
22	Batch apply inadeq key repairs	10	30-Apr	13-May											2
23	Table Load	5	14-May	20-May											
24	Table Normalize	10	21-May	03-Jun											
25	**Data Conversion**														
26	Find Redundant Data	1	01-Jun	01-Jun											
27	Find Bad Keys	1	02-Jun	02-Jun											
28	Load & Normalize Tables	3	14-Jul	17-Jul											
29	*TOTAL Programmer*							10	10	9	5	5	5	5	5
30	Choose among Redundant Vals.	20	03-Jun	30-Jun											
31	Fix bad keys	30	03-Jun	14-Jul											
32	Fill in missing Mstr fields	20	19-Jul	14-Aug											
33	*TOTAL USER*														

17-3 Project management spreadsheet.

charges. It is easy to put in escalators and to have labor rates change in a multiyear model. It is easy to add discount factors to compute a net present value.

A spreadsheet is too limited for most project management. The project manager must roll all the dates by hand when anything shifts. He or she must keep track of task dependencies manually—the spreadsheet will not complain if tasks are out of sequence. The spreadsheet model makes it hard to compute total staffing requirements. This simple example does not show DBA time because it would be hard to represent two kinds of labor

Note: The key to this spreadsheet is the cell formula which uses the task start and stop dates and the week-ending date to figure how many days for the task fall into each calendar week. All dates are expressed in spreadsheet date format. In this spreadsheet, to cut column width, rows 2 and 3 both contain the same dates. They are formatted as month names in Row 2 and as the day of the month in Row 3.

The key cell formula is the same in both Lotus and Excel. The entry for cell G5 is:

```
(MIN(G$3+1,$F5+1)-MAX($E5,G$3-4))*(G$3>=$E5)*(G$3-4<=$F5)
```

Taken by parts, this is what it does:

MIN(G$3+1,$F5+1) finds the earlier of the end of the week or the end of the task. It adds one day because the ending date is inclusive: the period Jan 3 to 7 is five days even though 7 - 3 = 4.
MAX($E5,G$3-4)   finds the later of the beginning of the task or the beginning of the week
(G$3 > =$E5)   equals 1 if the end of the week is later than the start of the task
(G$3-4 < =$F5)   equals 1 if the start of the week is earlier than the end of the task

so:
(MIN(G$3+1,$F5+1)-MAX($E5,G$3-4)) is the number of days worked in the week if there were any, but it a meaningless negative value if there were no days worked during the week.
(G$3 > =$E5)*(G$3-4 < =$F5) is a test of whether any days between the start and end of the task fell within the week. It equals 1 if there were, and 0 otherwise.
The whole expression says: Take this many days (if there were any), otherwise use zero.
The spreadsheet globals are set to show zero values as blanks.

The $ values in this cell formula anchor references to the top row (here row 3) for week ending dates, and the starting and ending date columns (here columns E and F). Once the formula is entered into one cell (G5 in this case) it can be copied down and across everywhere it is needed in the spreadsheet.

17-4   Notes to Fig. 17-3.

for the same task (here, mapping old data fields to new data fields and setting up tables). The total for programmer labor falls awkwardly within the conversion step in Fig. 17-3, because it is half done by programmers and half by users.

Spreadsheets coexist well with automated project management systems. After a little manipulation in a text editor, most project management tools can import the WBS printed to disk from a spreadsheet. On the back end, project management systems can usually write output in spreadsheet format for further manipulation.

There is more to project management than can ever be summarized in two dimensions, and spreadsheets are fundamentally two-dimensional media. Automated project management systems, because they have built-in intelligence about tasks, resources and calendars, the stuff of project management, can offer an infinite variety of two-dimensional reports to represent a project from every possible angle.

Automated project management systems

Automated systems like Timeline produce an infinite variety of reports that show every aspect of a project, the most important of which include:

- When are the major tasks scheduled, and when will the project end?
- How many and what types of people will be needed each week or month of the project?
- How much money is needed each month to pay outside vendors?

Figures 17-5, 17-6, and 17-7 show three of the seven major report formats from the Time-line Version 5 product.

Project management systems take a fair amount of administrative effort to use. The work should be done on any project, but it is often overlooked where there is no formal system. The supporting tasks include:

- Collecting actual cost data from accounting.
- Collecting actual labor usage data. This is a major manual effort in shops that do not have time accounting in place.
- Determining which tasks were completed and which ones started, during the week.
- Reconfirming dates and costs of outside events, such as when a hardware system will ship and how much it will cost.
- Revising the WBS and resource estimates for future tasks based on experience and changes in the design or project plan.

Project managers (PM) usually find it most convenient to assign and train an administrative person to run the system, but money is an issue. It is common to find that projects are not budgeted for administrative support. A project manager often has to convince his or her management that a project is more than a bunch of people working on the same job: it is an organization.

The PM cannot delegate the job of reviewing project management system reports. They provide news, good or bad, in small weekly doses that a PM can use to better control the project. The alternative is the "shock-and-surprise" method of management, wherein management keeps a stiff upper lip and sticks with a doomed schedule until the bitter end, when a major deadline is missed.

Whether the information is palatable or not, there is no doubt that the PM needs to know the impact that slippages today have down the line, on overall project costs and schedules. Time is of the essence in rescheduling resources such as new hires, hardware delivery, and other resources that are pegged to the schedule. It is better to delay a machine six months than have it arrive and sit idle.

How to present schedule and cost news to higher management is a political decision. When they realize they can get time and cost to completion figures on a periodic basis, management might ask for them. An automated system can improve a project simply by encouraging upper management to face facts.

A project management system uses the concept of earned value to answer the question that budget and accounting systems cannot address: how is a project doing? Earned value is the amount of work accomplished as a function of the effort expended. A project is healthy if it is 55 percent done and only 40 percent of the budget has been spent. It is in trouble if the figures are reversed.

Earned value takes slippages into account. A slippage can put a project ahead of budget but behind on earned value. Say the development software is delivered four months late. The project is ahead of budget because among other things there is no charge for the

Task Name	Resources	Status
Data Conversion Analysis		C
Confirm key field formats	AnnL	C
Map old data flds/new flds	AnnL	C
Map old recs to new tables	AnnL, DBA	C
Det prime source ea. fld	AnnL	C
Data Conversion Design		C
Dsgn redundant data elim proc	AnnL	R
Dsgn data purification proc.	AnnL	CR
Design batch conver modules	AnnL	C
Data Conversion Programming		C
Ident Redundant Data	PGram	
Load Redundant Data recs	PGram	
Select among redundant values	PGram	
Apply selected redund. values	PGram	
Ident. Inadequate Key pgms	PGram	C
Load Inadequate Key Recs pgms	PGram	C
Online Fix of Inadeq. key pgms	PGram	C
Batch apply inadeq key repairs	PGram	C
Table Load	PGram, DBA	C
Table Normalize	PGram	C
Data Conversion		C
Find Redundant Data	PGram	
Find Bad Keys	PGram	C
Choose among Redundant Vals.	User	R
Fix bad keys	User	CR
Load & Normalize Tables	User	C
Fill in missing Mstr fields	User	C

1992

17-5 Timeline project GANTT chart produced for Corel Draw.

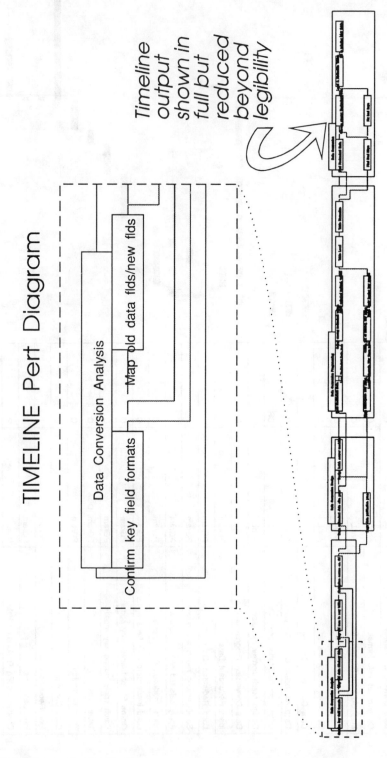

TIMELINE Pert Diagram

Data Conversion Analysis

Confirm key field formats

Map old data flds/new flds

Timeline output shown in full but reduced beyond legibility

17-6 Timeline Pert diagram.

Data Conversion Analysis
- Confirm key field formats
- Map old data flds/new flds
- Map old recs to new tables
- Def prime source ea. fld

Data Conversion Design
- Design redundant data elim proc
- Design batch conver modules
- Degn data purification proc

Data Conversion Programming
- Ident Redundant Data
- Load Redundant Data recs
- Select among redundant values
- Apply selected redund. values
- Ident Inadequate Key pgms
- Load Inadequate Key Recs pgms
- Online fix of inadeq. key pgms
- Batch apply inadeq key repairs
- Table Load
- Table Normalize

Data Conversion
- Find Redundant Data
- Choose among Redundant Vals
- Load & Normalize Tables
- Fill in missing Mstr fields
- Find Bad Keys
- Fix bad keys

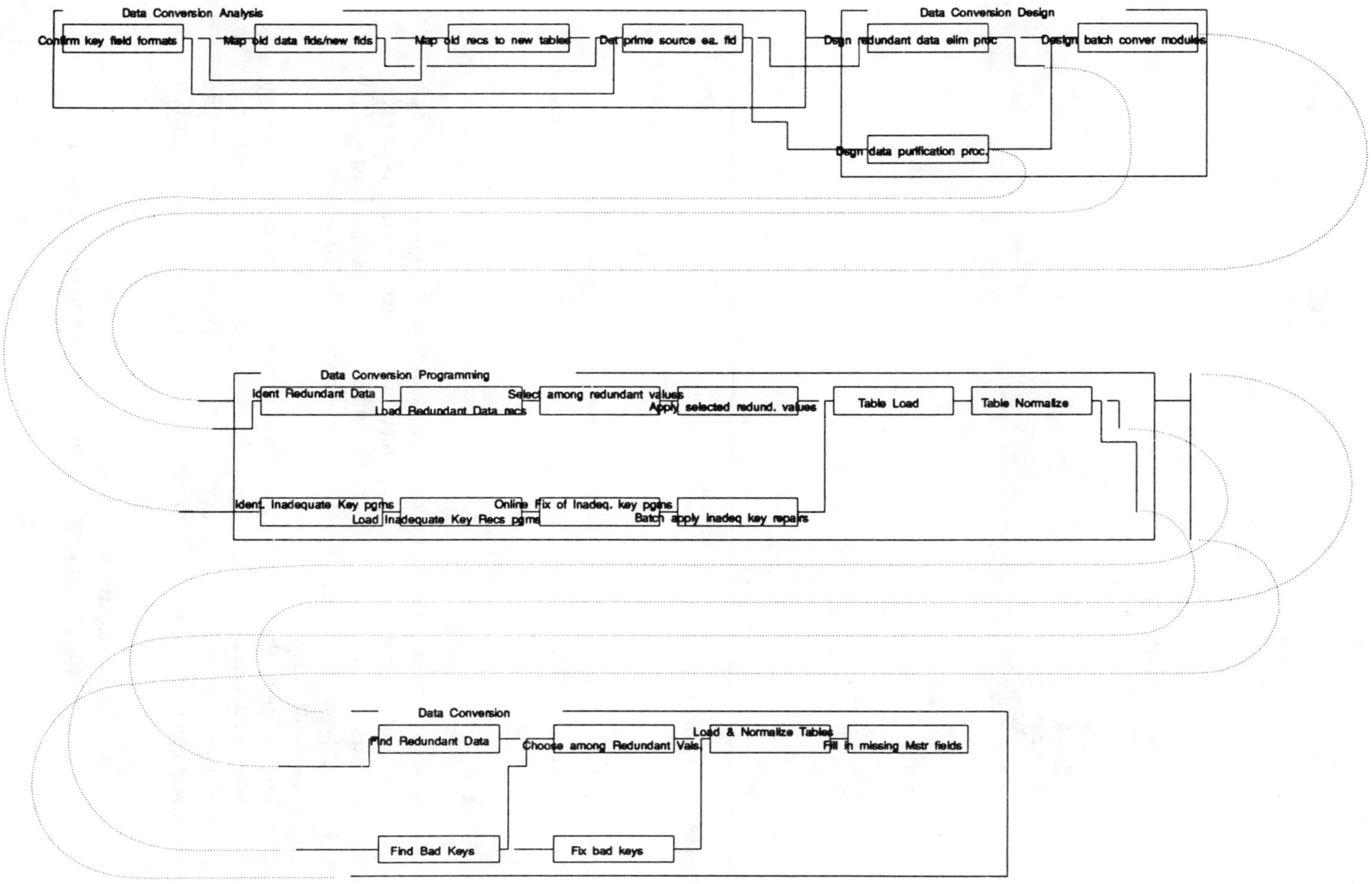

```
Schedule Name : Data Base Conversion
Responsible   :
As-of Date    : 18-Feb-92  9:00a       Schedule File : CONVERS



              92
              Mar Apr May Jun Jul
AnnL      2  ..#   .   .   .   .
          1.5..#   .   .   .   .
          1  ####  .   .   .   .
          0.5####  .   .   .   .
          0  --------------------

DBA       0.5.#   .   . ##    .
          0  --------------------

PGram     1  ..  ####   .   .#  .
          0.5.. ############   .
          0  --------------------

User      2  ..    .   .   . ####
          1.5..    .   .   . #####
          1  ..    .   .   . #####
          0.5..    .   .   . #####
          0  --------------------
```

17-7 Timeline histogram showing resource utilization schedule.

software. The earned value computation will show trouble: the programmers' salaries have been charged against the project for four months and there is no code to show for it.

Summary

Data processing projects are complex undertakings. It takes at least a spreadsheet to estimate the work involved in most projects of more than two or three months. As projects surpass two staff-years or so they involve more tasks and dependencies than most managers can track in their heads. It becomes cost effective to use an automated project management system to track cost and schedules.

The time and discipline that project management systems require are high enough that many shops are reluctant to use them. A management system represents insurance. The premium of time spent running the system is additional overhead on projects where all goes well. A project management system pays for itself in a number of ways when things go wrong:

- Earned value computations give an early warning.
- Cost and schedule to completion figures are the basis for a go/no go decision.

- Computed task schedules tell the manager how much to delay hire and buy decisions.
- Morale is preserved because team members know what is going on.

A systematic management system is a good counterbalance to a project manager's experience and intuition. It makes the best possible global projections on the basis of a series of detailed estimates.

18
Estimating

Management always asks the same questions. A satisfactory answer to "What good is this new system?" is immediately followed by "How much will it cost?" and "How long will it take?" A repeatable (and therefore predictable) process is step 1 in Watts Humphrey's prescribed path from chaos to a mature software process.

Personnel costs are usually the most significant factor in an ADP system development. They are always one of the most important to predict. Hardware resource requirements and the costs of hardware, software, and communications are usually less important variables. Estimating hardware and network requirements is a separate discipline which is not addressed here. Chapter 16 on sourcing discusses the process of locating vendors and getting prices.

Types and uses of estimates

A project sizing estimate is a type of model. It combines assumptions about the amount of work to be done and the productivity of the work force to project the amount of labor required to do it. The more effort goes into the model, the better the estimate is likely to be. The trick in estimating is to optimize the trade-off between the value of accurate information and the effort spent on modeling.

Strategy-phase estimates attempt to throw rough bounds around the cost of a proposed system to determine whether or not they are justified. They are crude by nature. Even the most basic measures of a system, the numbers of tables and processes, can only be estimated. Estimating devices used during the strategy phase should be equally unrefined. Rather than spend 10 minutes per module making estimates like the one shown in Table 18-1 it is enough to project "There will be about 100 tables which will need maybe 80 forms to update them. Of these forms, perhaps eight will be complex, 30 medium, and the rest simple. Assume one day for the simple ones, two for the medium ones, and a week apiece for the complex ones." The cost justification example in chapter 19 uses this level of estimate. Project management requires better estimates because:

Table 18-1 Computing an estimate for an SQL*Forms module.

Function Point	Count	Design Weight	Design	Code Weight	Code
SQL in query	1			12	12
Block (incl. CONTROL)	3	20	60	5	15
Field	35			5	175
Field-level function	7	5	35	30	210
Block-level function (suite of triggers @ block level & lower)	1	360	360	360	360
Form-level function (suite of triggers @ form level & lower)	1	480	480	480	480
Page	4	60	240	10	40
Called Form	1	30	30	10	10
TOTAL TIME (minutes)			1205		1302
TOTAL TIME (8 hr days)			2.5		2.7

- Schedules depend on accurate estimates of task duration.
- People are measured on how actual time spent compares with the estimate.
- Estimated-versus-actual analyses will be used to refine the estimating process.

Better information is available for estimating once a project is underway. The number of tables and modules within the system comes into clearer focus. Staffing patterns are established. The development environment is fixed. Productivity data is available from early tasks within the project. The capability for delivering better estimates develops in parallel with the need for them.

There are many things to estimate besides labor, among them transaction throughput, database size, processing workload and response time. The technique is broadly similar to estimating labor. The estimator applies standard factors to the estimated measures of various facets of the system to be developed. The size of a table, for instance, is a factor of the number of rows within the table, the number of columns within the row, the average number of characters per column (and null columns), the free space in the table, the volatility of the table, the block size of the DBMS to be used, the indexes to be used, and so on ad infinitum. The key points are that the manufacturer (Oracle) can usually provide formulas that are accurate enough for the purposes of estimation, and the system parameters are fairly self-evident statistics. Oracle CASE is sophisticated enough to prompt the analyst to provide the most useful of them.

Statistics to support estimation

Estimation as practiced is more art than science. It would be richer in science if software development shops used statistics from past projects when estimating for future projects. That is where project management, cost accounting, and configuration management disciplines are indispensable. A shop that maintains an historical database that correlates data available from these sources can confidently assess how much effort will go into developing another similar system. A software development shop that keeps no records has to rely on recollections and guesses. Historical data of interest at the module level include:

Data Item	Sources
Module language	CASE, project management
Subjective estimate of complexity	CASE, project management
Module size estimate (usually in function points associated with the language)	CASE, project management
Actual module size	Configuration management system
Estimated coding time	Project Management
Actual coding time	Time and cost accounting
Estimated testing time	Project management
Actual testing time	Time and cost accounting
Programmer experience with tool	Project management
Programmer seniority level	Personnel
Tool Version	Configuration management system

Historical data of interest at the system level include:

Data Item	Sources
Estimated number of tables	CASE entities
Actual number of tables	CASE tables/RDBMS data dictionary
Estimated number of columns	CASE attributes
Actual number of columns	CASE columns/RDBMS data dictionary
Estimated number of modules, by type and complexity	CASE functions, project management, analyst's estimate
Actual number of modules, by type and complexity	CASE module definitions, configuration management
Estimated numbers of synonyms, views, indexes, grants, and other database objects	Analyst's estimate
Actual number of database objects	RDBMS data dictionary
Estimated DBA and designer time spent on setting up tables	Analyst's estimate, project management
Actual DBA time	Time and cost accounting
Estimated system level tasks:	Project management system
• Project administration	
• Integration testing	
• Test data development and maintenance	
• Data purification	
• Installation	
• Training	
Actual time for above system-level tasks	Time and cost accounting
Estimated resource requirements:	Analyst's estimates

- Processor power
- Processor memory
- Disk storage
- Network bandwidth

Actual resource requirements   Various

Valuable as these statistics are, few shops would collect them simply to improve the quality of future estimates. The key fact is that most of these statistics are byproducts of management disciplines that support current products. Management must decide which statistics to keep in an historical database and allocate resources to build the apparatus for collecting the statistics. In a small shop, it might be as easy as maintaining a paper file of project histories with statistics that can be keyed into a spreadsheet.

Estimation techniques and metrics

How big is a module? A system? In olden days, and even yet in the Blue Kingdom, the answer is given in lines of code (LOC). Analysis of historical activity indicated that a programmer can write N lines of debugged code per day. The value of N typically ranged between 5 and 100 and may or may not have included comments. Using the COCOMO (constructive cost model) technique, an estimator would decompose a system into modules, estimate the number of lines per module, and divide by a productivity factor to estimate how long the job would take.

The LOC measurement falls apart when there is no source code. SQL*Menu and SQL*ReportWriter have no meaningful flat-file representation. Nobody writes forms in .inp file format. With CASE, even 3GL source code is produced by machine. Oracle demands different metrics.

Function-point analysis

Function-point analysis (FPA) is the technique of estimating coding effort as a function of the objects in a module. The FPA as defined by its originator, A.J. Albrecht, standardized on inputs, outputs, internal files, inquiries, and external interfaces to other systems. He devised a scheme that assigned weights to each of these factors. His formula to compute the programming effort involved in a module involves taking a sum of the function-point counts multiplied by the weights, then multiplying by a series of factors to adjust for technical complexity and environmental factors.

The kernel of the FPA technique makes perfect sense for Oracle. Albrecht's metrics apply to the 3GL environment and need to be replaced. More than that, different metrics turn out to be useful in estimating for different Oracle tools. Conveniently and not too coincidentally, the most useful function points turn out to be the kinds of things in which CASE is interested, like functions, tables, and columns. Table 18-2 offers suggested function points for Oracle development. It offers tentative weighting factors that have not been statistically substantiated and which would differ from shop to shop in any case.

Using the function points in Table 18-2 as a basis, here is how the time required to develop a master-detail form for land records would be computed. A master table of 30 columns contains one row for each plot of land in the county. A separate master table

Table 18-2 Suggested function points for Oracle estimating.

Product	Function Point	Weighting Factors (est. minutes per function point)	
		Design	Code
SQL statements in all products (see Note 1)	Column in SQL statement		1
	Tables in Joins	10	5
	Subquery	20	10
	Group By		6
	Connect By	20	20
	SQL Function		3
	Logical operation (AND or OR)		3
	Update Function	10	20
SQL*Forms	SQL in query or commit triggers (see above)		
	Block (incl. CONTROL)	20	5
	Field		5
	Field-level function	5	30
	Block-level function (suite of triggers @ block level & lower)	360	360
	Form-level function (suite of triggers @ form level & lower)	480	480
	Page	60	10
	Called Form	30	10
PL/SQL			
SQL*ReportWriter	SQL in query (see above)		
	Group	30	10
	Field	5	10
	Summary	30	15
	Page Header / Footer	30	15
	Report Header / Footer	30	15
	Paneling	30	10
	Matrix Report	60	30
SQL*Menu	Menu Option	5	5
	Substitution Parameter	20	10
	Role	30	30

Table 18-2. Continued.

Product	Function Point	Weighting Factors (est. minutes per function point)	
		Design	Code
Pro* Language module	Embedded SQL (see above)		
	Input/Output file or report	60	60
	External column or data field	10	10
	Processing Complexity (1-5)	60*P	60*P

Notes:
1. Most shops will use a reduced number of function points for SQL statements, perhaps classifying them as simple, moderate and complex.
2. The weighting factors presented here are not statistically derived
3. Each shop will need to establish its own function points and derive weighting factors through analysis of historical data.

contains one record for each landowner. A detail table of five columns shows what percentage of each plot is owned by each landowner.

The module to be sized is the SQL*Forms process which updates plot and percentage ownership records. It can call a separate form that maintains the landowner table. Here are the function points:

- 3 blocks (control, plot, and percentages).
- 35 fields.
- 7 field-level functions (edit input).
- 1 block-level function (ensure that percentage ownership records are not inserted or updated unless they total 100 percent).
- 1 form-level function (suite of triggers to maintain running total of ownership percent).
- 4 pages (3 for plot data, one for ownership percentages).
- 1 called form.
- SQL in query to get landowner information.

The process to compute the time to design and develop the form is shown in Table 18-1. It comes out to slightly over a week.

Simplicity is a virtue in estimating. There is not much economy in taking two hours to figure that a module will take four hours to code. The Oracle function points in Table 18-2 are rather involved. Many of them will be unknown during analysis and it may not be worth the bother to figure them out just to estimate development. Every shop needs to consider these types of measures to keep the estimating process simple:

- Stick to function points for which there is historical data available to support estimating.

- Consider using fewer and simpler function points for estimating during the early life-cycle phases of strategy and analysis
- Substitute judgment for quantitative methods for some function points, especially when seasoned people are available to make them.

It is just as important to be aware that these estimates apply only to actual development. The resources required for related tasks in the Work Breakdown Structure such as testing and documentation may be proportional to the size of the module. Other WBS tasks such as management might be established as a factor of the total development and, indirectly, of module size.

Environmental factors

Albrecht's FPA methodology multiplies raw weight by a number of corrective factors which took into account all of the variables shown in Fig. 2-3 such as the development environment, the quality and experience of the people involved and the required reliability of the system. These fudge factors are sufficiently numerous and their ranges sufficiently broad that they can be used in hindsight to justify almost any result.

Oracle itself cuts down on many of the variables. Oracle project managers will be better served by using their base weighting factors to work up estimates for the whole project and only then coming up with adjustment factors to make the result conform with their intuition. Put another way, they should respect the integrity of the process until they get a final number. Estimates cannot be very accurate before the biggest variable, personnel, is established.

Charles R. Symons (1988) and Y. Renee Lewis (1991) have updated FPA methodologies for relational systems. They take into account the lower productivity experienced in tightly integrated embedded-code environments. Lewis offers tables of factors that adjust productivity in an Oracle environment for:

- Required software reliability.
- Database size.
- Product complexity.
- Execution time constraints.
- Storage constraints.
- Required response time.
- Maintenance volatility.
- Analyst capacity.
- Programmer capacity.
- Application experience.
- Virtual machine experience.
- Programming language experience.
- Modern programming practices.
- Software tools.
- Required development schedule.

Although applying the factors systematically might seem at the time to be more work than is warranted, the estimator will find having them as a reference quite valuable. These environmental factors and the traditional input/output metrics of function point analysis are especially useful for Pro- language development of 3GL code.

Unequal comparisons

The constant change that goes with an Oracle environment handicaps an estimator. How does productivity change in going from Forms Version 2.3 to 3.0? How does CASE affect the amount of time for system testing?

Assuming that the function point analysis technique described above produces accurate results, the proper way to accommodate a change in the environment would be to continually revise the weighting scheme. The practical difficulties are that the development team is obviously on a learning curve with any new product, and of course there is no experience base by which to recalibrate the weights.

The most practical approach is to have an experienced developer use the new tool and come up with rule-of-thumb adjustments. Refine those with whatever figures the vendor can provide and the experience of shops with which you network through the Oracle users group to come up with working estimates. Sticking with estimating techniques and weights that apply to older tools produces conservative estimates because new tools almost always improve productivity. The estimating techniques and weights from the older tools serve well in a broad sense because they offset the developer's learning curve and the pervasive optimism that surrounds new tools.

Oracle rules of thumb

There is a lot of folk wisdom among Oracle developers and consultants that is worth repeating. As a rule of thumb: takes 2.25 times as much disk for an Oracle system as the tables and indexes themselves require. It is better to use lots of small disks than a few large ones. Many units provide many access heads and therefore faster access. They also make it possible to spread data files, indexes, and log files over multiple units in such a way that a single disk crash cannot wipe out both the database and the redo logs needed to recover from a crash.

The 80/20 rule applies in many ways. With the 80/20 rule, 80 percent of the database activity comes from 20 percent of the input forms, often much less than that. Also, 80 percent of the development effort goes into 20 percent of the forms and reports. These rules caution an estimator that balancing workload is not a matter of module counts. It is perfectly reasonable to assign a junior developer 20 forms that maintain validation tables against one backbone data entry form for a senior developer.

Summary

Estimating is an essential costing and project management discipline. Every investment decision must be based on estimates of the costs and returns. Scheduling and staffing are based on estimates of the workload.

Function point analysis makes more sense than estimating. This chapter identifies workable function point metrics for the major Oracle products. The figures for the workload represented by each function point are much more subjective. They change from version to version with Oracle's products and they are highly dependent on the skill and experience levels of the developers who use them.

The only reliable way to estimate future productivity is to project from the past. That takes discipline. It requires a project management system that carries function point statistics and sizing estimates for each module. Those must be paired with an accounting system capable of recording how much effort actually goes into each one. That provides raw data for input into a database or spreadsheet maintained by the software process coordinator described in chapter 10. The sum of a shop's experience over several projects provides the basis for future estimates.

19
Economic analysis and cost justification

Spreadsheets have been a godsend for scientific managers. It is now possible to justify every decision with figures. Most business cultures have codified these analyses to the point that anyone looking for a decision must have the spreadsheets to back it up, and most such presenters are well versed in the black art of lying with statistics. Savings and loans used spreadsheets to justify junk bond acquisitions.

Good spreadsheet technique acknowledges the fact that projections of the future are merely a model based on some set of assumptions. The skillful modeler isolates them as parameters instead of building them into the model. The measure of a successful model is that although advocates and opponents might disagree on the financial assumptions that go into a decision, they agree that the spreadsheet model faithfully projects what will happen if their side's assumptions are true.

There have been a number of books written on economic analysis in data processing. Barry Boehm's *Software Engineering Economics* is the classic. The treatment in this book is different in that it focuses on spreadsheet techniques to implement the analyses that other authors describe. Both this book and those that focus on economics have to assume a style of organization and management; here it is the methodologies outlined elsewhere in this book.

An excellent model can never overcome poor quality assumptions. Good forecasting goes hand in hand with good project management and cost accounting. The surest way to know how much effort it is to develop a form, install a LAN, or purify a data file is to extrapolate from the experience of prior projects. Financial analyses cannot be very accurate in organizations that lack the discipline of comparing forecast with actual results.

MIS directors have occasion to use cost models during every life-cycle phase, from planning strategy for a system to converting out of it. The most concentrated use is early in the project life, before they commit to a course of action. Early in the project is where spreadsheets are of the most use. Later in its life, the project will be subject to management by project management and accounting software.

This chapter shows an actual spreadsheet model. The reason for making the example so large, aside from realism, is to show the types of items that belong in a typical cost model. A modeler should use it as a reference by exclusion, checking carefully for lines in this example do not have parallels in the model being developed.

What to model

Financial models are built to support decisions. Continuing with the status quo is usually an implicit alternative. A selection model is designed to select the best among several alternatives to the status quo, but a justification model usually deals with only one.

A business cannot base its decisions solely on the output of a financial model. There are aspects of business such as employee safety and customer satisfaction that frequently cannot be directly equated with money. Others, such as degrees of risk, relate to money in a way that is difficult to quantify. The easiest way to handle these factors is to list them explicitly as subjective factors and exclude them from the financial analysis.

Simple models focus on one project at a time and to assume unlimited resources. Parker, Trainor, and Benson in *Information Strategy and Economics* go into making real-world trade-offs among multiple projects competing for finite resources. Most of the time it works best to leave resource constraints out of a spreadsheet model and list them along with the unquantifiable factors. The equations are difficult to implement in a spreadsheet.

The life cycle of a software system is the period between its conception and its re-placement by something else. An ideal model would evaluate the total life-cycle costs and benefits of every alternative. The further you look into the future, however, the less likely events are to unroll as projected. New technologies and changes in the business will have an increasing impact on the utility of any piece of software. Most models assume a soft-ware life cycle of three to six years. Even at that, it is good practice to assign discounted weights (over and above the cost-of-money discount) to out-year costs and benefits in recognition of the increased likelihood that events will make them moot. The key factors in performing a financial analysis of a single system are to:

- Establish an evaluation period.
- Model cost and benefit factors that can be reduced to numbers.
- Identify unquantifiable costs and benefits.
- Identify risks and resource constraints.

These data provide the decision makers with as much quantifiable information as is available and put it into a context that includes the significant factors of management judgment.

The time factor in economic analysis

The promise of a dollar next year is not as good as a dollar in the hand this year. The number that establishes how much it is worth is called the *present value discount rate*. If the discount rate is 10 percent, a dollar next year is worth 90.9¢ today (90.9¢ plus ¹⁄₁₀ of 90.9¢ = $1.00). Discount rates compound for multiyear models, yielding a set of discount factors like those shown in Fig. 19-1. The promise of a dollar in two years at a discount rate of 10 percent is 82.6446¢. That amount at 10 percent compounded interest will yield a dollar after two years.

	Dis-count Rate			Years in the future				
		1	2	3	4	5	6	7
1	5	0.952381	0.907029	0.863838	0.822702	0.783526	0.746215	0.710681
2	6	0.943396	0.889996	0.839619	0.792094	0.747258	0.704961	0.665057
3	7	0.934579	0.873439	0.816298	0.762895	0.712986	0.666342	0.622750
4	8	0.925926	0.857339	0.793832	0.735030	0.680583	0.630170	0.583490
5	9	0.917431	0.841680	0.772183	0.708425	0.649931	0.596267	0.547034
6	10	0.909091	0.826446	0.751315	0.683013	0.620921	0.564474	0.513158
7	11	0.900901	0.811622	0.731191	0.658731	0.593451	0.534641	0.481658
8	12	0.892857	0.797194	0.711780	0.635518	0.567427	0.506631	0.452349
9	14	0.877193	0.769468	0.674972	0.592080	0.519369	0.455587	0.399637
10	16	0.862069	0.743163	0.640658	0.552291	0.476113	0.410442	0.353830
11	18	0.847458	0.718184	0.608631	0.515789	0.437109	0.370432	0.313925
12	20	0.833333	0.694444	0.578704	0.482253	0.401878	0.334898	0.279082

The spreadsheet formula used to compute these discount factors is the same in Lotus and Excel. The entry in cell B2 is

```
(1+.01*$A2)^-B$1
```

which represents the equation

$$(1 + \text{discount rate})^{-\text{number of years}}$$

The dollar signs in the equation anchor the discount rate and year number so the equation can be copied throughout the full rectangle of values.

19-1 Present-value discount factors at discount rates between 5 and 20 percent.

The discount rate in a financial model can represent expected inflation, bank interest or the expected return on alternative investments. Bank interest as reflected by long-term treasury bills is the easiest to establish and most frequently used. Inflation is usually lower and the return on alternative investments is usually higher.

A high discount factor favors projects with short-term paybacks because it weights current expenses much higher than out-year returns. Referring to Fig. 19-1, a dollar seven years from now is worth 71¢ at a discount rate of 5 percent but only 28¢ at a discount rate of 20 percent. This arithmetic suggests that rapidly growing companies that expect a high return on their investments must justify long-term ADP projects on factors such as competitive advantage rather than cost.

Risk calculus

Risks must be analyzed subjectively. Some cancel each other out and some are multiplicative, like the risks of development time per form and accuracy of projection of numbers of forms. Figure 19-2 shows that if there is a 100 percent difference between the low and

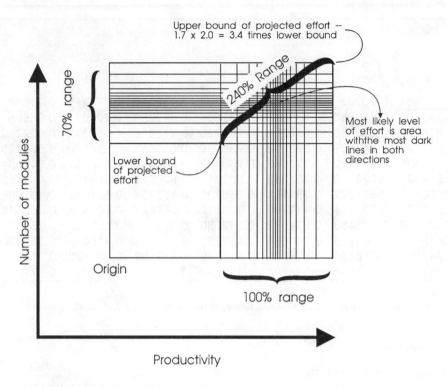

Individual probabilities are represented by the X and Y axes.
The combined probability is represented by the area of
rectangles having one corner at the origin

19-2 The compounding effect of multiple risks. Individual probabilities are represented by the X and Y axes. The combined probability is represented by rectangles with one corner at the origin.

the high estimates of the time it will take to write a form and a 70 percent difference between the low and the high estimates of the number of forms in the system, the result is a 240 percent difference between the high and the low estimates for programming the forms.

When two independent risk elements are multiplied together like this, the combined risk is statistically greater than either risk taken independently. However, because the likelihood of both factors being at their extremes is low, the compound risk is lower than the factor of the two would imply. The two factors here, number of modules and time to program one module, are truly independent. If each has a 10 percent chance of being at the top of the range, the combined chance is only 10 percent of 10 percent, or 1 percent.

Risks do not always multiply, and in fact they sometimes offset one another. Application system performance and hardware cost are two areas of risk. Spending more on hardware will usually result in faster equipment that will decrease the risk that the system will not perform.

It is difficult to come up with a range of risk on a single factor such as productivity.

Even if it were possible, the mathematics involved to statistically compute the compound risk in a project is beyond the skill of most project managers. Analysts and project managers can, however, subjectively look at the levels of risk in each part of a project and how those risks relate to one another to assess the relative level of risk in a particular alternative. Comparing the risks in separate alternatives is an important criterion for choosing among them.

Project managers have to take more than project risk into account. They also face professional risk. Doing a project in Oracle with an expected level of effort of 10 staff months with a 40 percent margin for error could take between 6 and 14 months. An alternative could be doing it in C with an expected level of effort of 20 staff months with a 15 percent margin of error—between 17 and 23 months. Who looks worse, the PM who comes in at 14 months rather than the expected 10, or 23 months instead of the expected 20?

Projects in the Oracle environment of rapidly evolving high-productivity tools are inherently more difficult to size than projects in a stable 3GL environment. The payoff is that even in the worst case, Oracle usually takes less time than the other alternatives. The Oracle MIS director and project manager have to recognize and accept the uncertainty which comes with progress if the PM is to be evaluated fairly.

Costs and benefits

There are hundreds of reasons to implement data processing systems and as many different benefits. The cost side is more predictable. Data processing systems are built of similar software and hardware elements and all fit a life-cycle model. Figure 19-4 is an example showing typical cost elements within a development.

Cost avoidance is the largest benefit of many systems. It is given in today's world that most of a company's core systems will be automated. Doing away with the payroll or general ledger system is not an alternative; these functions are a sine qua non of being in business. Whether to register avoided costs on the cost or benefit side of the ledger is a matter of style. Figures 19-3 through 19-5 show the benefits as negatives on the cost side.

Structuring a spreadsheet financial model

A financial model is a computer program, not an arithmetic problem. It has to be written as such. An arithmetic problem has one right answer, and the objective of the problem solver is to find it as quickly as possible. A financial model or a computer program produces a unique answer for each set of input, and must be written in such a way that the variables can be easily changed. The elements of a model are:

- Input   Assumptions that apply to every alternative in the model.
            Assumptions peculiar to individual alternatives.
- Process   Formulas that express what individual items will cost.
            Formulas to consolidate and discount costs.

- Output   Details of the alternative, to prove the model.

                      Bottom-line figures comparing the alternatives.

                      Optionally, graphs showing how alternatives compare.

A model takes design just like any computer program. The major questions are what the independent variables will be and what the output will look like.

Use of variables

Most computer programs accept input as transactions, but the input data for spreadsheet model is contained in cells within the spreadsheet itself. A good design identifies these inputs by grouping them together where they can be easily seen and changed. They are also known as independent, or global variables. Formulas in which the variable is used refer to the master location.

Figure 19-3 shows the global variables for a model grouped together within a pension system financial model spreadsheet. A user can readily see that they can change the discount rate assumption or the hourly rate for an analyst and rerun the model.

Figure 19-4 is the bottom line—the output of the model. It presents a succinct comparison of the alternatives in a printable format. The cell formulas used to compute the results are behind the scenes. They are no longer of interest once the modeler accepts the fact that they work.

Figure 19-5 shows the local variables and a copy of the global variables in a dependent spreadsheet that computes costs and benefits for a single alternative. It repeats the practice of isolating the variables where the programmer can easily find and change them instead of burying them in the formulas.

Figure 19-6 shows the cells where detailed computations are performed. The cell formulas reference variables that are global to the module and local to the spreadsheet for the single alternative. Examining a single cell, the formula for defining screen functions is:

$$= 1/LABH*(SCDS*SCNS + SCDM*SCNM + SCDC*SCNC)$$

instead of

$$1/170 * (2*46 + 6*20 + 20*4)$$

Pension System Model						
Parameters		Administration	25			
Discount Rate	6.00%	Analyst	45			
Labor Inflation Rate	4.00%	Program Manager	50			
Labor Hours/Month	170	Programmer	35			
		User Management	45			
		User Staff	25			

19-3 Parameters in the pension system financial model.

Cost/Benefit Summary						
	1992	1993	1994	1995	1996	1997
Cost Summary (1000s of actual $)						
Enhance Current System	489.6	509.2	529.6	550.7	572.8	595.7
Oracle CASE Reimplement	950.3	550.2	234.9	244.3	254.1	264.2
Discount factor = 6.0%	1.0000	0.9434	0.8900	0.8396	0.7921	0.7473
Cost Summary (discount $)						
Enhance	489.6	480.4	471.3	462.4	453.7	445.1
Oracle	950.3	519.1	209.1	205.1	201.2	197.4
Cumulative cost (discount $)						
Enhance	489.6	970.0	1441.3	1903.7	2357.3	2802.5
Oracle	950.3	1469.4	1678.5	1883.6	2084.8	2282.3
Benefits (1000s of actual $)						
Enhance						
Oracle	0.0	0.0	0.0	20.0	30.0	30.0
Discount factor = 6.0%	1.0000	0.9434	0.8900	0.8396	0.7921	0.7473
Benefit (discount $)						
Enhance						
Oracle	0.0	0.0	0.0	16.8	23.8	22.4
Cumulative benefit (discount $)						
Enhance	0.0	0.0	0.0	0.0	0.0	0.0
Oracle	0.0	0.0	0.0	16.8	40.6	63.0
Net Present Value (cumulative benefits less costs)						
Enhance	-489.6	-970.0	-1441.3	-1903.7	-2357.3	-2802.5
Oracle	-950.3	-1469.4	-1678.5	-1866.8	-2044.3	-2219.3

19-4 Pension system model—summary table.

The cell, incidentally, is highlighted in approximately the middle of Fig. 19-6 under Design . . . Design Modules . . . Screens. The variables it uses are shown in Figure 19-5:

- There are 170 labor hours in the month (LABH).
- It takes two hours to design a simple screen, and there are 46 of them (SCDS & SCNS).
- It takes six hours to design a moderate screen, and there are 20 of them (SCDM & SCNM).
- It takes 20 hours to design a complex screen, and there are four of them (SCDC & SCNC).

This way when the modeler updates the parameters section shown in Fig. 19-3, every appropriate formula automatically picks up the new values.

Pension System Model

Imported Parameters

Parameters		Labor Rates	
Discount Rate	6%	Admin Spt	25
Labor Inflation Rate	4%	Analyst	45
Labor Hours/month	170	Programmer	50
		Project Manager	35
		User Management	45
		User Staff	25

Labor Rates Table (derived from base rate & labor inflation tables)

Year	1	2	3	4	5	6
ADM	25	26	27.04	28.12	29.25	30.42
ANAL	45	46.8	48.67	50.62	52.64	54.75
na	0	0	0	0	0	0
PM	50	52	54.08	56.24	58.49	60.83
PROG	35	36.4	37.86	39.37	40.95	42.58
UMGT	45	46.8	48.67	50.62	52.64	54.75
USTF	25	26	27.04	28.12	29.25	30.42

Local Variables

Local Variables	Simple	Moderate	Complex
Hours to prepare & conduct an interview	8		
Hours to analyze a transaction function	4	12	40
Hours to design a screen	2	6	20
Hours to program an SQL*Forms module	4	8	40
Hours to analyze a report function	1	3	6
Hours to design a report	2	4	12
Hours to design a subroutine	4	12	40
Hours to program a ReportWriter module	3	8	24
Hours to analyze a batch function	4	12	40
Hours to design a batch function	8	24	60
Hours to program a batch function	8	36	80
Hours to program a subroutine	8	16	60
Numbers of item types			
Interviews	11		
Screens	46	20	4
Reports	75	35	20
Batch processes	15	15	5
Subroutines	0	5	5

19-5 Pension system model—parameter section of dependent spreadsheet for Oracle CASE alternative.

	Mos. Effort /year	1 1992	2 1993	3 1994	4 1995	5 1996	6 1997
Work Breakdown Structure (Conceived in strategy phase. Strategy is sunk cost, so start with analysis							
Project Management and Overhead							
Install project management system	0.25	0.25	0	0	0	0	0
Develop WBS	0.5	0.5	0	0	0	0	0
Run project management system	1.25	1.25	1.25	0	0	0	0
Project Mgmt & Reporting	4	4	4	0	0	0	0
Order/Install Oracle CASE and Sun/Solburne work station	1.5	1.5	0	0	0	0	0
Hiring / personnel management	0.5	0.5	0.5	0	0	0	0
Contractors: Locate, evaluate and manage consultants	0.5	0.5	0.5	0	0	0	0
Project Secretary	3	3	3	0	0	0	0
Quality control		0	0	0	0	0	0
Maintain project-specific standards to supplement installation standards	0.25	0.25	0.25	0	0	0	0
Coordinate quality checking performed by team members themselves	0.25	0.25	0.25	0	0	0	0
Develop and manage user walk-throughs and acceptance tests	0.5	0.5	0.5	0	0	0	0
Configuration management		0	0	0	0	0	0
Establish project CM procedures	0.75	0.75	0	0	0	0	0
Establish libraries & procedures	0.5	0.5	0	0	0	0	0
Perform configuration management function	1	1	0.1	0.1	0.1	0.1	0.1
Acquisition		0	0	0	0	0	0
Locate vendors for hardware, software & integration services	0.25	0.25	0	0	0	0	0
Development environment: Solicit bids & award business	1	1	1	0	0	0	0
Production environment: Solicit bids & award business	1.5	0	0	0	0	0	0
Analysis		0	0	0	0	0	0
Prepare to reengineer existing system		0	0	0	0	0	0
Analysts read system documentation	1.5	1.5	0	0	0	0	0
Pull table definitions into Oracle CASE	1	1	0	0	0	0	0
Compl defs of curr entities & attributes w/constraints	1.5	1.5	0	0	0	0	0
Interviews	0.518	0.518	0	0	0	0	0
Executive management (2)		0	0	0	0	0	0
Employee records (4)		0	0	0	0	0	0
Employer records (2)		0	0	0	0	0	0
Pension and Benefits (3)		0	0	0	0	0	0

19-6 Pension system model—detail labor hour development of Oracle example.

	Mos. Effort /year	1 1992	2 1993	3 1994	4 1995	5 1996	6 1997
Work Breakdown Structure (Conceived in strategy phase. Strategy is sunk cost, so start with analysis							
Compl defs of all entities, attributes and relationships. Expect 80 tables, 300 attributes.	1.5	1.5	0	0	0	0	0
Define functions.		0	0	0	0	0	0
Hierarchical decomp of fns to module level		0	0	0	0	0	0
Screen Processes	1.718	1.718	1.718	0	0	0	0
Report Processes	0.882	0.882	0.882	0	0	0	0
Batch Processes	1.294	1.294	1.294	0	0	0	0
Write business rules for commonly used algorithms,	1.5	0	0	0	0	0	0
Walk through with users		0	0	0	0	0	0
Individual area reviews of data definitions and business rules	0.5	0.5	0.5	0	0	0	0
Final walk-thru with all participants.	0.25	0	0	0	0	0	0
User involvement during analysis: interviews, feedback sessions, walkthrus, etc.		0	0	0	0	0	0
User Management	0.75	0.75	0	0	0	0	0
User Staff	3	3	0	0	0	0	0
Design		0	0	0	0	0	0
Develop screen and report formatting standards	1.5	1.5	0	0	0	0	0
Design user documentation plan	1	1	0	0	0	0	0
Design standard help facility	2	2	0	0	0	0	0
Convert CASE analysis into design	0.5	0.5	0	0	0	0	0
Design Modules		0	0	0	0	0	0
Screens	0.859	0.859	0.859	0	0	0	0
Reports	1.559	1.559	1.559	0	0	0	0
Batch Processes	2.294	2.294	2.294	0	0	0	0
Subroutines	0.765	0.765	0	0	0	0	0
Define development and object system hardware, software and communications requirement	1	1	0	0	0	0	0
Design bridge software for transition. Estimates are:		0	0	0	0	0	0
50 table conversions	2	0	0	0	0	0	0
15 batch programs to find data anomalies and correct them automatically or suggest resolutions	2	0	0	0	0	0	0
15 simple forms for online correction of anomalies	0.75	0	0	0	0	0	0
10 reverse bridges to support continuing use of existing system.	0.75	0	0	0	0	0	0
Develop test plan		0	0	0	0	0	0
Test data for all tables, testing major module logic and business rules	1.5	1.5	1.5	0	0	0	0

19-6. Continued.

Work Breakdown Structure (Conceived in strategy phase. Strategy is sunk cost, so start with analysis	Mos. Effort /year	1 1992	2 1993	3 1994	4 1995	5 1996	6 1997
User interaction during design: feedback sessions, walkthrus, etc.		0	0	0	0	0	0
User Management	0.5	0.5	0.5	0	0	0	0
User Staff	2.25	2.25	2.25	0	0	0	0
Analysts	0.75	0.75	0.75	0	0	0	0
Implement		0	0	0	0	0	0
Establish development environment		0	0	0	0	0	0
Hardware	0.5	0.5	0	0	0	0	0
Operating System	1	1	0	0	0	0	0
Utilities (editor, tape utility, backup/restore, configuration management)	0.5	0.5	0	0	0	0	0
Oracle products	1	1	0	0	0	0	0
Programming -- modifying CASE generated code & writing subroutines	na	0	0	0	0	0	0
Screens	PROG	8.82	9.173	0	0	0	0
Reports	PROG	17.24	17.93	0	0	0	0
Batch	PROG	18.55	19.29	0	0	0	0
Subroutines	PROG	6.65	0	0	0	0	0
Develop user training and documentation	ANAL	11.48	11.93	0	0	0	0
Acquire & install object hardware.	PROG	5.95	6.188	0	0	0	0
User interaction during programming: feedback sessions, walkthrus, etc.	na	0	0	0	0	0	0
User Management	UMGT	5.738	5.967	0	0	0	0
User Staff	USTF	12.75	13.26	0	0	0	0
Analysts	ANAL	7.65	7.956	0	0	0	0
Programmers	PROG	11.9	12.38	0	0	0	0
Transition	na	0	0	0	0	0	0
User training	ANAL	5.738	5.967	0	0	0	0
Execute one-time conversion and purification programs	USTF	8.5	8.84	0	0	0	0
Parallel & acceptance test	na	0	0	0	0	0	0
Analyst	ANAL	0	0	0	0	0	0
Programmer	PROG	0	0	0	0	0	0
User management	UMGT	0	0	0	0	0	0
User Staff	USTF	0	0	0	0	0	0
Production	na	0	0	0	0	0	0
Clerical staff effort using the system	USTF	255	212.2	165.5	172.1	179	186.1
System maintenance effort	na	0	0	0	0	0	0
Programmers	PROG	142.8	18.56	19.31	20.08	20.88	21.72
Analyst/designers	ANAL	91.8	15.91	49.65	51.63	53.7	55.84

19-6. Continued.

	Resource	Total Costs (1000s of dollars)					
		1 1992	2 1993	3 1994	4 1995	5 1996	6 1997
Work Breakdown Structure (Conceived in strategy phase. Strategy is sunk cost, so start with analysis							
Project Management and Overhead	na						
Install project management system	PM	2.125	0	0	0	0	0
Develop WBS	PM	4.25	0	0	0	0	0
Run project management system	ADM	5.313	5.525	0	0	0	0
Project Mgmt & Reporting	PM	34	35.36	0	0	0	0
Order/Install Oracle CASE and Sun/Solburne work station	PROG	8.925	0	0	0	0	0
Hiring / personnel management	PM	4.25	4.42	0	0	0	0
Contractors: Locate, evaluate and manage consultants	PM	4.25	4.42	0	0	0	0
Project Secretary	ADM	12.75	13.26	0	0	0	0
Quality control	na	0	0	0	0	0	0
Maintain project-specific standards to supplement installation standards	ANAL	1.913	1.989	0	0	0	0
Coordinate quality checking performed by team members themselves	PM	2.125	2.21	0	0	0	0
Develop and manage user walk-throughs and acceptance tests	ANAL	3.825	3.978	0	0	0	0
Configuration management	na	0	0	0	0	0	0
Establish project CM procedures	PM	6.375	0	0	0	0	0
Establish libraries & procedures	PROG	2.975	0	0	0	0	0
Perform configuration management function	ADM	4.25	0.442	0.46	0.478	0.497	0.517
Acquisition	na	0	0	0	0	0	0
Locate vendors for hardware, software & integration services	PM	2.125	0	0	0	0	0
Development environment: Solicit bids & award business	PM	8.5	8.84	0	0	0	0
Production environment: Solicit bids & award business	PM	0	0	0	0	0	0
Analysis	na	0	0	0	0	0	0
Prepare to reengineer existing system	na	0	0	0	0	0	0
Analysts read system documentation	ANAL	11.48	0	0	0	0	0
Pull table definitions into Oracle CASE	PROG	5.95	0	0	0	0	0
Compl defs of curr entities & attributes w/constraints	ANAL	11.48	0	0	0	0	0
Interviews	ANAL	3.96	0	0	0	0	0
Executive management (2)	na	0	0	0	0	0	0
Employee records (4)	na	0	0	0	0	0	0
Employer records (2)	na	0	0	0	0	0	0

19-7 Pension system model—expanding labor hours into detailed cost.

		Total Costs (1000s of dollars)					
	Reso urce	1 1992	2 1993	3 1994	4 1995	5 1996	6 1997
Work Breakdown Structure (Conceived in strategy phase. Strategy is sunk cost, so start with analysis							
Pension and Benefits (3)	na	0	0	0	0	0	0
Analysts	ANAL	5.738	5.967	0	0	0	0
Implement	na	0	0	0	0	0	0
Establish development environment	na	0	0	0	0	0	0
Hardware	PROG	2.975	0	0	0	0	0
Operating System	PROG	5.95	0	0	0	0	0
Utilities (editor, tape utility, backup/restore, configuration management)	PROG	2.975	0	0	0	0	0
Oracle products	PROG	5.95	0	0	0	0	0
Programming -- modifying CASE generated code & writing subroutines	na	0	0	0	0	0	0
Screens	PROG	8.82	9.173	0	0	0	0
Reports	PROG	17.24	17.93	0	0	0	0
Batch	PROG	18.55	19.29	0	0	0	0
Subroutines	PROG	6.65	0	0	0	0	0
Develop user training and documentation	ANAL	11.48	11.93	0	0	0	0
Acquire & install object hardware.	PROG	5.95	6.188	0	0	0	0
User interaction during programming: feedback sessions, walkthrus, etc.	na	0	0	0	0	0	0
User Management	UMGT	5.738	5.967	0	0	0	0
User Staff	USTF	12.75	13.26	0	0	0	0
Analysts	ANAL	7.65	7.956	0	0	0	0
Programmers	PROG	11.9	12.38	0	0	0	0
Transition	na	0	0	0	0	0	0
User training	ANAL	5.738	5.967	0	0	0	0
Execute one-time conversion and purification programs	USTF	8.5	8.84	0	0	0	0
Parallel & acceptance test	na	0	0	0	0	0	0
Analyst	ANAL	0	0	0	0	0	0
Programmer	PROG	0	0	0	0	0	0
User management	UMGT	0	0	0	0	0	0
User Staff	USTF	0	0	0	0	0	0
Production	na	0	0	0	0	0	0
Clerical staff effort using the system	USTF	255	212.2	165.5	172.1	179	186.1
System maintenance effort	na	0	0	0	0	0	0
Programmers	PROG	142.8	18.56	19.31	20.08	20.88	21.72
Analyst/designers	ANAL	91.8	15.91	49.65	51.63	53.7	55.84

19-7. Continued.

	Reso urce	1 1992	2 1993	3 1994	4 1995	5 1996	6 1997
Total Costs (1000s of dollars)							
Work Breakdown Structure (Conceived in strategy phase. Strategy is sunk cost, so start with analysis							
TOTAL SYSTEM COST, BY YEAR (1000's) OF MOVING TO CASE		950.3	550.2	234.9	244.3	254.1	264.2
BENEFITS OF RE-IMPLEMENTING WITH CASE							
50% likelihood of attracting IFCWB pension processing					20	30	30
Option: Enhance Current System							
Costs same as ongoing -- take from above							
Clerical staff effort using the system	USTF	255	265.2	275.8	286.8	298.3	310.2
Compl defs of all entities, attributes and relationships. Expect 80 tables, 300 attributes.	ANAL	11.48	0	0	0	0	0
Define functions.	na	0	0	0	0	0	0
Hierarchical decomp of fns to mdule lev.	na	0	0	0	0	0	0
70 Screen Processes, 4 complex, 20 moderate	ANAL	13.14	13.67	0	0	0	0
130 Reports, 20 complex, 35 moderate	ANAL	6.75	7.02	0	0	0	0
35 batch processes, 5 complex, 15 moderate	ANAL	9.9	10.3	0	0	0	0
Write business rules for commonly used algorithms,	ANAL	0	0	0	0	0	0
Walk through with users	na	0	0	0	0	0	0
Individual area reviews of data definitions and business rules	ANAL	3.825	3.978	0	0	0	0
Final walk-thru with all participants.	ANAL	0	0	0	0	0	0
User involvement during analysis: interviews, feedback sessions, walkthrus, etc.	na	0	0	0	0	0	0
User Management	UMGT	5.738	0	0	0	0	0
User Staff	USTF	12.75	0	0	0	0	0
Design	na	0	0	0	0	0	0
Develop screen and report formatting standards	ANAL	11.48	0	0	0	0	0
Design user documentation plan	ANAL	7.65	0	0	0	0	0
Design standard help facility	ANAL	15.3	0	0	0	0	0
Convert CASE analysis into design	PROG	2.975	0	0	0	0	0
Design Modules	na	0	0	0	0	0	0

19-7. Continued.

	Reso urce	1 1992	2 1993	3 1994	4 1995	5 1996	6 1997
		Total Costs (1000s of dollars)					

Work Breakdown Structure (Conceived in strategy phase. Strategy is sunk cost, so start with analysis

	Reso urce	1 1992	2 1993	3 1994	4 1995	5 1996	6 1997
Screens	ANAL	6.57	6.833	0	0	0	0
Reports	ANAL	11.93	12.4	0	0	0	0
Batch Processes	ANAL	17.55	18.25	0	0	0	0
Subroutines	ANAL	5.85	0	0	0	0	0
Define development and object system hardware, software and communications requirement	ANAL	7.65	0	0	0	0	0
Design bridge software for transition. Estimates are:	na	0	0	0	0	0	0
50 table conversions	ANAL	0	0	0	0	0	0
15 batch programs to find data anomalies and correct them automatically or suggest resolutions	ANAL	0	0	0	0	0	0
15 simple forms for online correction of anomalies	ANAL	0	0	0	0	0	0
10 reverse bridges to support continuing use of existing system.	ANAL	0	0	0	0	0	0
Develop test plan	na	0	0	0	0	0	0
Test data for all tables, testing major module logic and business rules	ANAL	11.48	11.93	0	0	0	0
User interaction during design: feedback sessions, walkthrus, etc.	na	0	0	0	0	0	0
User Management	UMGT	3.825	3.978	0	0	0	0
User Staff	USTF	9.563	9.945	0	0	0	0
System maintenance effort	na	0	0	0	0	0	0
Programmers	PROG	142.8	148.5	154.5	160.6	167.1	173.7
Analyst/designers	ANAL	91.8	95.47	99.29	103.3	107.4	111.7
		489.6	509.2	529.6	550.7	572.8	595.7

19-7. Continued.

Lotus is slightly different from Excel in that a range name within a formula is only considered absolute if it is prefixed with a dollar sign. Also, Lotus recognizes a formula without its being prefixed by an equal sign. In 1-2-3, the above formula would be:

$$1/\$LABH*(\$SCDS*\$SCNS + \$SCDM*\$SCNM + \$SCDC*\$SCNC)$$

As a programming technique, the variable names are carried right next to the variables themselves in the apparently empty cells in Fig. 19-5. Both Lotus and Excel have functions that automatically assign text to adjoining cells. When the model is complete, as the example is assumed to be, the programmer hides the variable names because they have no meaning outside the spreadsheet.

Physical organization of the spreadsheet

The major considerations in laying out a spreadsheet model are to group logically related items together and to make the column widths right for reporting. Whether to put the model entirely in one large spreadsheet or split it into one per alternatives depends on its size. There is a point at which the economies of separating the details of individual alternatives into separate spreadsheets outweigh the bother of knitting them all together.

Global variables and final results belong in the upper left corner, the easiest part of a spreadsheet to get to. They can have individually tailored column widths if they are side by side. Summary graphs like the one shown in Fig. 19-8 belong with the summary numbers.

Locate the variable data associated with individual alternatives close to the formulas that use them. Again, putting them side by side means they can have separate column width definitions. Figures 19-5, 19-6, and 19-7, the detail section of this example, happen to be located one over the other and therefore share columns.

Any large spreadsheet involves referring to data in one area from another. It is generally a good idea to have it display in both places. In this example the global variable data shows up once where it can be printed out with summary data from the model, and again where it can be printed out with the details of a single alternative. The summary costs of the Oracle alternative in this example appear at the bottom of that detail area and again in the summary area.

Cell formula techniques

Even a modest-size spreadsheet like the one in the example here is a labor to program unless you reuse generic formulas. The most critical device is the one that compares start and stop dates within the same row as the formula with the period date in the same column as the formula to determine whether or not there is any activity within a time period for the line item. Chapter 17 shows how that is done.

This example assigns a labor category to each task, as shown by the resource column in Fig. 19-7. To take inflation into account, each resource has a unique cost for each period in the model. The labor rates in this model are shown in Fig. 19-5. The detail formulas in Fig. 19-7 perform a spreadsheet lookup function (here VLOOKUP) to determine how much the assigned resource costs for the year associated with their cell.

Summary

The spreadsheet example in this chapter is a model for constructing a financial model. The input parameters (Fig. 19-3) are consolidated and easy to find. The output (Fig. 19-4) is concise and located next to the input. The most convenient way to view it might be a graph (Fig. 19-8). The body of the spreadsheet, containing the detailed computations, is located on separate, linked spreadsheets as in this example. Alternately, the computations can be located down and away from the input and answers in the same sheet.

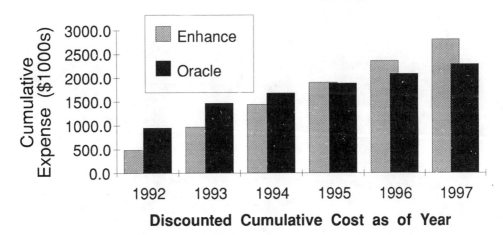

Comparison of Cumulative Costs (discounted) of Enhancing Present System and Reimplementing Using Oracle CASE

19-8 Excel spreadsheet chart comparing two alternatives.

The detail portions of the spreadsheet (Figs. 19-5 to 19-7) are self-contained in that they echo values copied from the input area in the master spreadsheet. The idea is that the modeler can debug the detail sheet without constantly referring back to the master.

A systems development cost model almost always ties to a work breakdown structure. The example here is carried forward from the WBS in Figs. 17-2 and 17-3. Though the examples in this chapter look rather bulky, they actually represent a fairly small project. It is important to recognize in advance how large a model will be. Models get clumsy when they outgrow their foundations the same way data systems do.

Bibliography

Aguayo, Rafael, *Dr. Deming, the American who Taught the Japanese about Quality,* Simon & Schuster, New York, 1991.

Barker, Richard, *CASE*Method Entity Relationship Modelling,* Addison-Wesley, Berkshire, England, 1989.

Barker, Richard, *CASE*Method Tasks and Deliverables,* Addison-Wesley, Berkshire, England, 1990.

Boehm, Barry, *Software Engineering Economics,* Prentice-Hall, Englewood Cliffs, NJ, 1981.

Booch, Grady, *Object Oriented Design,* Benjamin/Cummings Publishing, Redwood City, CA, 1991.

Brooks, Frederick P. *No Silver Bullet: Essence and Accidents of Software Engineering, Computer,* Vol. 20, No. 4, April 1987, pp 10–29.

Drucker, Peter F., *Management,* Harper & Row, Claremont, Calif., 1974.

Eggerman, W.V., *Configuration Management Handbook,* Tab Books, Blue Ridge Summit, PA, 1989.

Hall, George, *Strategy, Systems and Integration,* Tab Books, Blue Ridge Summit, PA, 1991.

Hay, David, "Data Modeling: Conventions of Thought." a series of articles in *Oracle User Resource.* New York City, Adirondack Information Resources.

Humphrey, Watts S., *Managing the Software Process,* Addison Wesley, Pittsburgh, PA, 1989.

Hursch, Jack L. and Carolyn J., *Working with Oracle Version 6.0,* Tab Books, Blue Ridge Summit, PA, 1989.

Lewis, Y. Renee, "An Adaptation of Function Point Analysis and COCOMO for Estimating the Cost of Application Development using SQL*Forms," *International Oracle User Week Proceedings,* 1991.

Martin, James, *Information Engineering, Design and Construction,* Prentice-Hall, Englewood Cliffs, NJ, 1990.

Parker, Marilyn M., Trainor, H. Edgar, and Benson, Robert J., *Information Strategy and Economics,* Prentice-Hall, Englewood Cliffs, NJ, 1989.

Peters, Thomas J. and Waterman, Robert H., *In Search of Excellence,* Harper & Row, New York, 1982.

Rogers, Ulka, *Oracle A Database Developer's Guide.* Yourdan Press Computing Series, Annandale, NJ, 1991.

Seibert, Graham, *Working with Oracle Development Tools,* Tab Books, Blue Ridge Summit, PA, 1991.

Symons, Charles R., "Function Point Analysis: Difficulties and Improvements," *IEEE Transactions on Software Engineering,* Vol 14, No. 1, January 1988.

Index

D

RE